THE RED ANGEL

Elaine Black, secretary of the International Labor Defense, a communist organization, today was sentenced to six months in the county jail, the first woman to be so punished for radical activity. She is shown at left, in custody of Matron Rita Copeland.

THE RED ANGEL

THE LIFE AND TIMES OF ELAINE BLACK YONEDA, 1906-1988

by

Vivian McGuckin Raineri

International Publishers New York

This book is dedicated to
Karl and his and Elaine's family;
and to my family:
My mother Muriel
and
My father "Mac"
in loving memory
and to
My brothers and sisters:
Ed, Muriel, Ginny and Hank

First Edition, 1991

Manufactured in the United States of America

Library of Congress Cataloging-in-Publication Data

Raineri, Vivian McGuckin.
The red angel : the life and times of Elaine Black Yoneda / Vivian McGuckin Raineri.
p. cm.
Includes bibliographical references and index.
ISBN 0-7178-0688-X : $19.00. — ISBN 0-7178-0686-3 : $9.95 (pbk.)
1. Yoneda, Elaine Black, 1906-1988. 2. Social reformers—United States—Biography. 3. Radicals—United States—Biography. 4. Communists—United States—Biography. 5. Labor movement—United States—History. 6. Japanese Americans—Evacuation and relocation, 1942-1945. 7. Japanese Americans—Civil rights. I. Title.
HQ1413.Y66R35 1991
303.48'4'092—dc20 91-15038
[B] CIP

CONTENTS

PART TWO

PART FOUR

Preface

Elaine Black Yoneda was a remarkable woman whose contribution to labor and civil rights in the 1930s, mostly in San Francisco, establish her place in labor and Left history. Indeed, if that history began and ended in that tumultuous decade it would be a story worth the telling. However, Elaine never let up. She lived a long productive life, and as long as she had breath, she fought for people's rights and a better world. People with whom she worked loved her militant fighting spirit. Her honesty and consistency resulted in friendships and alliances that so often crossed political lines.

She is of the stuff that legends are made: "When we remember Elaine, we remember Joe Hill," San Francisco Labor Council Secretary Walter Johnson said at her memorial on August 28, 1988. "We can rejoice that she lived her whole life as she did and contributed to the great tradition of American radicalism," wrote novelist and historian Alexander Saxton.

Elaine first put her indelible mark on history at a time of great turmoil and drama. It is a big history and I came to believe ever so strongly that it was essential to show as much of that history as possible to provide background and demonstrate the turbulent atmosphere of those times – from Elaine's perspective as she saw and lived it. This book makes no pretense of providing a complete history, but those parts of history and those vignettes that Elaine experienced and upon which she made her mark.

Elaine was a product of those times; what molded her as a political person and a fighter were the struggles of the Left for bread and justice and the fighting spirit of people, both in her own country and in the world. In the thirties, she found her place of struggle in the International Labor Defense.

For purposes of Elaine's story, the history of the thirties is best reflected in the publications of the International Labor Defense itself – and first and foremost, its wonderful pictorial monthly, the *ILD Labor Defender*. These provided the main source for general historical background as well as detailed records of many cases and issues of that time. This material is so woven into the narrative that I have used citations only when it seemed to be of particular benefit to the reader. The *Western Worker* and the *Waterfront Worker* – and beginning in 1938, the *Peoples World* – were also invaluable and unique resources; there is simply no place else where this history of people's struggle is available. I have used other unabashedely "Left" sources in order to keep close to Elaine and to reflect her outlook and her politics. These and other sources are all listed in the Bibliography.

The Red Angel is an interweaving of many sources. For Elaine's early life and her work with the ILD in the 1930s, there is, above all, the indispensable oral history done in February and March, 1976, and March, May and June, 1977, by Lucy Kendall for the Women in California Collection of the California Historical Society. An interview done with Elaine on October 4, 1977, on the Petaluma Jewish Community by Kenneth Kann helped with the chicken farming episode as well as other experiences during that period. Elaine's own files were invaluable. The important material on the ILWU Women's Auxiliary came from her files.

Unfortunately, many of her personal ILD records were lost during the Yoneda's incarceration in Manzanar. Much of the material from that experience is drawn from her testimony before the Commission on Wartime Relocation and Internment of Civilians in August 1981, and the oral history conducted on March 3 and 4, 1974, by Arthur A. Hansen for the Japanese-American Project of the California State University at Fullerton.

I have used these sources plus additional descriptive material and quotations from various speeches, lecture notes and newspaper interviews with Elaine and Karl, family correspondence and newspaper articles. I shall refrain from thanking the FBI for the 600 pages of files they provided under the Freedom of Information Act.

I express appreciation to Bancroft Library, University of California, Berkeley; The Labor Archives and Research Center of San Francisco State University; the Niebyl-Proctor Marxist Library for Social Research, Berkeley; Meiklejohn Civil Liberties Institute, Berkeley; and Noyo Hill House, Fort Bragg, California.

Karl Yoneda's confidence in me was essential to this book. I also want to thank the Elaine Black Yoneda Memorial Book Committee that originated this writing project and whose encouragement was invaluable as well as heartening. *The Red Angel* was conceived by people active in the San Francisco Bay Area Labor History Workshop who formed a Book Committee specifically to see that Elaine's place in history would be remembered. In addition to Karl, members of the Book Committee are committee chair Don Watson, June Fisher, Professor Robert Cherny, Jean Pauline, Lisa Rubens,

Martha Winnaker, and I. Alicia Matzger, organizer for ILWU Warehouse Local 6, came enthusiastically on to the Book Committee in late 1990 and became an invaluable addition. While Book Committee members provided suggestions, I alone am responsible for the facts as presented and the interpretation and analysis of events.

This history originally was conceived as a self-published project to say something about Elaine's life and to record the impressions and tributes that her friends, relatives and co-workers wanted to express. When it was decided to publish commercially, we considered these tributes an integral part of this work as they provide fine, true and touching insights into Elaine that complement the history and highlight her experiences and interactions with others. I have woven them chronologically into the narrative. I wish to thank each of the contributors for enriching Elaine's story.

Thanks also to those who generously provided research data from their own files, to those who helped me deal with the intricacies of my computer, kept me supplied with little yellow stickums that I used by the gross, and understood my need for time and solitude in order to get this book done.

Through the narrative I have tried to "glue" all this material together in a coherent and readable fashion. I have endeavored to make this history as accurate as possible and with a class conscious view of events consistent with Elaine's life and work. Elaine was a complex person, and quite consciously did not allow her innermost feelings to be explored as she related her experiences. That is unfortunate. Yet her deeds are the best indicator of her proud spirit and fine talents.

I knew Elaine for a number of years. I loved her honesty, her compassion, her anger, her passion for life, for the struggle, for justice, for Karl. She was very feminine, loved pretty clothes, high-heeled shoes, lovely colors. I see her smiling, her head turned to Karl, a pretty beaded comb in her snow-white hair. I loved her for herself and I loved Elaine and Karl as a couple, partners, strong warriors, loyal companions, lovers.

Vivian McGuckin Raineri
April 1991

Illustrations

THE RED ANGEL

PART ONE

1.

Childhood and Youth

Arrival

In the late 1890's, Nathan Buchman and Mollie Kvetnay were child laborers in a match factory in Mozyr, Russia, a city on the Ukraine-Byelorussian border halfway between Minsk and Kiev. A family story tells of a strike that erupted in the factory when the owners replaced adult workers with children at much reduced wages. When Nathan, 13 years old, and Mollie, only 11, agitated in the factory and joined the strikers, they were blacklisted.

In 1902, 20-year-old Nathan fled Czarist Russia. Strikes and agrarian uprisings were intensifying. A revolution was in the making. Nathan and Mollie were members of the Jewish Workers Alliance (the Bund), a Marxist organization of mostly young revolutionaries. To escape conscription into the Czar's army, Nathan fled, choosing the New World of the United States of America. He had to leave his sweetheart Mollie behind. It took more than two years, working at odd jobs, including a short stint as a miner in Pennsylvania, to save enough money to send for Mollie.

She arrived in New York City in October of 1905, and a year after that – on September 4, 1906 – on the Lower East Side, a daughter was born. They named her Rose Elaine and endowed her at birth with a heritage of revolutionary politics.

Nathan took a job in the Ingersoll watch factory in Waterbury, Connecticut, working a 54-hour week and going to barber school at night. Here a second child, Abraham (Al) was born – Elaine's "Connecticut Yankee." In 1910, with 4-year-old Elaine and the toddler Al, they moved to Brooklyn where Nathan opened his barber shop. They arrived shortly after the New York waist and dressmakers, led mostly by Russian immigrants, brought a major strike in the garment industry to a successful conclusion.

Entrepreneurs

Nathan's was a 4-chair barbershop, considered large in those days. But he maintained a union shop with a union card in the window. He and Mollie were active in the Socialist Party. The young Buchmans had emigrated at a time of increasing labor activism in the U.S.; 30 million immigrants, mainly workers, swelled the population between 1900 and 1920 – 13 million of them landing between 1900 and 1914. Nathan and Mollie were among those able to attain modest prosperity as small entrepreneurs, in contrast to most immigrant workers who went straight into factories and mines. Elaine reminisced that Nathan was "working his way up."

A significant section of organized workers espoused the cause of socialism. A resolution presented by militant Socialists at the 1902 American Federation of Labor (AFL) convention called upon the AFL to "advise the working people to organize their economic and political power to secure for labor the full equivalent of its toil and the overthrow of the wage system." It received 4,171 votes to 4,899 opposed. In 1905, the Industrial Workers of the World (IWW or "Wobblies") was founded – its aim to organize workers on an industrial, rather than craft, basis; it openly proclaimed its goal to abolish the capitalist system.

There were strikes in the coal and copper mines, on the railroads, in the woods, and in the great textile factories. Employers countered workers' militancy with an aggressive open shop campaign led by the National Association of Manufacturers (NAM) and the National Civic Federation, the latter purportedly representing management, labor and the "public"; steel magnate Andrew Carnegie and others of his class represented the "public." "Convinced that it was folly to fight it, [Samuel] Gompers and other labor statesmen joined the National Civic Federation, formed in 1900, dominated by the country's largest monopolists."[1] Gompers was the organization's main labor representative. He told a Congressional hearing on February 11, 1904, that the aim of trade union officers was "by every means . . . to avert and avoid contests and conflicts." While Gompers ordered strikers under his jurisdiction to return to work, rebellious workers throughout the country went on strike, often taking matters into their own hands.

Conflict was rife and barbers were not immune from class hostilities. Down the street from Nathan's shop was a non-union barber through whose window a brick would occasionally be hurled. The neighbors said he didn't pay his workers a fair wage.

While Nathan built his barber business, Mollie helped the family finances by modeling in a shirtwaist factory. "Mollie was very beautiful... a perfect 36," Elaine recalled. Mollie joined the Garment Workers Union and worked only in union shops.

Back to Russia

In late 1911, Mollie took 5-year-old Elaine and 2-year-old Al to visit her parents in Mozyr. Nathan's parents and most of his family were by now in the U.S., but Mollie never forgot her father's plaintive cry when she left home: "My little bird, where are you flying to?" The trip required the not uncommon practice of purchasing false papers, for Nathan was a wanted man in Czarist Russia. Therefore, false identities had to be established for Mollie and the children.

On the way to their ship in New York's harbor, the unorthodox Buchmans stopped at City Hall and were finally legally wed. "Free love [was] very prevalent in those days," Elaine explained.

The trip helped Nathan to build up his barber business without the expense of a family. However, the original plan to stay in Russia for two years faded after nine months. Mollie saw her daughter becoming more and more spoiled. While Mollie and Nathan tended to indulge her, to her grandparents Elaine was princess of the house. She learned to speak Yiddish, soon refusing to speak English at all. The grandparents catered to Elaine's every childish desire, while she rebelled against working with her mother on the first reader Mollie had brought along. Mollie feared that Elaine would lose English completely. Also, the rumblings of World War I were in the air, a bad time to be away from Nathan and home.

Those were memorable months for Elaine. She long remembered the farm with its large house, bathing with the women in the river, the sweet jam and halvah. She rode in the back of her grandfather's horse-drawn wagon as he brought logs to the match factory – the same factory where her parents had worked as children. Before sundown on Fridays, everything came to a halt to prepare for the Sabbath in the grandparents' orthodox home. The candles were lit. Mollie, however, persisted in her non-religious ways. "Well, you haven't changed," her mother observed. "I don't intend to change," Mollie replied.

Pogrom

During the high holidays an aunt and her eight children visited the farm, when suddenly the children were rounded up and hidden in the basement and on top of grandmother's big oven in the kitchen. It was a pogrom! "We were told to lie still and not even to cough if it choked us because something terrible was happening... They were attacking Jews... We lay there... it was endless laying under the covers... the stove wasn't lit because of the holiday." The attacks stopped short of the farm, probably because it was mostly surrounded by Gentile farms. Afterwards, Elaine heard the adults talk about whose farms had been burned down, who was wounded, and how close the attacks had come. Her parents' atheism had been kindled during childhood by "the plundering and killing when the pogroms came." They had wondered, "Why did God allow it?" The Bund, in which they had been active as teenagers, engaged in armed self-defense against the pogroms.

Life in Brooklyn

The Buchman's Brooklyn home was strictly non-religious. However, religious practices were kept by Elaine's paternal grandparents in Manhattan, and by some of the other relatives. Family relationships were very friendly, and there was a tolerance for the various religious practices among the households. Elaine's parents permitted no religious observances in their home. The only time her father ever slapped her was when she went to the synagogue to hear the shofar, a ram's horn blown on the New Year and Day of Atonement. "The kids said it made a different sound from anything we had ever heard." Nathan ordered: "nothing to do with any organized religion until I was eighteen." Then, he said, she could even become a nun!

May Day was special. Nathan locked up the barber shop and the family joined the festivities; a day of picnicking and marching in the big parade. Workers marched behind their union banners, Bakers' Union members in white aprons and hats and carrying a challah (a bread twist that Jewish people baked as a symbol of their trade). Elaine also went with her parents to rallies for Socialist Party candidates "who ran and [sometimes] even got elected... "

Her parents sent her to Socialist Sunday School, held in Labor Lyceums or Socialist Party centers. Elaine supposed that the "basics of socialism" were taught but, "I really don't remember." She did

Mollie, Elaine (age 2) and Nathan Buchman in New York City

remember that when the Labor Lyceum in Brooklyn burned down, the children cried. All week long they looked forward to the singing and social activity.

World War I

Elaine celebrated her eighth birthday in 1914, shortly after Europe plunged into war. She attended Public School 178 in the primarily Jewish Brownsville section of Brooklyn. Mollie and Nathan opposed the war as imperialist and inimical to the interests of the working class of all nations. A special convention of the Socialist Party voted to oppose the war.

Mollie and Nathan were glad that no family members were of draft age when military conscription went into effect in 1917.

Workers' wages remained static during the war while inflation ran rampant. In defiance of union leadership and employer charges of "treason," workers undertook almost 5,000 rank and file strikes, and most of these were won. But the rich got richer; the war made 20,000 new U.S. millionaires.

In Brooklyn, pre-teenager Elaine shivered in her unheated school. Due to the wartime coal shortage, Public School 178 was amalgamated with another school; each day Elaine walked two miles to attend. Once, during a blizzard, she got stuck in a big snow bank, and was saved when "somebody saw my feet sticking out." In her spare time, like many girls, she tried her hand at knitting khaki scarves for the soldiers. She also continued the piano lessons her mother insisted upon, despite Elaine's rather lackadaisical attitude toward them. Little was expected of Elaine as help around the house. "Immigrant parents seemed to want to shield their children from a hard life, didn't want them exposed to the oppression and exploitation they had suffered in their [own] very young years."

In far-off Russia, the Bolshevik revolution triumphed on November 7, 1917. In the United States, Socialist leader Eugene V. Debs proclaimed, "The day of the people has come." The Germans surrendered in Europe and on November 11, 1918, the armistice was signed. The "Great War" was over.

New York to California

All across the United States, a wave of strikes engulfed the nation in 1919 and the Left was charged up with new vigor. There were strikes by railroad workers, clothing workers in New York and several other eastern cities, New York City dock workers, a general strike in Seattle in support of shipyard workers, and the Lawrence, Massachusetts, strike of 32,000 textile mill workers. Some of the strikes failed, due to employer-government collusion, buttressed by the police and the courts, plus – in some cases – union leadership betrayal and corruption. In others, however, wage increases and a shorter workweek were won. By September 22, when 365,000 steel workers took on the great steel trust, it took four months for the combined power of the corporations and government, and sabotage by the Gompers leadership, to break it. In October, a strike of 500,000 coal miners was defeated.

As government repression increased, the Socialist Party foundered. The split between the left and right wings deepened. In Brooklyn, where Nathan and Mollie maintained membership, the Left prevailed, joining with other like-minded locals of the party throughout the country to formally organize a Left Wing Section of the Socialist Party.

Divisions were rife as another Left grouping decided to organize a Communist Party and yet a third split off to form the Communist Labor Party. Nathan and Mollie decided to leave the Socialist Party and join the new Communist Party founded in Chicago on September 1, 1919; they were charter members. Within two years, the two Communist parties merged.

By mid-1919, independent political action in the form of farmer and labor parties was emerging in some 20 states, while in North Dakota, the Non-Partisan League had embarked upon a radical farmer-labor program and captured control of both state legislative houses. Among League accomplishments was the creation of a state-owned bank as well as the best mine safety laws in the country.

Palmer Raids

The Palmer raids were the government's answer to the postwar upsurge of labor and the Left. The country had to be saved from "Bolshevism" and made safe for the open shop. The great "red scare" was on. On January 2, 1920, agents of the Department of Justice, under orders from Attorney General A. Mitchell Palmer, swept down upon homes, offices and union halls in some 70 cities across the country. They struck in the night, arresting thousands, creating terror against men, women and children. Mass deportations of foreign-born workers followed, due process of law being ignored. For the Left, the period was a time of simultaneous retreat and reorganization, as many people dropped away from the movement. The new Communist parties were only semi-legal.

Mollie and Nathan decided to move to California when the school year ended. With a friend from Russia, Mollie went into the candy store business to save up money for moving expenses and to pay off the piano she was buying on credit for Elaine and Al. Nathan prepared to sell the barber shop to his partner.

Elaine graduated from the eighth grade in June of 1920. Already she smoked, sneaking cigarettes so her parents wouldn't know. Her hair was bobbed; she had long since cut off the golden curls that dangled down her back. Without really knowing what was happening – Mollie "didn't discuss that with a child" – Elaine was maturing into a young woman. Mollie – remarking in Yiddish – "It is not nice," bound Elaine's developing breasts with tea towels to make her flat, Elaine being "rather bosomy from the age of eleven."

In July with their two children, a piano and a sewing machine, the Buchmans moved across the country to Lemon Grove, California, a small town near San Diego. Elaine, almost 14, was spoiled and ornery. She had never been assigned regular household chores, knew nothing about cooking, and could "care less" about the piano although she became quite proficient from the nine years of lessons. A rebel at heart, Elaine was determined to do things her own way.

Silk Stockings from Paris

The school in Lemon Grove was a small country school, and it was there that Elaine first experienced anti-Semitism. As the only Jewish student, she "got into quite a few arguments over being Jewish and for the first time, had to meet anti-Semitism head on." Her parents told her that stories and stereotypes were manufactured in order to keep people divided.

The Buchmans didn't stay long in Lemon Grove, moving to San Diego where Nathan, increasingly plagued by rheumatism that made barbering hard on his legs, bought a small dry goods store. He kept on the payroll as saleswoman, store manager, and buyer, a Mrs. Fischer, a Mexican-American widow who had worked for the previous owner. As always with his employees, he paid union scale. San Diego was a Navy town and Mrs. Fischer had been married to a sailor. She knew the wholesale houses and Elaine enjoyed going with her on buying trips; Elaine even learned a little Spanish.

The store was large enough to have separate clothing departments for women and men. Best of all, "there were silk stockings from Paris with arrows and butterflies and things like that," Elaine said, "a full line of hats and very exquisite shoes, as well as yardage." Mollie worked in the store with Nathan and designed and sewed clothes for her young daughter. She was a fine self-taught seamstress and had always made Al's shirts and Elaine's dresses. Elaine was well-dressed. "If I saw some hand-painted georgette that I wanted and it would take three yards to make me a dress . . . the three yards were ordered. And mother would sew." Her parents "didn't believe that the lot of the worker was to go around in rags . . . "

For three years Elaine attended San Diego High School. She didn't have any particular socialist leanings, nor did she read much.

Both parents were members of Friends of Soviet Russia. In 1921, Ella Reeve "Mother" Bloor, in San Diego to address a meeting in support of the Russian revolution, stayed at the Buchman home. Elaine was going on 15 then and went to the meeting although she "didn't know what it was all about, but I went," she said. "It was quite a big meeting for San Diego." That marked Elaine's first direct awareness that her parents supported the Russian revolution. Mollie was active also in the Women's Council, a left-wing organization mainly composed of Jewish women; the meetings were conducted in Yiddish. Mostly they did supportive activities for the Soviet Union, petitioning the U.S. government to recognize the young socialist state.

Economic Crisis

The wake of conversion from war to peacetime production brought a sharp economic crisis in 1920–21. Wages were cut by as much as 50 percent, easy for the employers to get away with as workers competed for jobs; 3,500,000 were unemployed. Strikes were broken, trade unionism was in crisis, and the National Association of Manufacturers established an Open Shop Department to counter an expected rise in workers' militancy. It was into this situation that the Trade Union Educational League (TUEL) was born. Organized in November 1920, it took some time for TUEL to take hold, but by 1922 it was bringing new vigor and unity into a divided labor movement.

TUEL was "that effective meeting place of radicals and middle-of-the-roaders, of Communists and moderates who could not stand the sell-out policies of the AFL . . . the source of the militant trade union activity of the time. Workers rallied to it by the tens of thousands . . . "[2] TUEL did not form opposing unions, rather its aim was to transform the existing trade union movement into a militant fighting force capable of waging successful struggle and to make inroads against craft unionism. The influential Chicago Federation of Labor was already on record for the amalgamation of craft unions into industrial unions. And while Mollie and her Women's Council friends petitioned for recognition of the Soviet Union, so did many of the nation's largest unions.

On November 21, 1920, the American Labor Alliance for Trade Relations with Russia was founded by New York trade unions. AFL unions were prominent in this endeavor to "remove all obstacles to trade with Russia... and establish complete and unrestricted relations with Russia." Going against this current in his own organization, however, AFL President Samuel Gompers charged that trade between the two nations would provide "an unlimited opportunity to corrupt the world with propaganda."

Elaine didn't participate in or concern herself with the political activities going on in her home. When there were meetings in the house, she would go to her room and do her homework. "I really didn't know a good deal of what was going on." As time went on, she became wrapped up in her own rebellion. She and a girl friend wanted to go into nurse's training together, but Mollie and Nathan refused to sign a consent form. "They said do something else, or go on to college, but not into nursing. They wanted me to become a teacher, or even a doctor but they didn't want their daughter carrying bed pans." Elaine was defiant. "If you are not going to let me be a nurse, I won't bring home a diploma." And she didn't, quitting high school in her senior year.

The San Diego store did well enough for the Buchmans to move in 1923 to the more metropolitan Los Angeles where Nathan purchased another ready-to-wear store on Whittier Boulevard. Their apartment was in back of the store and Elaine and Al had rooms of their own. This larger store also had a County Library section that Elaine helped keep in order, occasionally helping out in the store as well. She enrolled for secretarial training at Woodbury Business College, graduating from the nine-month course in three-and-a-half months.

2.

Work and Marriage

Elaine Gets a Job

Later that year, through the school's employment service, Elaine got her first job. It was at the Darby Hotel, a plush residential hall on West Adams Street. She was 17 and impressed, as "most of the guests were lords and ladies, some from England . . . " She remembered a countess, too. The hotel "didn't look like much from the outside, but inside was such splendor and riches that I had never been exposed to." Elaine sat at a desk in an area where art exhibits were sometimes held. She had never before been to an art show and even the richness of the picture frames "just floored" her. She had her own dining table and a waiter who catered to her needs. The bowls of fruit on the tables were renewed each day, and it always stuck with her that it "obviously wasn't the same fruit that had been there the day before." Elaine was aware of the waste of good food and she and a hotel waiter talked about it. "Although there was no depression at that time, we knew there were poor people."

Elaine maintained "an even keel" with the hotel's swank clientele. "The guests had no complaints about my appearance. I must say that, in those days, if I had a lilac dress I had lilac shoes and if it was brown, it was brown shoes. I was quite a clothes horse . . . The gloves, the hat, and everything else had to match." Mollie still made most of her outfits and they were "very elegant."

Elaine continued to live at home and was largely wrapped up in her own life, with little awareness of the political and social ferment stirring around her. However, this ferment would soon envelop her life.

Millions Cry for Justice

In San Quentin prison, located at the edge of San Francisco Bay near San Rafael, Thomas J. Mooney and Warren K. Billings were confined in tiny cells. In one of the most shameful frameups in labor history, they had been convicted of murder in the July 22, 1916, San Francisco Preparedness Day Parade in which eight persons were killed. Mooney was a labor agitator and organizer whose attempts to organize streetcar men had won him the enmity of the Chamber of Commerce, which was determined to keep the open shop in San Francisco. He was sentenced to death by hanging, Billings to life imprisonment. Throughout the United States working people took to the streets in protest, while across the world in Petrograd, Russian workers demonstrated for Mooney in front of the American Embassy. The ringing cry for justice was taken up by millions around the world. Between the international movement and the threat of a general strike on the West Coast – Mooney's death sentence was twice postponed and then commuted to life imprisonment. A national Free Mooney-Billings Congress held in January 1918, in Chicago, brought together 1,400 delegates to plan a defense strategy.

Across the country, in South Braintree, Massachusetts, labor organizers Nicola Sacco, shoemaker, and Bartolomeo Vanzetti, fish peddler, awaited execution. They were anarchists accused of committing the April 15, 1920 payroll robbery of the Slater and Morrill Shoe company during which the paymaster and a guard were killed. The Sacco-Vanzetti case, like Mooney-Billings, aroused the ire of the international working class; protests and demonstrations were held in cities and villages around the world.

But the oldest – and probably loneliest – labor prisoner in the United States, James B. McNamara, was largely forgotten in these years. McNamara was convicted in 1911 of the October 1, 1910 bombing of the *Los Angeles Times* building in which 21 persons were killed. This was a time described later by the *People's World* as one "of bitter labor conflict, in which open-shoppers, headed by the *Los Angeles Times*... and the Merchants and Manufacturers Association, were trying to break the unions, [and] an explosion wrecked the new building of the *Times,* causing loss of life." Convicted with McNamara was Matt Schmidt, sentenced to life imprisonment, and McNamara's brother John who got 15 years.

In a deal with the prosecution recommended by Clarence Darrow, McNamara's lawyer, writer Lincoln Steffens, and some labor leaders, McNamara – to "save the labor movement" – was persuaded to change his plea from not guilty to guilty, a move that turned public opinion vehemently against him. That the general public had an abhorrance for violence as exemplified by the dynamiting of the *Times* was undoubtedly a factor in radical labor's abandonment of it as a class weapon. Employers, however, continued to instigate and pay for organized violence and murder against working people. Indeed, such violence was institutionalized in the system. As the years progressed, James B. McNamara was to become the most respected and beloved of all labor prisoners. His warmth and courage and defense of prisoners' rights became legendary.[1]

There were also such cases as that of 57 Communist leaders indicted in Bridgman, Michigan in early 1923 for such crimes as "illegal assembly." And there were many others, each having its separate defense committee and each rallying people across the nation and, in some cases, across the world to protest.

Marriage and a Baby

The Young Workers League had come into existence in May 1922, formed out of several socialist and communist youth groupings. After they moved to Los Angeles, Mollie and Nathan urged Elaine to attend a meeting of the YWL; she acquiesced, not anxious to do so but willing to see what it was about. There she met Edward Frances Russell, Jr., a young machinist whose father had a long history in the labor movement, from the Knights of Labor and the Wobblies in the early days to organizing for the Machinists Union. A friend and co-worker of Mother Bloor, he had been tarred and feathered in the South as he went from town to town organizing.

Young Ed was like Elaine, not much interested in the Young Workers League or the Trade Union Educational League in which his father and some of his friends were active. He and Elaine empathized with each other's non-involvement in politics. It may have been, Elaine said, that "our non-interest was our mutual interest at the time." At any rate, the vivacious Elaine and handsome Ed were attracted to each other and soon decided to get married.

Elaine quit her job and on January 12, 1925, she and Ed were married at the Los Angeles City Hall. Mollie and Nathan were not pleased but did not intervene.

Elaine and Ed were determined to "go our own way – perhaps because it was contrary to what our parents wanted. We would just forego 'the movement' and set up a home of our own. However, the furnished room where they set up housekeeping "wasn't much of a home," and they soon moved in with her parents (as they were to do off and on for the next few years). They were never asked to pay rent while living with Mollie and Nathan, though Elaine did help out some in the store. Elaine was a young housewife who knew not how to keep house, cook or iron; Ed taught her how to iron – no doubt to keep him in pressed shirts. At first she stayed home while Ed drove a milk truck. When he got home from work, he wanted the table set and dinner ready.

This got pretty boring for the free-spirited Elaine. In 1926, wanting "some money for what I wanted to do," she got a job as a salesgirl selling yardage in a department store on Fifth Street. It was non-union; hours were long and wages low. Elaine got pregnant that same year, and on July 27, 1927, a daughter, Joyce, was born.

Tears for Sacco and Vanzetti

On August 23, 1927, after seven years of national and international protest, Sacco and Vanzetti were executed. Their names had become sacred to working people throughout the world, their case a bitter indictment of U.S. injustice. The great Socialist leader Eugene V. Debs, shortly before his own death in 1926, denounced the "capitalist courts of Massachusetts (which) have had them on the rack day and night, devouring the flesh of their bodies and torturing their souls . . . " Vanzetti's own words written in a letter to his son four months before he and Sacco were executed were to become immortal: "If it had not been for this thing I might have lived out my life talking at street corners to scorning men . . . this last agony is our triumph!"

The Buchman household mourned the deaths. "Eddie and I were very distressed. I wasn't in the movement, but I cried when the news came over the radio," said Elaine.

Staying home and taking care of the baby "probably" satisfied her in that period. Mollie continued to make Elaine's clothes and now made Joyce's as well. By October 1929, when the stock market crashed, Ed was working as a machinist, promoted to the position of foreman at one of Hollywood's film studios. With overtime he made as much as $80 per week, big money for those days.

Eddie joined the Fraternal Order of Elks and Elaine became an Elkette – "I was still the fashion chart." They moved into their own place in a bungalow court and engaged in a busy social life. For most people, however, the "roaring twenties," had faded to a moan.

3.
"Don't Starve—Fight!"

Enter the Thirties

While Elaine and Ed lived in relative comfort, TUEL delegates met in national convention to reorganize as the Trade Union Unity League (TUUL) in September of 1929, a month before the stock market crash. The trade unions were in decline despite a decade of struggles. The TUEL had attempted—with gains and losses—to work within the existing AFL unions. It had widespread support from rank and file workers as it led strikes in defiance of national AFL leadership. In all of its activities, TUEL sowed the seeds of industrial unionism. One of its most important victories was winning a shorter work week for thousands of New York furriers. The TUEL was constantly attacked as a "Communist conspiracy" both by employers and most AFL leaders.

The main emphasis of the new TUUL was to organize the unorganized on an industrial basis. Of 690 delegates at its founding convention, 72 were women and 64 were Black workers. Black workers had increased in the industrial work force but were excluded from most unions; in 1925 the American Negro Labor Council was formed to fight discrimination in the labor movement. Women TUUL delegates urged special attention to organizing the nation's 8,500,000 women workers. Rose Wortis, International Ladies Garment Workers Union (ILGWU) leader, was elected TUUL secretary and steel organizer and Communist William Z. Foster its general secretary.

By 1930 the economy was almost at a standstill. Factories, mines and mills closed. Millions were jobless and hungry, wages were cut to the bone, workers and farmers were evicted from their homes and farms, and shanty towns called "Hoovervilles" sprang up everywhere. While President Hoover promised that "prosperity was just around the corner" and Chambers of Commerce provided the unemployed with apples to sell on street corners, people became more desperate. They began to take the law into their own hands. One action was to move evicted families back into their homes and apartments; while spontaneous in the beginning, this was the beginning of an organized anti-eviction movement that was to sweep the country. An angry people surged into the streets. The rumblings of discontent grew louder. The Communists put out a call: "Don't Starve, Fight!"

The Imperial Valley Strike

Nowhere was the slogan "Don't Starve, Fight!" more applicable than in the nation's harvest fields and orchards. Here workers earned starvation wages and labored under inhuman conditions, while growers pitted racial and nationality groups against each other. In California's Imperial Valley, the new TUUL, in line with its policy of industrial unionism, organized the Agricultural Workers Industrial League which, for the first time in farm labor history, effectively organized across racial and nationality lines. Response in the fields was enthusiastic and, according to the *Daily Worker* of January 6, signaled "... the beginning of mass rebellion by all the scores of thousands of bitterly exploited Mexican, Filipino, Hindu, Japanese, and Chinese agricultural laborers who slave for the big open-shop fruit growers and packers under conditions bordering closely on peonage."

As union organizing spread from field to field, some 5,000 workers became involved; they demanded a pay hike, an end to piecework, elimination of the labor contract system, and recognition of field workers' "job committees." The unity achieved was historic. The Communist Party, plus an organization several years old, the International Labor Defense (ILD), mobilized support for a strike call while the growers stockpiled tear gas and guns against the revolutionary union. A "Workers Defense Corps" guarded the union headquarters.

The strike movement was to be broken by the sheer numbers and brutality of the police and vigilante forces aligned against it, but the threat that it represented to the growers was clear. The ethnic composition of strike leadership reflected the new and bold unity among the workers. Arrests came in April as the union was attempting to organize a conference of all agricultural workers in the Imperial Valley. Rank and file unionists and leaders met on April 14 to plan the conference.

ILD organizer Frank Spector described that meeting in a *Labor Defender* article he wrote later that year from prison:

> One after another the workers spoke, each in their own language. They told of starvation and sickness of their wives and children, of constant wage-cuts, of the long hours of bitter toil under a scorching sun . . . of the readiness to fight under their union's militant guidance. Suddenly the door burst open. Into the hall rushed an armed mob of policemen, deputy sheriffs and privately hired thugs, with revolvers and sawed-off shotguns . . . Out of this mob stepped Sheriff Gillette, chief gunman of the Imperial Valley bosses. Ordering the workers to throw up their hands . . . [there was] a frenzied search of the 108 workers . . . they were chained in groups. Then the mob, with a brutal display of force, threw them into huge trucks [and] . . . into the El Centro County jail.

The following months saw deportations of some Mexican workers and release of others, while the Imperial Valley became an armed camp. "Criminal Syndicalism" charges were brought against nine men, all Communists. They were Danny Roxas, Eduardo Herrera, Emilio Alonzo, Braulio Orosco, Tetsuji Horiuchi, Carl Sklar, Oscar Erickson, Frank Spector, and Lawrence Emery. They were all found guilty. Alonzo was deported to Argentina; all the others were sentenced to long prison terms. After serving two-and-a-half years, Horiuchi was ordered deported. Because deportation to Imperial Japan meant prison or even death, the ILD arranged for the voluntary departure of Horiuchi to the Soviet Union.

The strike marked the first use in California in the 1930s of the Criminal Syndicalism Act against farmworker organizers; it marked also the bravest attempt yet to organize farmworkers across color and nationality lines into one union.

Out of this initial effort, the militant Cannery and Agricultural Workers Industrial Union (CAWIU) was born.

"You May Be Next"

John Dos Passos described the Imperial Valley situation in a *Labor Defender* article:

> The interests which own the State of California are at work to outlaw the Communist Party . . . and through the Communist Party they are at work to outlaw any working class movement whatsoever.

> The conviction of Imperial Valley strikers in the spring of 1930 . . . marked the first revival of the state's Criminal Syndicalism Act since it was used to smash the IWW from 1919 to 1924. In the trial at El Centro all the familiar figures of dicks and frameup experts reappear, even to Lt. Hynes, chief red-baiter of the Los Angeles police force who won his spurs by his zeal as a stool pigeon in the San Pedro dock strike run by the IWW in 1925. . . . This situation must be faced . . . every time a radical organizer or a striking worker is sent up for . . . [a] bitterly long term . . . it's that much easier to slip the noose around the next man's neck. You may be next . . .

Elaine didn't know it yet, but soon she would be committing her life to the defense of organizers like those described by Dos Passos.

The International Labor Defense

The International Labor Defense was founded on June 28, 1925, to coordinate the legal defense of arrested and jailed labor and political activists, its birth mandated by the need for one national permanent defense organization. The ILD had a militant program:

- The ILD organizes for mass struggle against capitalist class justice in all its forms.
- It fights for the unconditional freedom of all class war prisoners.
- It mobilizes the masses for material aid and comfort to class war prisoners and their dependents.
- It fights against national oppression and lynchings of Negroes.
- It fights for the defense of foreign born workers, against deportation and for the right of political asylum.
- It fights for freedom of speech, press and assembly for workers and for the right to organize for self-defense.
- It fights against injunctions and all anti-labor laws.
- It organizes the international solidarity of the working class.
- It publishes an illustrated monthly magazine, the *Labor Defender,* and utilizes the entire labor press for publicity and for the mobilization of mass support for its program.

By 1930, the ILD had attracted both famous and rank-and-file supporters to its cause; some were or became Communists. Elizabeth Gurley Flynn, Alfred Wagenknecht, J. Louis Engdahl, Louis Colman, Sasha Small, Rose Pastor Stokes and William L. Patterson were among the early national leaders. Its monthly pictorial magazine, *The Labor Defender,* was an attractive informational and agitational journal. It seemed as if everybody who was anybody on the Left in those years affiliated with the ILD. Its National Committee of 43 included in 1927: Upton Sinclair, Eugene V. Debs, Clarence Darrow, Scott Nearing, William Z. Foster, Bishop William M. Brown, Alice Stone Blackwell, Charles E. Ruthenberg, Robert Minor, Rose Baron, James P. Cannon, Ralph Chaplin, Harrison George, and William F. Dunne. "Mother" Bloor, whom Elaine had met in 1921, was one of the many organizers who fanned out over the nation, appearing wherever workers went on strike and needed defense. "We must not fail these fighters, our defenders, those who go to the front," Bloor said of her work with the ILD.

The *Labor Defender* maintained an impressive staff of contributing editors in the United States and foreign countries. These included American novelists, social critics, and reporters as well as some of the best-known writers of other nations. Among the distinguished group who wrote for the *Defender* were Henri Barbusse, Langston Hughes, Jack Conroy, John Dos Passos, Maxim Gorki, Josephine Herbst, Ludwig Renn, Lincoln Steffens, Hugo Gellert, Albert Deutsch, R. Doonping, Waldo Frank, Mike Gold, John Howard Lawson, Conrad Komorowski, Grace Hutchins, "Mother" Bloor, George Maurer, and Joseph North.

In 1927 – as the ILD perceived that "international solidarity was becoming more than ever a necessity" – it affiliated with International Red Aid (IRA), an organization founded in Moscow in 1923. The IRA had sections in 70 countries with a total membership of over 14,000,000 and was, the ILD said, "the only international working class defense organization."[1]

In the Soviet Union – where it was known as MOPR* – International Red Aid was described as "the organized expression of the active revolutionary class-solidarity of the toilers of all countries . . . [it] carries out within the revolutionary and liberation movements of the exploited workers and peasants in the capitalist and colonial countries practical red aid and unifies them in their struggle."[2]

Predecessor of International Red Aid was International Workers Aid (Internationale Arbeiterhilfe), founded in Berlin in September 1921 to aid the famine-stricken Soviet people in the early days of the Soviet state and to provide industrial and technical assistance.

---

*Acronym for Society for the Aid of Revolutionary Fighters

Its purpose enlarged after 1923 to support workers' struggles in capitalist and colonial nations. Among its founders and supporters were Clara Zetkin, Albert Einstein, Romain Rolland, Martin Anderson Nexo, Anatole France, Henri Barbusse, George Bernard Shaw, W. Munzenberg and many other prominent people; many of these became active in the IRA. The organization's central committee was located in Berlin until 1933 when it could no longer function under Nazi terror. It moved to Paris and ceased to exist in 1935, but its national sections joined existing anti-fascist popular front organizations or helped to create new ones. IRA affiliates throughout the world played a central role in mobilizing anti-fascist protest, defending trade unionists and rallying support for victims of racist and national oppression. In the pages of the *Labor Defender,* writers representing the world democratic movements told the stories and made the appeals that moved thousands of U.S. trade unionists to action. International Red Aid was a pioneer in the field of human rights on a global scale.

4.

The Transformation of Elaine

Elaine's First Demonstration

Ed's father and his trade union friends kept after him. They asked, "how come we weren't in the movement?" Elaine listened to the discussions. "Ed, of course, knew more about it than I did." While Elaine's background was sheltered, she was aware of having been "exposed to some of the things that were happening in the movement... On the other hand, I had whatever I wanted. I was a spoiled brat."

Nathan and Mollie, meanwhile, felt the effects of the depression; business waned and creditors got tough.

Ed and Elaine agreed to meet another couple after an unemployed demonstration in downtown Los Angeles. They would all then go on to dinner and a show. Elaine, however, refused to participate in the demonstration. She argued about the role of the police, claiming that when they reacted, it must be because they were provoked by demonstrators. "It's probably the things you're saying, and maybe somebody is kicking them or something," Elaine argued. She thought the police couldn't be as bad as people said they were.

The plaza, site of the demonstration, was a shambles when Elaine and Ed arrived. Their friend was nowhere to be seen, although his wife soon showed up. She had heard that some people had been arrested. Elaine and Ed walked with her to the office of the ILD.

The ILD office was dark, but the Communist Party office was in the same building and there they found the husband and about 25 others excitedly exchanging experiences. Among them was a group of Japanese men; one was being congratulated by the others. It seems, Elaine said, that he "saw this cop who was about six feet tall coming at a worker from the back with his club raised. He used jujitsu and floored the big cop." Some demonstrators had been arrested and put into a patrol wagon. But, with the big policeman temporarily out of action, those arrested simply got up and walked away. Among the group of Japanese men was a young man named "Karl Hama."* Elaine was destined to meet him again. It was clear that he noticed her.

Elaine urged her friends, "Let's go, let's go! We have our reservations at the restaurant."

"At the height of the depression, I was worried about the reservations . . . and dressed in a semi-evening gown – a cocktail gown of layers of georgette with rhinestone trimming, rhinestone belt. I don't know whether the slippers were silver or not, but they blended in with the rhinestones, to say the least . . . I kept saying, 'Let's go, let's go.' "

"Just a minute, just a minute," their friend delayed them.

"And just as I was saying again, 'Let's go. We are going to be late,' the door was flung open."

"You're not going anywhere!" a voice announced.

Enter "Elaine Black"

It was the Red Squad carrying sawed-off shotguns. An older woman refused to sit down when ordered to by the police. Elaine was shocked. "They took her and tossed her up against . . . [a] chair so that it broke under her, and she just lay on the floor, in great pain." The police started taking names. Eddie's nickname was Blackie and when the police asked Ed for his and Elaine's names, Elaine quickly broke in, "Eddie and Elaine Black." Ed followed suit; it would have meant his job if he had given his real name. A cop pulled at Elaine's hand. " . . . I was wearing my wedding ring and the diamond solitaire . . . he turned my hand and it really hurt . . . " "What did you say your name was?" "Elaine Black." And that was how "Elaine Black" was born! Elaine used the name thereafter and so did Ed when he joined the TUUL.

Elaine and Ed were finally released. It was clear to the police that "we were going someplace, and I was obviously overdressed" (for a demonstration). A cop said, "You can go but don't ever let us catch you with these red Russian bolsheviks again," recalled Elaine. "Actually, I don't know if there were any Russians there . . . it looked to me like there were more Japanese." The friend who had escaped from the paddy wagon was re-arrested.

---

*Karl Yoneda used the name "Hama" in his political work to protect family members who lived in the Los Angeles area.

The Red Squad was led by Captain William F. "Red" Hynes who began as an undercover agent for the Los Angeles Police Department in 1922. By 1930, police intelligence bureaus, encouraged by the FBI's J. Edgar Hoover, flourished in cities across the country. Hynes was the most infamous of the local Bolshevik hunters and the L.A. "Red Squad" was noted for its brutality. Before long, Elaine would see a lot of Hynes and the Red Squad.

Unemployment Demonstration

As unemployment grew into the millions, the TUUL and the Communist Party undertook to organize the frustration and rage of hungry jobless people. Unemployed Councils were the form; they rose in cities and towns, in neighborhoods and blocks. They demanded food for hungry children, unemployment benefits, anti-eviction statutes, anti-discrimination measures, no pay cuts, health care, maternity benefits, and housing for the homeless.

March 6, 1930, was set as a day of national protest, and hundreds of thousands surged into the streets in New York City, Detroit, Chicago, Pittsburgh, Milwaukee, Minneapolis, Philadelphia, Cleveland, Youngstown, Boston, Seattle, Denver, San Francisco, Los Angeles – in at least 30 cities and towns across the country.

Elaine got a babysitter for Joyce and went downtown to watch the demonstration. It was one of the biggest protests in Los Angeles' history and, said Elaine, "hundreds were arrested and beaten – some were almost clubbed to death." Nationwide, March 6th marked the historic day that the unemployed and homeless – poor farmers, Black workers and sharecroppers in the deep South, miners in Appalachia – all became a strategic political force to be reckoned with. Elaine, too, would never be the same.

She approached the rally site near City Hall at Main and First streets. There was an orange juice stand set up in a nearby parking lot. From across the street Elaine noticed that an elderly woman was holding a glass of juice. Suddenly six plain clothesmen – Elaine learned afterwards that they were members of the Red Squad – converged upon the woman. "She didn't provoke the police ... They just swooped down on her and dragged her away, the glass she had in her hand was shattered." They twisted her arms behind her back and "threw her into a patrol wagon." Elaine heard her appeal to the police to stop hurting her and ask why they were arresting her. "Her voice rose, and I thought, my God, she wasn't doing anything... She wasn't tossing leaflets up in the air... [or] saying let's take over City Hall. She had a glass of beverage to her mouth." Elaine was shaken. When she found out that the ILD would defend the woman, she knew she had to take a stand. She went to the ILD office and offered herself as witness for Lillian Silverman, a garment worker.

"I Shouldn't Remember What I Was Wearing"

"Well, I must say they sort of looked out of the corners of their eyes at me. Here is a young woman, obviously well-dressed in the middle of the depression... offering her services out of the blue as a witness... I shouldn't remember what I was wearing, but I had a sort of cossack hat of mock caracul, a short jacket of the same material, a blue dress that was bordered with the same material. Therefore I had brown shoes, a brown purse and brown gloves that blended in with the caracul. It wasn't exactly brown, but a sort of camel color. The height of fashion at the height of the depression."

They took Elaine's name and address and when Silverman was put on trial on charges of refusing to move on, disturbing the peace and rioting, Elaine – who had never before been in a courtroom – did testify. She was 23 years old. She was incredulous as "Red" Hynes told the court that Elaine was "a well-known Communist and getting Moscow gold. And this is under oath. I just didn't know what he was talking about. I was not a member of the Communist Party and didn't become one for another year . . . the judge was very partial to the prosecution."

The judge asked, "Supposing this country was at war with Russia. Whose side would you be on?" "I would have to know who the attacker was first, and then I would decide." Elaine added later, "Now if I had known anything about court procedure, I would have told the judge he was out of order. It had nothing to do with the case... " When she was asked about Eddie, who was working on March 6 and wasn't at the protest, "I got on my high horse. 'If you want to question him, subpoena him.' " The ILD people and the spectators were impressed. This woman caught on fast. She had a quick mind and a tongue to match.

Elaine Joins the ILD

Elaine thought Silverman would get off. How could any jury convict her? But it did. For Elaine that was the last straw. She joined the ILD on April 1, 1930, becoming a member of the Tom Mooney Branch. The movie industry hit a slump; Eddie was laid off and they moved back in with her folks. He joined the Unemployed Council; she went to work in a grocery store and started going more regularly to ILD meetings. This pattern continued for almost a year. Then Elaine was offered a job in the ILD office. ILD organizer Ida Rothstein told the staff they needed a trained office worker, one who would not be scared to go into a police station and ask questions and post bail. Elaine fit the bill; she took the job while Rothstein got complaints from "people in the [Communist] party as well as the ILD district council; how come she hired someone so inexperienced and so young to be in charge of the office?"

Rothstein stood by her decision, recognizing that this young woman had innate qualities of leadership, spoke well, and would not be easily intimidated. The job paid $10 a week, slightly less than the grocery. She went to work for the ILD on February 9, 1931. It was at a time when beatings, jailings, and murders of workers by company thugs, police and vigilantes were intensifying across the country. Three Black men were shot to death on August 4, 1931, as they participated in an anti-eviction struggle in Chicago; five workers, including two Young Communist League members, were killed at the Detroit hunger march in March, 1932; two Textile Workers Union officials were deported to England. Workers were brutalized and killed on picket lines and in unemployed demonstrations.

Elaine's job, like that of all ILD staff, was

> To defend workers who are arrested, not for any crime, but for union, political, or working class organizational activity. It also opposes and fights for repeal of all laws designed, not to suppress crime, but to enable the financial interests to use the courts against labor. Its function is to provide legal defense, bail, mass campaigns, prison relief and aid to the families of prisoners.*

Those arrested were urged to telephone the ILD, which defined itself as "the legal department of the working class – the organized

---

*from ILD Statement of Purposes

machinery behind which workers are united to defend the class interests. An injury to one worker is an injury to the whole working class."

> The prisoner who sits behind bars imposes a special obligation not only on ILD members, but on all toilers . . . they must be shown that they are not forgotten. They are hemmed in by stone walls and steel bars, closed off from the outside world. The barbaric prison regime of the United States does not recognize the existence of political prisoners . . . the ILD sends relief regularly each month to the political prisoners in jail . . . [to] make life in jail more endurable . . . [it] sends relief every month to the families of political prisoners and of those who have been killed in the class war.*

Branches adopted prisoners and prisoners' families, wrote letters to them, sent them money for incidentals to make prison life a bit easier, and conducted a special winter relief campaign to provide Christmas gifts, especially for prisoners' children. They organized visits to prisoners and delegations to prison wardens and commissions demanding that prisoners be allowed to receive letters, books and newspapers.

In 1933 the organization of children's ILD branches was undertaken, the most important function being "to counteract the poisonous influence of the schools, which teach our children to hate the organizations of the working class, to be ashamed of its heroes who are sent to jail for fighting their battles." "Young Defender" groups were established. Members wrote poems and drew pictures for the "Young Defenders Corner" in the monthly *Labor Defender*. They marched in parades, wrote letters to political prisoners and corresponded with children in foreign lands. In San Francisco, when the Youth Defenders held an integrated demonstration protesting discrimination against Blacks at Doug's Barber Shop in the Fillmore district, three carloads of police attacked, arresting four youths and beating others.[1]

Working-Class Defense

Elaine educated herself about the legal defense movement. She learned that the need for working class defense and relief in the

*From ILD Statement of Purposes

United States was as old as the 1776 revolution. ILD literature told her that as long ago as "the great strike movement of 1877, small defense groups came into being but none of them were permanent. None of them had any clear program or policy except defense of the one or more victimized workers – usually strikers." That pertained to the Haymarket Square martyrs of 1886 in which the defense movement "died with . . . heroic speeches on the scaffold," as well as to the 1892 Homestead Steel strike that resulted in acquittal of strike leaders and strikers – thanks in large part to a $75,000 defense fund contributed by the AFL – but which left the labor movement bereft of any kind of permanent defense structure. This was true of the 1903 defense committee formed around the Western Federation of Miners; the union leaders were acquitted, but despite thousands of dollars collected, the defense movement collapsed when the case was over.

This was the general rule, the single exception being the Mooney Molders Defense Committee. "When the next act of terror made it necessary to organize a defense for the victims, all the terrific work of gathering forces had to be done from the beginning. Debs, Joe Hill, Mooney, Billings, McNamara, Ettor, Giovinetti, the leaders of the Lawrence textile strike, Sacco-Vanzetti – all these leaders of the working class faced trial with defense committees behind them, but different ones in each case."

The "common and basic defect" of all of these committees was the "belief that it was possible for a worker to get justice in a ruling class court." The ILD set a more militant course which included mass protests and pressure on the court system. "We defend our prisoners in these courts because the system under which we live forces us into these courts. But we know what they are. We have no illusions."

The ILD replaced the Workers Defense Union, the National Defense Committee and the Labor Defense Council – the earlier organizations composed of IWW members, Socialists, and liberals – but none of which had set up a national apparatus. "The class struggle was growing fiercer every day. Victims increased in number. A permanent, national organized defense movement became a vital necessity," and so the June 1925 national conference establishing the ILD out of the remains of existing defense committees and, especially, the trade union movement, was a great success.

From exile in the Soviet Union, William D. "Big Bill" Haywood said the ILD was the "Red Cross of the labor movement." It was, he said, "the duty of every American worker to support" it. "Voices from prison – the graves of living men," he said, "will come to thank you for your deeds." By the early 1930s when Elaine joined up, the ILD had 800 branches in 47 states.

Elaine learned the organizational structure of the ILD. The basic unit was the branch; a designated number of branches formed sections which in turn united into districts. National conventions were held every two years; these elected a national executive committee that appointed a smaller body to function on a daily basis between executive committee meetings. The only compulsory duty of members was to pay dues. Employed members paid 20 cents per month; the unemployed paid two cents per month.

Ruling-Class Terror

ILD activists were never allowed to rest on their laurels. General Secretary J. Louis Engdahl, after a tour of some of the large districts in July-August, 1930, was critical that branches were not adequately meeting national and international crises. "The growing unemployment continues to arouse and sharpen the discontent of the impoverished masses. The resulting protest meets more and more ruling class terror. It takes the form of attacks by the police, lynchings, injunctions, deportations, mob attacks and the creation of new extra-legal organizations, such as the American Fascist Association and Order of Black Shirts."

It was, he said, a period of "intensified war preparations" accompanied by "a new barrage against militant workers" with thousands of new arrests. ILD organizers, he said, must "root the organization in the workshops of the nation," and must "combat lynching, race discrimination and all forms of Jim Crowism," do better work among the youth and foreign-born, and develop better work among farmers – especially in the South.

Engdahl urged "the rousing of the whole organization in support of the oppressed masses, especially in aid of the rising revolutionary struggles in the colonial and semi-colonial countries and the colonies of American imperialism [the Philippines, Cuba, Virgin Islands, Hawaiian Islands, Puerto Rico]."

Working for the ILD, Elaine would find, was an all-consuming job but she would fit in and grow with it. She was a "natural."

Posting Bail for "Karl Hama"

On February 10, 1931, the day after Elaine went to work for the ILD, there was another unemployed demonstration at City Hall. Among those arrested was the young Japanese-American, "Karl Hama," a farm worker organizer active in the unemployed movement, and director of the Los Angeles ILD office. Karl was a young revolutionary born in 1906 in the U.S. but educated in Japan. To escape being inducted into the Japanese Imperial Army, he returned to the U.S. in December 1926, and joined the Communist Party in 1927.

At the demonstration, Karl had been viciously beaten up by police. The ILD people searched the jails but didn't find him. A photo series in the *Los Angeles Times* showed Karl holding up a sign, "Our Children Need Food," a plainclothesman approaching him from behind. The next frame showed him lying on the ground, the third being lifted up, bloodied and unconscious. A French seaman who helped the fallen Hama was later deported for taking part in the "Red" demonstration.

On the third day after the demonstration, "Red" Hynes called the ILD and said, "Come and pick up the Jap, he's dying anyway." Elaine and Anna Kanatz, member of the ILD Bail Fund Committee, rushed to the jail, posted bail, and took the badly-injured Hama to a doctor. "He was a bloody mess," Elaine said. "The bandages had not been changed on his head. Everything was still covered with blood."

The two women "stood out like shining stars," Karl recalled. The meeting in jail marked the first time that Elaine and Karl exchanged words, although she had glimpsed him a year earlier in the ILD office and Karl had seen Elaine and Ed at meetings. Karl was found guilty of "disturbing the peace" and served 90 days in jail. He was intrigued by Elaine and wrote her a poem while in jail; it spoke of her "big smiling eyes . . . youthful gestures" and "fighting spirit."

The Scottsboro Case

On March 25, 1931, in Scottsboro, Alabama, nine young Black men, ranging in age from 13 to 20, were jailed on a rape charge. Clarence Weems, Clarence Norris, Andy Wright, Haywood Patterson, Olin Montgomery, Willie Robertson, Ozzie Powell, Roy Wright, and Eugene Williams were quickly tried and convicted in a rabid lynch mob atmosphere. Eight of the nine were sentenced to death in the electric chair. On April 2, the *Daily Worker* in New York and on

April 4, the *Southern Worker* published in Chattanooga, Tennessee, carried stories on the racist frameup.

The ILD immediately demanded a stay of execution and sent New York Attorney Joseph R. Brodsky to work with Irving Schwab, also of New York, and George Chalmers of Chattanooga to stop the legal lynchings. Under the direction of General Secretary J. Louis Engdahl, the ILD launched a national and international campaign to save the lives of the youths. While the defense committee broadened out in the next few years and there were struggles for control of the case – mainly with the NAACP – the ILD and the Communist Party led the mass campaign. Protests erupted all over the world.

Brodsky was soon to become the ILD representative on the executive committee of the American Section of the International Juridical Association (IJA) which provided – through the years – comprehensive review and analysis of the Scottsboro case in the pages of the *IJA Bulletin.*

The *IJA Bulletin* in the United States long outlasted the life of the organization's German founder. Dr. Alfred Apfel founded IJA in 1931 in Berlin to fight fascist repression. It was he who pursuaded the brilliant New York lawyer, Carol King, to establish a U.S. section. "Within a few months, the American Section had an office and an executive committee drawn from across the country including Carol King, secretary; her associate Sol Cohn, treasurer; Osmond K. Fraenkel, representing the American Civil Liberties Union; Joseph Brodsky, representing the ILD; Roy Wilkins, representing the NAACP; a group of highly respected professors and scholars . . . and a number of writers . . . "[2]

Dr. Apfel was arrested in Berlin in early 1933. The word came that the "international head of the IJA had died in custody, apparently as a result of torture."

The IJA preamble put it solidly in the political Left:

> Present America offers the example of a country discarding traditions of liberty and freedom, and substituting legislative, administrative and judicial tyranny. This country, once known to the world as the haven of refuge of oppressed peoples, now excludes, or deports, those daring to voice unpopular opinions; with a Constitution supposed to protect freedom of expression, it now persecutes and imprisons its political dissenters . . .

Its program was complementary to that of the ILD:

> . . . combat repressive legislation and resist increasing executive, judicial and Administrative oppression; support progressive legislation; support the defense of political prisoners, especially in the courts; expose and attack abuses in the administration of the law; combat oppression for political opinion, color, race, creed, sex, or religious belief of lack thereof . . . support workers and their organizations seeking to ameliorate and improve their conditions and against the forces of the state wherever the latter aligns itself on the side of special privilege; help establish in this country and throughout the world social and legal justice . . . [3]

The IJA became an important resource for progressive lawyers.

Scottsboro Mothers

Five Scottsboro mothers worked closely with the ILD to save their sons. Ada Wright, mother of Andy and Roy Wright, had never traveled outside of Tennessee when she accompanied Engdahl on a tour of Europe in 1932. International Red Aid arranged meetings in Germany, France, Belgium, Holland, England, Norway, Sweden, Denmark, Czechoslovakia, Austria and the Soviet Union. In Germany, fascist officials forbade meetings in Cologne, Frankfurt and Munich. In Leipzig, Hanover, and Berlin, meetings were broken up. In Leipzig a German worker was shot for demonstrating. German newspapers attacked Albert Einstein and Thomas Mann for supporting the protests. Bulgaria and Belgium deported Mrs. Wright and Engdahl while Czechoslovakia drove them out and England tried to deny them visas. U.S. embassies in all of these countries received scores of demands for justice for the Scottsboro youths. The long strenuous tour ended in the Soviet Union. Totally exhausted, Engdahl contracted pneumonia and died there on November 21. He was 48 years old.

William L. Patterson, ILD national secretary and *Labor Defender* editor, was asked to head the ILD during Engdahl's absence. He took charge of the defense campaign after Engdahl's death. So massive in scope and so exposing the nature of Southern racism did the case become that *The Jackson County Sentinel* of Jackson, Mississippi, said the Scottsboro Boys defense campaign was "the most dangerous movement launched in the South in many years."

Later, based on the Scottsboro case, the White Legion of Alabama would propose a bill "which would make it impossible for an out of the state lawyer to practice in the state of Alabama to the extent of embarrassing our courts and juries." One "embarrassment" was the courageous act of 15 Black residents of Scottsboro who dared challenge the southern court system that convicted the Scottsboro youths by testifying in 1933 that they were as qualified as whites to be grand jury members.

The mothers continued to tour, leading marches and delegations, speaking at churches and rallies. In New York City in 1933, they led 100,000 May Day parade marchers. On May 6, there was a Scottsboro March on Washington:

> Upon their arrival in Washington, the marchers, now 3,000 strong, lined up four abreast, with arms linked, and marched to the White House, where a delegation composed of James Ford, William Patterson, and Ruby Bates demanded to see the President. They were received by Presidential Secretary Louis Howe, who announced that the President was "too busy" to discuss the case with them. The marchers thereupon proceeded to the Capitol, where the delegation presented a twenty-four-part civil rights bill, mandating an end to discrimination, peonage, and lynching, to the Vice-President and Speaker of the House, and demanded "congressional action for the unconditional release of the Scottsboro boys."[4]

Patterson wrote later that "from the very start the Scottsboro defense was mass defense, supplemented by the best available legal defense – but mass pressure, nationally, internationally, mass pressure of Negro and white united in protest against the vicious lynch frameup of nine innocent Negro boys." In the first year of the case, the ILD three times won stays of execution; by 1934, six stays had been won.

Elaine Promoted

The Mooney-Billings case was reaching a plateau when the Scottsboro case started. Mooney's death sentence had been converted to life imprisonment; he remained under life sentence in San Quentin, Billings in Folsom. And in Kentucky, in "Bloody Harlan County," so-called because of the violence used against striking miners by thugs, vigilantes and police, terrorism reigned and mine leaders were jailed on charges of murder; the Harlan County case became another national focus of the ILD.

Elaine recalled the atmosphere in Los Angeles as "a mass violation of civil rights. The right to speak, to assemble, the right to petition were all being violated by the Red Squad. Working at the ILD you were constantly under threat of being invaded by the Red Squad. Several times they did come in and make a shambles of the place."

A *Labor Defender* article termed this "undercover warfare." A constant "snooping into people's homes and activities. A constant combing of the city goes on, with 31 stoolpigeons and a Red Squad on the job, to identify and frame-up all active, militant class conscious workers... Let any one make a radical statement... take part in a demonstration, or attend a left-wing or communist meeting ... and a dick is on your heels... And then the head of the Intelligence Buro, Lieut. Wm. F. Hines... has you on his list. His men are spying in every organization..."

Elaine soon became ILD district secretary. Her job was to keep track of and inform ILD district organizer Ida Rothstein or ILD worker Lillian Goodman who had been arrested, where they were jailed and what was the bail. The ILD never used bail-bond brokers. Bail money was raised by loans as small as $5 as well as comparatively large loans from people who had equity in property; funds were put into a revolving fund. Police often charged leftists with "suspicion of criminal syndicalism," a felony that carried no bail; the police could keep people in jail for 72 hours just on "suspicion."

The Criminal Syndicalism Act had been adopted in California on April 30, 1919, to attack the IWW; throughout the 1920s it was used to harass the Left and became a major legal device to clamp down on Communists and labor. The statute read:

> Section 1. The term "criminal syndicalism" as used in this act is hereby defined as any doctrine or precept advocating, teaching or aiding and abetting the commission of crime, sabotage (which word is hereby defined as meaning wilful and malicious physical damage or injury to physical property), or unlawful acts of force and violence or unlawful methods of terrorism as a means of accomplishing a change in industrial ownership or control, or effecting any political change.
>
> Section 2. Any person who:
>
> 1. By spoken or written words or personal conduct advocates, teaches or aids and abets criminal syndicalism or the duty, necessity or propriety of committing crime, sabotage, violence or any unlawful method of terrorism as a means of accomplishing a change in industrial ownership or control, or effecting any political change; or

2. Wilfully or deliberately by spoken or written words justifies or attempts to justify criminal syndicalism or the commission or attempt to commit crime, violence or unlawful methods of terrorism with intent to approve, advocate or further the doctrine of criminal syndicalism; or
3. Prints, publishes, edits, issues or circulates or publicly displays any book, paper, pamphlet, document, poster or written or printed matter in any other form, containing or carrying written or printed advocacy, teaching, or aid and abetment of or advising criminal syndicalism; or
4. Organizes or assists in organizing, or is or knowingly becomes a member of any organization, society, group or assemblage of persons organized or assembled to advocate, teach or aid and abet criminal syndicalism; or
5. Wilfully or by personal act or conduct, practices or commits any act advised, advocated, taught or aided and abetted by the doctrine or precept of criminal syndicalism, with intent to accomplish a change in industrial ownership or control, or effecting any political change; Is guilty of a felony and punishable by imprisonment in the state prison not less than one nor more than fourteen years.
Section 3. If for any reason any section, clause or provision of this act shall by any court be held unconstitutional, then the legislature hereby declares that, irrespective of the unconstitutionality so determined of such section, clause or provision, it would have enacted and made the law of this state all other sections, clauses and provisions of this act.
Section 4. Inasmuch as this act concerns and is necessary to the immediate preservation of the public peace and safety, for the reason that at the present time large numbers of persons are going from place to place in this state advocating, teaching and practicing criminal syndicalism, this act shall take effect upon approval by the governor.*

Charges lesser than criminal syndicalism carried bail of varying amounts. Sometimes when arrests were heavy, it took time to raise bail. "There was no instant getting out of jail," Elaine said. "You had to stay in – sometimes overnight, sometimes longer."

*The Criminal Syndicalism Act is still on the books in California

5.
Commitment

Elaine Joins the Communist Party

"Workers! Prepare Your Defense!" was a 1931 ILD slogan. There was "greatly increased terror, strikes, lynching..." What was necessary, the ILD said, was development of a "class struggle defense policy" built "from the bottom up" and the "character of the ILD as an independent class organization must be clarified." The ILD emphasized many times that it was only "through a broad united front from below that we will be able to win and maintain leadership in these struggles..." There was the problem of arrests running "into hundreds and thousands daily," and it was not always possible to provide sufficient legal help; therefore a self-defense strategy for those capable of defending themselves also needed to be developed.

Elaine was still new to ILD work in the fall of 1931 when the Los Angeles chapter decided to organize a broad defense conference; 100 organizations, including 26 AFL unions, sent delegates. The conference decided to hold a mass meeting on October 30 at the Philharmonic Auditorium around the Scottsboro, Mooney-Billings, and Harlan County cases. This was an ambitious project – the Philharmonic was Los Angeles' largest hall.

Thousands of leaflets were prepared and distributed; Elaine was impressed by the hard and effective work of the Communists in the ILD, especially the women. Most of the women she worked closely with were Communists – among them Ida Rothstein, Sadie Goldstein and Anna Kanatz. Elaine knew, too, that women Communists had been prominent in establishing the ILD itself. Rose Baron and Anna Damon, ILD national secretary, were among them; Elizabeth Gurley Flynn was already a legend in the Left and labor movements although she didn't join the Communist Party until 1937. These were spirited and highly capable women; Elaine was like that, too.

Holliday Cullimore, in her University of California Women's Studies Senior Thesis, *Communist Women Activists in the Interna-*

tional Labor Defense in the 1930s: Standard Bearers of Feminism, wrote:

> Communist Party Popular Front activism . . . was central to the radicalism in the thirties, and provided the stage on which many women activists performed during the thirties. This form of political activism provided women with an arena in which to put forth demands for social, material, and political justice in the face of the depravity presented by the depression.
>
> In the ILD, these women sought to achieve such goals by working to secure civil rights and justice for radicals, labor unionists, and ethnic and national minorities who were subject to fierce anti-communism, anti-unionism, racism and anti-immigrant sentiments.

While "these women did not take up the banner of feminism," Cullimore concluded, "their actions show that they kept the feminist standard flying by providing continuity, and laying the groundwork for the revival of feminism thirty years later." Cullimore was especially appreciative of Elaine's "fervor," which never left her, as we shall see.

Elaine joined the Communist Party on October 14, one week before the Philharmonic meeting. She was recruited by ILD District Organizer Ida Rothstein, a Russian émigré, also known as Ida Roth. Ida was a "forceful speaker – forthright . . . each word a pearl," Elaine said. A former needle trades worker, Rothstein had a long history of trade union organizing, including going to the mine fields and organizing miners as the legendary Mother Jones and Mother Bloor had done. Elaine considered Ida "viable and forceful," a woman who "participated in all the unemployed marches and demonstrations . . . a woman who dedicated her life to the betterment of mankind."

"Then," said Elaine, "having been at the conference and seeing the work of the party at that time, and having been called a Communist all the time at trials and in the newspapers, I joined . . . [but] to say it [the ILD] was all Communist was not so. You didn't have to be a Communist to be a member of the ILD, to work for it, to become a paid official, and to continue working for it." Elaine joined "because of the activity I saw of the Communist Party in the unemployed movement, in the fight against deportation, and I saw that they were the ones who were the most harassed . . . I thought there must be something there that the employer class wanted to see decimated. So I decided I would be a Communist." Eddie also joined.

"Agit-Prop"* and Youth Groups

Miriam Sherman worked with Elaine in those early days. Sherman's father was an active party member and their home a "meeting and eating place for comrades." A Young Communist League (YCL) member, Sherman became active in the ILD at the time of the Scottsboro case and "went to churches and organizations to raise money for their defense. We even had a traveling drama [agit-prop] group which performed in the open air, in parks, on street corners... and I was the collection speaker. We had street corner meetings all over Southern California, and circulated petitions, sent telegrams, raised money for defense, and... organized youth groups of the ILD... we had three lively functioning youth groups in L.A. and it was during this time that Elaine was giving leadership to this campaign.

"We also had the task," Sherman said, "of organizing defense of those arrested by the local Red Squad, those who were beaten up leading delegations to City Hall to protest the denial of free speech to the unemployed councils. Elaine told me that when she saw that the people working with her on the top committee of the ILD were Communists, she decided that joining the Communist Party was a good idea. She learned that the Communists were in the forefront of those struggles, and they were the most devoted and sincere."

Police Riot

Two thousand people showed up for the Philharmonic meeting. The ILD had made the arrangements and paid the $400 rent, quite expensive for those days. The Red Squad was there when Elaine arrived. "I went into the lobby, and Hynes met me: 'There's not going to be any meeting.' " As other committee members began to arrive and people milled around in the street, Hynes was shoving the protesting Elaine out of the building. It was getting dark. Suddenly the police launched a massive tear gas attack, lobbing over 100 tear gas bombs into the crowd. People were scattering to escape the fumes.

Elaine started walking up Hill Street, but screams from Pershing Square – across from the auditorium – drew her back. On a street corner, members of the Red Squad were beating a short little man "no bigger than I was." Elaine rushed over, put herself between the

---

*Agitation and Propaganda

police clubs and the man because they "had him down on his knees already, as short as he was, and I took some of the blows." She also fought back, kicking the policeman. The next thing she knew she was thrown into an open touring car. One of three arrested men in the back seat was the little fellow she had tried to defend. "The driver was Charles Evans, smallest man on the Red Squad who "wanted to show he was the toughest and he probably was . . . [for] beatings and smashing heads. He always wore gloves . . . brass knuckles under them." He hit Elaine; "I don't know how many blows I got . . . " The man Elaine had tried to defend said to Evans: "Ain't you ashamed, hitting a lady?"

"She ain't no lady," Evans replied, and hit Elaine in the breast. "I felt those brass knuckles and was pretty sore for a long time."

Reuben "Ruby" Winger was the man Elaine defended, although she didn't know him until they were on trial together. Later she said, "Yes . . . I kicked a cop that was beating Ruby; I turned around and kicked and probably hurt him, but that was the only area I could reach and I was trying to keep him from hitting Ruby's brains out . . . Sure, I kicked but it was after I'd seen an illegal act being committed."

What happened in the Square was in fact a police riot. The *Los Angeles Times* account said:

> With tear gas drenching Pershing Square while police, swinging night sticks, engaged in a furious battle with 1500 Communists and their sympathizers, downtown theater crowds numbering many thousands last night witnessed one of the most spectacular Red riots in years as plainclothes men and uniformed officers broke up the asserted Communist "Mooney-Harlan (Ky.) miner mass meeting and demonstration" scheduled for the Philharmonic Auditorium. "Red" Hynes told the Times that his department was not concerned with "protecting any asserted rights of known enemies of our government or with their fantastic and hair-splitting free speech rights."

The Betsy Ross Case

Elaine was taken to the Hill Street station. Other arrested women were being booked as she arrived. The L.A. *Times* identified them as Sylvia Cooper, Mrs. Tony Wiser, Sadie Klein and Betsy Ross. Elaine heard one of the women tell the booking officer that she was born in Poland; that worried Elaine. "That meant a Jewish woman would be deported to Poland for participating in a U.S. demonstration for Mooney, for the Harlan miners, for the Scottsboro Boys." Elaine refused to give her name and gave the ILD office as her address, hoping others being booked would take the cue and not answer questions about their citizenship.

Red Hynes was called in. "He said, 'So you won't . . . say who you are.' And he pulled me into another room. They had Eddie . . . in that room, beating him, he was a bloody mess. They said, 'You're going to look like that if you don't answer questions.' And they took me back. Hynes said, 'You're a flag waver.' I said, ' . . . then my name is Betsy Ross.' So the case became known as the Betsy Ross et al case, alias Elaine Black."

The arrested women were thrown together into solitary confinement with steel walls on all sides; their shoes were taken away. It was cold; there were no bunks, no blankets. All were charged with suspicion of criminal syndicalism, refusing to move and disturbing the peace. They were held 72 hours on the criminal syndicalism charge, then the charges were reduced to bailable misdemeanors. Bail was posted on the third day. The men's lot was similar: Eddie was charged with battery. Paul Walton, Reuben Winger and Louis Douglas were charged with disturbing the peace.

Walton was a young man referred to in the *Times* article as an "asserted Negro Communist" who had "climbed one of the taller palm trees in the park and sought to evade the [police] rush. He was sighted and efforts of police to dislodge him failed until a 'ten strike' with a gas bomb brought him skidding down the rough trunk."

The police removed Walton's shoes. "They had him treed and were making pulp out of his feet and legs," Elaine said. For the rest of his life, he walked with canes. The police version of the "riot" was that they "were forced to use tear bombs and night sticks to suppress the disturbance."

"Pressing forward in the face of a screaming mob," said the *Times,* "the officers drove the 'defense squads' through Pershing Square with the gas, until they reached Sixth Street, which was obliterated with the low-hanging and eye-smarting gas."

The Trial

The "Betsy Ross" case was Elaine's first trial as a defendant. She and Walton were among the four defendants who represented themselves. Leo Gallagher, well-known civil rights attorney, defended the others.

When Elaine's turn came, she entreated the jury: A finding of guilty would mean violating basic democratic rights of redress and petition. The public meeting had been called to petition for the freedom of a man named Mooney, wrongfully imprisoned for many years, for support of striking miners of Harlan County, Kentucky, who were being framed for murder, for the Scottsboro Boys – one only 13 years old – who had left their homes to look for work and found themselves framed for rape.

The courtroom was used as a forum to defend civil rights, free speech and assembly. Elaine emphasized to the jury that the meeting was to be held in a private auditorium for which rent had been paid. "We weren't allowed to go in," she told the jury. "The police stopped us. The tear gas was so thick there that night that the Biltmore Hotel had to be emptied. People didn't know what it was all about. Hundreds were exposed to the gas. They wouldn't have known there was such a meeting going on if the police hadn't violated the right to assemble."

The jury was out for a long time. All defendants were found innocent except the four who had defended themselves. The judge granted a motion for a new trial; the "Betsy Ross" case was eventually dismissed on appeal.

A Gutsy Lady

Elaine and Ed's marriage began an on-again, off-again thing. The final separation came in July 1932, when Joyce was five years old. Both Elaine and Ed were active in the movement. He participated in unemployed demonstrations and hunger marches. Elaine's work in the ILD was a 24-hour responsibility that often took precedence over her family life; that took its toll, as did Ed's increasing drinking. And when Ed was unemployed, it was a struggle just to keep food on the table; Elaine's salary of $10 a week couldn't do it. They wouldn't have made it at all had they not lived with Elaine's folks – a factor, however, that also made married life more difficult. They were finally divorced in January 1934.

Nathan lost the store; for lack of ready cash, his creditors closed his business. He put the few thousand dollars he and Mollie had left in the bank. Two weeks later, like banks throughout the country during the depression, it went broke. Nathan scraped enough money together to buy a small truck and sold candies and tobacco wholesale to groceries, drugstores, and cigar stands.

In the meantime, Elaine and Karl Yoneda often found themselves at the same meetings. He was in charge of bundle orders for the ILD *Labor Defender*. That meant ordering and distributing bundles of the paper to various groups for sale and distribution. He also helped to organize a Japanese branch of the Unemployed Council, was on the District Bureau of the ILD, and was active in anti-deportation struggles of Japanese activists. He continued to be inspired to write poetry to Elaine. She said later that she did not know "whether he was in love with me from the start . . . " During the "Betsy Ross" case, he penned the following lines:

Charged with "disturbing the peace" and "unlawful assembly"
She stands in the courtroom defending herself with calmness
Jotting down every word the prosecutor says about her
She occasionally turns to the "gallery" with a smile
How great she looks, her young body concealed in a black dress . . .
Comrade Elaine Black
Your lips represent proletarian emancipation and
Your bewitching eyes light the path of struggle
Your wavy hair signifies a banner of revolutionary triumph and
Your little delicate hands will shake hands of victory marchers
You are our leader, comrade and eternal revolutionary companion . . .

Remembering Elaine in those days, Miriam Sherman found especially wonderful her "bubbling enthusiasm, her unbounded dedication to the cause of justice, peace and freedom, and her total faith in the power of the working people. She was not only a member of our family," Sherman said, "she belonged to the world's family."

Exciting, Exhausting Days

Those were exciting, exhausting days for Elaine. National unemployment climbed toward 17 million. Every day saw new attacks on hungry, jobless people. Evictions were rife, and the unemployed councils moved furniture back into apartments and homes as soon as sheriff's deputies moved it out. There were constant rallies, marches and demonstrations. The ILD, with Tom Mooney's approval, launched a combined Mooney-Scottsboro-Harlan County appeal.

On July 11, 1932, Angelo Herndon, Black Young Communist League member, was arrested in Atlanta, Georgia, for his work with that city's Unemployed Committee. Main evidence against him was a leaflet addressed to "Workers of Atlanta! Employed and Unemployed – Negro and White . . . Men and Women of Atlanta." The flier urged the unemployed to demonstrate against the "fakers [who] grow fat off our misery . . . " by going to the county courthouse to prove "there is plenty of suffering in the city of Atlanta . . . demand immediate relief! Organize and fight for unemployment insurance at the expense of the government and bosses! Demand immediate payment of the bonus to the ex-servicemen."

Herndon was charged with "inciting Negroes to insurrection," – an old Georgia slave law – tried, found guilty, and sentenced to 18 to 20 years in prison; in Georgia that meant the chain gang. The campaign to free Herndon became another major national and international ILD crusade. Atlanta lawyers Benjamin J. Davis, Jr. and John Geer were in charge of his legal defense, although others, including Carol King of New York, also became involved. But it was the two native Georgians who risked the wrath of the KKK, putting their lives on the line. Davis moved to New York later and in 1944, was elected to the New York City Council, the city's first Black Communist City Councilman. (Peter Cacchione was the first Communist N.Y. City Councilman, first elected in 1941.)

Raids on Radicals

That same month, July 1932, 25,000 World War I veterans marched to Washington, D.C., in a national Bonus March, demanding promised service pay. They set up camp in Anacostia Flats. U.S. troops attacked the veterans and their families with tear gas and bayonets, killing two. This attack sounded the death knell for President Hoover's reign. Franklin D. Roosevelt won the 1932 election and would be sworn into office on March 4, 1933.

In the nation's farmlands, the economic crisis was as severe for farmers as it was in the cities for workers. Over one million farmers lost their farms in the early thirties. In the South, in defiance of Ku Klux Klan law, Black and white sharecroppers joined forces in the Sharecroppers Union.

In Los Angeles, not only was ILD headquarters attacked but

Elaine's home was invaded and wrecked. On January 15, 1932, a mass raid on a meeting of Communist Party members in Long Beach resulted in over 100 arrests. Of these, nine were Japanese Issei,* one was Greek and one a Hindu; they were all ordered deported by the Immigration Service. Because deportation to Japan and Greece could mean imprisonment or even death for them, the ILD arranged for them to be granted asylum in the Soviet Union.

Elaine and Karl worked together with Anna Kanatz and Sylvia Wexler to raise money for the fares. In addition to the ILD campaigns in the city, there were strikes of farmworkers in the lush agricultural valleys where vigilanteeism proliferated; the criminal syndicalism laws were a boon to the big ranchers as well as to the L.A. Red Squad. Anti-radical raids were becoming commonplace.

On the brighter side, the 1932 Olympic Games, held in Los Angeles that July, provided an exciting opportunity to dramatize the Tom Mooney case. While President Hoover was chairman of the American Olympics Committee, a National Counter Olympic Committee had been set up with Mooney designated as honorary chair. The crowd at the Olympic stadium was stunned when six young people, members of the YCL, doffed their outer clothing, leaped over the rail, and jumped into the arena. " . . . On the front and back of their shirts blazed in crimson letters the words 'FREE TOM MOONEY . . . ' they dashed around the track, 100,000 spectators . . . held spellbound at their courage and audacity . . . " As the four men and two women circled the track, in the stands a huge banner was unfurled by two more youths: FREE TOM MOONEY! They carried it to the front of the judges' stand where they stood as "throughout the grandstands leaflets by the thousands were hurled in all directions . . . 'FREE TOM MOONEY!' " The runners completely circled the track before "an army of heroic policemen, armed to the teeth, surrounded the young Communists, captured them without firing a single shot and took them away handcuffed . . . "[1] as Mooney sympathizers cheered. The six – Ann Davis, Jess Shapiro, Meyer Baylin, Edward Palmer, and Ethel and Russell Dell – were charged with suspicion of criminal syndicalism. The story circled the globe.

Black poet Langston Hughes, then living in the Soviet Union, wrote a poem for Mooney:

---

*Born in Japan

... all over the earth today
The workers speak the name ...

... the sound vibrates in waves

From Africa to China,
India to Germany
Russia to the Argentine,
Shaking the bars,
Shaking the walls,
Shaking the earth ...

Of course, the man with the title of governor
will be forgotten ...
On the scrap heap of time—
He won't matter at all.
But remembered forever will the name:

TOM MOONEY ... [2]

ILD Victories

Karl was arrested, then released, on February 11, 1933, when Hynes' Red Squad raided the John Reed Club in Hollywood; a special "Japan Night" was being celebrated. The police destroyed paintings and smashed furniture. Especially horrifying to Elaine was the mutilation by gunfire of a mural of the nine Scottsboro youths. "Each one had a bullet hole in the head."

The following day a delegation including Karl, Leo Gallagher, and members of the ACLU went to City Hall to protest. The City Council ordered them ejected. As they were being thrown out of City Hall by some 60 members of the Red Squad, Gallagher was so badly beaten that an ambulance had to be called, and Karl was dragged to a basement room where cops beat him so severely that he suffered internal injuries. Other men and women, too, were beaten unmercifully. However, the "delegates fought against their ejection and [Red] Hynes suffered a cut cheek and bruises," the *Western Worker* reported. Karl went to his sister's to recuperate.

By this time "I was attracted to Karl and I think he was attracted to me," said Elaine.

Elaine worked very hard in all of these cases. There were "almost daily arrests with the unemployed demonstrations, the evictions ... putting back furniture for the people who were evicted, going to

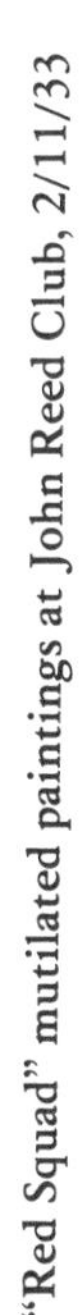
"Red Squad" mutilated paintings at John Reed Club, 2/11/33

whatever welfare agencies were available . . . there were constant arrests and constant going to the jails and putting up bail. It wasn't just an eight-hour shift. It was being on call 24 hours."

But the ILD was winning victories. "Mass-defense! That was the reason for the startling victories gained by the ILD . . . " said the *Labor Defender.* The ILD defended more than 5,000 workers in a one-year period of an "unparalleled number of arrests; deportations of workers who were not citizens . . . [and] Provocations and actual frameup cases against Negro workers . . . " The victories and partial victories included snatching – for the third time – the Scottsboro youths "temporarily from the chair," and convincing the U.S. Supreme Court to review the case. It also included winning not guilty verdicts in various labor and civil rights cases, and – working with the Committee for Protection of Foreign Born – winning asylum for two foreign-born workers, one a Venezuelan, the other Chinese.

Meanwhile, in Northern California four foreign-born residents of Jackson, in the Mother Lode mining country, were held in San Francisco for deportation. They had been arrested for marching in the May Day demonstration. Their homes were invaded and searched for "seditious literature." And across the Bay in Oakland, three men and a woman were arrested for speaking at an unemployed demonstration in front of the City Charities office. The struggles were never-ending, but the ILD could be counted on to swing into action.

Elaine "genuinely enjoyed the challenge of fighting an oppressive system and . . . communicated a vibrant warmth to all her co-workers," said Dorothy Ray Healey. And she learned. Always a gutsy lady, quick on the uptake, she was on her way to becoming a brilliant tactician. Her ringing voice was increasingly heard in the courtroom. Stylish always, she wore a proper hat and gloves and carried all four feet eleven inches of her – feet firmly planted in little high heels – with a smart air of knowing who she was and where she was going.

6.

To San Francisco

A Home with Karl

When an opening came up in the San Francisco ILD office, Elaine asked to be transferred. "I thought I needed a change of scene." Elaine was also beginning to get involved with Karl, and "I wasn't quite sure whether or not I was prepared to fight on another front – mixed marriage – and whether or not it was the right thing to do." Perhaps in San Francisco, she could figure things out, make a new home. Elaine left Los Angeles in April 1933. Joyce remained with her grandmother Mollie for three more years, spending vacations with Elaine.

On May 26, Elaine returned to the ILD office after a demonstration at the Hall of Justice. There was Karl. They looked at each other and whatever reservations Elaine had about their relationship dissolved. Karl had come to San Francisco to be the editor of *Rodo Shinbun,* Communist Party Japanese language paper, whose editor had been deported. He and Elaine moved in together that very day, defying the anti-miscegenation laws. They always considered May 26, 1933, as their anniversary date although legal marriage came later.

Ida Rothstein also came to San Francisco that year to work for the Communist Party as Fillmore Section organizer. She remained active in the ILD, and she and Elaine maintained a close relationship. Rothstein "was arrested many times, and harassed, but she kept right on."*

New Spirit in the Air

The year 1933 was a watershed year for resistance to despair and hopelessness. An angry people had watched the nation come to an

*In the 1950s, Ida Rothstein was killed by a hit-run driver

Karl and Elaine, spring 1933

economic standstill and the landslide vote for Roosevelt spelled a new day to millions of Americans. A new spirit was in the air, but the people remained hungry, jobless and homeless. Thousands of workers joined established AFL and independent unions. Across the country, significant numbers in auto, steel, the packinghouses, textile, mining and agriculture joined TUUL unions whose credo was the organization of "revolutionary industrial unions where there are no unions and in industries where the unions are corrupt and impotent."

There were strikes in auto, the shoe-making industry, the needle trades, mining, the packinghouses and agriculture. Particularly noteworthy was the 1933 strike of Detroit auto workers led by the

TUUL Auto Workers' Union; they won a shorter workweek and a more equitable pay scale. In May several thousand St. Louis, Missouri women nutpickers – most of them Black – struck the city's 16 R.E. Funsten pecan factories. The TUUL Food Workers Industrial Union, led by Communists, supported the women's demands, but the leadership came from Black women and for the first time, Black and white worked together on union committees. During the strike, which was won in spite of a fierce red-baiting campaign by the company, 11 TUUL unions were established and 100 women, mostly Black, joined the Communist Party.

The employers, vigilante groups, police and Red Squads took heed of all this militancy. They set up company unions, increased their use of scabbing, spying, informing, red-baiting, deportations, lynchings, mob violence, police attacks, and jail. The manufacture of armaments – guns and ammunition of all descriptions, tear gas, bombs and armored cars – to use against striking workers and jobless demonstrations became a big and profitable business.

Class Struggle in the Courtroom

Obviously, "class struggle begun on the streets or in the shop . . . [and] carried into the courtroom" required a new set of defense tactics and ILD National Secretary William L. Patterson – a lawyer himself – explained in the May 1933 *Labor Defender:*

> A lawyer has to concern himself only with the juridical aspects of the case. He is not asked to engage in the political defense of the accused, but his legal defense . . . It is not the lawyer who represents the working class in the capitalist courts. The ILD is the representative of the working class as is also the defendant. The lawyer is not engaged in the class struggle as a defender of working class interests nor does the sale or contribution of his services . . . make him one. It is the worker defendant who uses the court as his forum. It is he who introduces the social and economic questions so vital to an exposure of the court as a weapon of class rule. It is not the lawyer who politicalizes the defense struggles led by the ILD, but his legal defense which is politicalized by the ILD. A lawyer under the direction of the ILD is fighting for the constitutional rights of Negroes and of white workers as well, thus helping to politicalize the case . . .
>
> The center of support must be shifted from reliance upon "justice" dispensed in capitalist courts to reliance upon mass pressure . . . that

pressure must be supplemented by legal defense . . . [which] must be of the most expert character."

Tom Mooney Case

In San Francisco Elaine jumped into the struggles. The Mooney case continued to demand attention. One of Elaine's most vivid memories of that time was a big rally in Portsmouth Square in May 1933. A national Free Tom Mooney Congress had been held in Chicago that month; it was also the month that Mooney had expected to have a new day in court in San Francisco. Based on an unused murder charge in the original indictment, a new trial had been set. While a verdict here would not legally have altered his sentence, he saw it as an opportunity to expose the frameup.

Portsmouth Square, as described by Orrick Johns, sloped toward Kearney street, making a natural amphitheater that faced the Hall of Justice where Mooney was expected to be in court.

> By eight-thirty, the lower slopes of the 'amphitheater' are filled. The sidewalks lined. Farther up some workers crowd into place. They are coming by the thousands.
>
> Inside the hall there is breathless excitement, panic . . . Bluecoats line the corridors. Machine guns hide behind windows . . . Then begin the shouts. "Free Tom Mooney." Now the square reverberates with the shouting. The sound roars through the halls and chambers of the building. The lackeys of the law are alarmed. This is something new. The masses are taking part in the trial of a worker . . .
>
> . . . The Cossacks get busy. Mounted bulls spur toward the crowd, leap up the stone coping, charge on children and women. The demonstration breaks up slowly, faced with insurmountable odds. The workers separate, form again, shouting "Free Tom Mooney!" They gather in the street on the side of the square still shouting slogans.[1]

The mounted police rode into the crowd and for the next two hours, demonstrators were chased down, beaten, clubbed, and arrested. For Elaine it was "the first time in my life . . . [I was] run down by cops on horses who were swinging their clubs left and right; there were many who were bruised that day." Police on horses shoved people up against buildings and cars. A horse towered over Elaine, pressing her against a building wall; she was caught underneath, frighteningly aware that the man sitting on the horse "could really smash [her] brains out . . . "

Mooney was denied the right even to be in the courtroom that day. The judge blamed the demonstrators. The indictment on the one remaining charge was eventually dismissed and Mooney was robbed of his last legal redress to a court trial.

Elaine got very involved in the Mooney campaign, organizing meetings and raising funds. Everywhere, Mooney's name was a household word. The ILD organized a meeting for Mary "Mother" Mooney and Ada Wright, mother of two of the Scottsboro youths; it also arranged a joint international tour for the two mothers and called for "thousands and thousands of Negro and white workers to [come to] the defense of the boys. Workers in the factories must be reached . . . They should be told of the actions of the Cleaners and Dyers in Philadelphia who carried through a half hour Scottsboro protest strike."

An ILD pamphlet summed it up:

> Arising out of a ten year war of the California employers against all working class organizations, fought with a bitterness and a fury scarcely surpassed in all the history of the class struggle, the Mooney-Billings frameup has become the symbol of capitalist terror and suppression of the working class and its leaders.

Mooney saw himself as "the symbol of labor struggling for its rights." U.S. labor, he said, "is being shoved headlong into a state of peonage . . . while a few international bankers are becoming the crowned kings of the world . . . the fight for my freedom can become the center around which the workers will rally in their desperate struggle against unemployment, wage cuts and starvation."

In spite of desperately hard times, contributions to Mooney's defense actually increased, with most coming in nickels and dimes.

Elaine and Anita Whitney

Elaine worked often in the Mooney-Billings defense movement with Anita Whitney, charter member and elder stateswoman of the Communist Party. Though born with a silver spoon in her mouth, Whitney opted for a life of radical activism. Their paths crossed frequently, and she and Elaine became fast friends. Whitney, Elaine said, "was a gentle person who saw the need of bettering the conditions of workers." And as related by writer-historian Lisa Rubens, Anita Whitney "was particularly active with the ILD, raising money and visiting people in jail. One of the few Party members to own a car, she drove to Black cotton-growing communities in Fresno and Blythe, close to the Arizona border; to Filipino and Mexican harvesting camps in Coachella and Salinas. She spoke against segregation and for guaranteed wages and workers' compensation . . . The more she studied communist theory and party literature, the more she became convinced of the fundamental conflict between classes."[2]

Anita often acted as Elaine's "chauffeur," driving her to out-of-town meetings and rallies. "She was on the picket line, I was on the picket line. We would get arrested together," Elaine recalled. Whether defending political prisoners like Mooney or labor organizers in the succession of farmworker unions, Elaine was learning not only what it took to be a good ILD worker, but a Communist as well. Whitney was one of her teachers.

Leo Gallagher Goes to Germany

Elaine learned about international solidarity through the ILD's affiliation with International Red Aid. She was shaken when on June 22, 1933, – the year that Hitler seized power in Germany – IRA President Clara Zetkin died. Long marked for death by the fascist regime in Germany, Zetkin lived in exile in Moscow. She died there, blind and ill, but active until the end. A co-worker of Lenin, Zetkin was one of the world's leading Marxist revolutionaries. She developed much Marxist theory on the woman question and was the originator of International Women's Day, celebrated all over the world on each March 8th.

" . . . The work she started," said a tribute in the *Western Worker,* "will continue without flagging for a moment, carried on by the thousands of women trained, and the hundreds of thousands inspired, by Comrade Zetkin, to take her place."

In 1932 Zetkin had issued a stirring appeal to the world to "Save the Scottsboro Black youths from the pyre of the electric chair." A few days before her death, Zetkin called for an international "cry of indignation" against the German regime of barbarism where "tens of thousands have been thrown in jails, prisons and concentration camps."

> I urge you to take up as your own cause the cause of the fighters and the sufferers of fascism. Fie to the shameful persecution of other

races, particularly the indescribable shame of the Jewish pogroms! Toilers of all nations and races! Answer the Jewish pogroms in Germany with the struggle against fascism . . . Anti-fascists in all countries! I call upon you, together with the International Red Aid, to fulfill your solemnity of international solidarity.

"Wir Werden Nicht Vergessen" (We Will Not Forget), the ILD said. "The ranks of the working class the world over have lost a valiant and courageous leader." Women were both trained and inspired to take Zetkin's place in all manner of struggles. Elaine was one of them.

The U.S. ILD forged strong ties of anti-fascist solidarity before 1933 was over. ILD attorney Leo Gallagher, close co-worker of Elaine's, sailed for Europe, his destination Germany, where he would aid the defense of four Communists accused of burning the Reichstag. Before his departure, Gallagher warned: "I must have the mass support of the workers in the U.S. while I am in Germany. Without this my efforts will be futile."

One of those accused in the Reichstag fire was a Bulgarian named Georgi Dimitrov. On the day the trial started, anti-fascist protest demonstrations were held in front of German consulates in U.S. cities. The New York rally forced the consulate to close for the day.

Arrested in Germany, even though he held a power of attorney from Dimitrov, Gallagher was jailed, then expelled as an "enemy of the state." He undertook a European tour on behalf of the Reichstag fire defendants. By December, when the fascist court was forced to acquit him, Georgi Dimitrov had become famous the world over for his defiant and brilliant self-defense and exposure of the fascists.

7.

Vigilante Terrorism

Agricultural Workers Organize

Elaine's workload during 1933 increased at a rapid pace as strikers and union organizers took on California's big ranchers. In the state's fields, orchards and packing sheds, the Cannery and Agricultural Workers Industrial Union (CAWIU), successor to the TUUL, organized thousands of Mexican, Filipino, Japanese, Black and white workers. In 1933 the CAWIU often worked with the 10,000-member Confederacion de Uniones de Campesinos y Obreras del Estado de California. Desperation forced strike action in the state's verdant fields and orchards; peach pickers couldn't even eat on the $1.50 they were paid for 10 hours of picking and even that sometimes was cut to $1.00 or less.

As workers organized, so did the big farmers. In the Imperial Valley, "Cradle of Vigilantism," the Associated Farmers was formed that year to smash the union drive by means of coordinated statewide campaigns of terrorism. They often teamed up with the American Legion and others dedicated to "stamping out all un-American activity among farm labor." So systematic and violent was this antiunion drive that Carey McWilliams labeled it "the rise of farm fascism."[1]

Even in face of all the terror, however, farm workers' gains amounted to millions of dollars. Never before or since have there been so many farm workers on strike; waves of strikes hit 65 percent of the state's total crops. Between April and December, 1933, strikes involved 50,000 workers in 37 recorded and numerous unrecorded strikes in fruit, vegetables, and cotton. The CAWIU was the main union involved, providing militant leadership. Strikers sustained unprecedented violence and scores were arrested.

The ILD issued a new digest of instructions. "The recent struggles in the agricultural fields throughout California confront the ILD with the necessity for changing its methods to cope with the existing situation. We must be aware that these struggles are only preliminaries that will be followed by much fiercer combats." It instructed local branches of the ILD to immediately contact the strike committee of the union involved when a strike broke out, to help build morale through guaranteeing the strikers the best possible legal defense, assisting the organization of rank and file defense committees, keeping up to date on arrests and making sure strikers knew their rights when arrested, staying in touch with workers' families, and arranging for prison relief. Local publicity to win community support was also emphasized, as well as the organization of mass meetings and fund raising.

Posting Bail in Stockton

Elaine worked like a seasoned pro as strikes spread from one valley and crop to another valley and crop. At its peak, the ILD bail fund that Elaine coordinated reached $200,000, raised almost entirely from small loans and donations.

One particularly brutal strike was in the grape vineyards of Lodi; 11 strikers were arrested on conspiracy charges. Elaine needed to get to Stockton to post $1000 bail for strike leader Louis Yamamoto, but the town was cordoned off by vigilantes. Bail had to be posted with the Justice of the Peace at his home. The ILD car containing Elaine, farm worker organizer Pat Chambers and two other men was stopped at a roadblock by armed vigilantes. "They had been deputized. They wore stars but they had their pickhandles and sawed-off shotguns," Elaine said.

"Where are you going?" one demanded. "We're going to the Justice of Peace." "What are you going for?" Elaine grabbed the hand of the man sitting next to her. "We're going to get married and these are our witnesses." The vigilantes smiled, wished the happy couple good luck and let them pass. On arrival at the Justice of the Peace, Elaine posted the bail. "I thought he was going to have apoplexy. He turned purple."

Using her wits was Elaine's stock in trade, but all ILD workers had to learn this, she said. "We had to be alert and meet [the situation] head on. If I had said we were going to bail . . . [somebody] out, they could have killed us for that $1000 . . . They could have said they found the car overturned; they could do here in California like they did in the South all those years, with lynching and dumping bodies that you didn't find for years."

Cotton Strike

On October 4, 1933, a strike by cotton pickers from Tulare County on down to Bakersfield paralyzed the cotton industry. First a boycott of the ranches, then a strike involved 18,000 workers picketing on a vast 114-mile strike front. It lasted for 24 days, during which 19 new CAWIU locals were established. The workers were asking $1.00 per cwt. of cotton picked, up from 60 cents. There were mass arrests and roundups and, in Tulare, strikers were held incommunicado in a hastily constructed stockade. The Northern and Southern California districts of the ILD were both directly involved in the cotton strike. They raised bail for the arrested, made funeral arrangements for the murdered, organized protest meetings, and helped families left destitute.

It was a brutal strike. "And there were vigilantes," said Elaine, "and killings when vigilantes shot into a union hall." On October 12, in Pixley, ranchers surrounded the union hall and riddled it with gunfire, killing two. A third striker was killed at Arvin.

The massive arrests in the agricultural fields meant that ILD workers had to get to those areas, "going by bus or by train . . . [or] hitching rides because funds were low." The big ranchers with state and local governmental help continued their violent assaults on farmworkers, their halls, their homes, and their civil rights. When the ACLU attempted to hold a free speech meeting in Brawley, a "mob of ranchers . . . rounded up the visitors, threatened them with death, drove them from town at pistol-point and fired on them a few miles outside of the city." The visitors were "students, teachers and preachers" on a "good will tour" organized by the ACLU in order to receive "an inkling of the hardships and cruelties that the Imperial Valley workers are subjected to daily." When ACLU Attorney A.L. Wirin dared to come to town with an injunction to safeguard workers' rights, "he was promptly kidnapped and beaten and dumped far out in the desert."[2]

Most ferocious were the attacks on Mexican workers and their families. They burned workers out and used tear gas on men, women, and children. During the lettuce strike, a baby died when a camp of 2,000 lettuce pickers and their families was attacked with tear gas bombs. Strike leaders were railroaded to jail as were those who organized strike support; those convicted on criminal syndicalism charges drew long sentences and joined other and older political prisoners in San Quentin and Folsom.

A Lynching in San Jose

Elaine had vivid memories of the 1933 mob violence in San Jose, California. On the night of November 26, Thomas Thurmond and John Holmes, both white, were dragged from their jail cells by a screaming mob, lynched from a tree in the square across the street from the jail, and set afire. The two men had confessed to kidnapping and murdering the son of a San Jose department store owner. They had been held in San Francisco until moved to the San Jose jail. Governor James Rolph ignored the local sheriff's plea to send in state troops and gave his blessing to the lynch mob, declaring the following day that "it is the best lesson California has ever given the country," and commending "the patriotic citizens for the good job they did." A souvenir post card was sold on the streets of San Jose with a photograph of Thurmond's dangling body, the hanging tree in St. James Park surrounded by the mob.

The *Western Worker* termed the lynching "capitalist cultural degeneration . . . " The spokesmen for capitalism, it said, "were not really concerned with the lawlessness and savagery of the mob . . . they want to hold in reserve this savagery and mob spirit [for use] against the workers . . . "

The ILD demanded Governor Rolph's impeachment, and quickly organized a protest meeting in the same park. Two weeks later, 2,000 protesters came to San Jose. They heard John D. Barry, columist for the *San Francisco News* charge "there was connivance between the police and the hoodlums to carry through the lynching . . . there was ample opportunity to take them out of prison before the lynchers reached it . . . "[3] Jack Warnick spoke for the ILD whose position was "that this was . . . what was happening to the Negroes in the South . . . how many lynchings there had been . . . and did we want to emulate what took place in the South? . . . It was on that basis that we took up the issue. . . . Hecklers were far outnumbered by the protesters," Elaine said.

San Jose was not allowed to easily forget the hanging atrocity, being chosen as the site for a January 21 Western Regional Conference Against Lynching and Fascism. Purpose was to "lay the basis for an active campaign against terrorism against workers."[4] It was attended by 136 delegates from 11 western states. Poet Langston Hughes spoke for the League of Struggle for Negro Rights, and delegates "enthusiastically greeted the decision . . . to wage the broadest fight against lynching and other forms of terror that are spreading throughout the country," the *Western Worker* reported. There were, the paper noted, a good representation of Filipino, Chinese and Japanese delegates.

A similar conference in Portland, Oregon, drew 102 delegates, while in the deep South – in Birmingham, Alabama – 176 delegates participated in an anti-lynch conference. Meetings like these were organized across the country in response to a nationwide escalation of lynch terror.

8.

Voices from Prison

Prisoner Relief

The ILD organized monthly visits to Tom Mooney and Warren Billings as well as other labor prisoners in San Quentin and Folsom. A letter to the ILD from Mooney expressed gratitude for its support. "I will always try to live up to the highest traditions of the working class," Mooney wrote. Billings said the ILD was "the truest, staunchest friend."

"We had men, too," Elaine said, "like Matt Schmidt and James B. McNamara." They had been in prison since 1911, longer than any other labor prisoners in the U.S. McNamara was known as "Uncle Jim." He was sent to the "hole" many times for fighting for human rights within the prison's walls. For a time, Elaine was his sole contact with the outside. Schmidt was released on parole in 1939. McNamara died in prison in 1941.

The ILD in Northern California kept in touch with some 30 prisoners, providing each with $5 per month for incidentals, and fighting for their mail rights and to get reading material, including union newspapers, into the prisons. Nationwide, there were more than 250 labor prisoners. The ILD's "Prisoners' Relief Fund" helped to support prisoners' families "until their breadwinner is restored to them". What the $5 per month meant to prisoners was expressed by Billings: "It gives us hope as well as comfort – for it is something to look forward to – something we can depend upon – and it gives us a feeling of 'economic security,' for it assures us that we won't have to be begging other prisoners for smokes or stamps."

Another prisoner project was caring for the children of political and labor prisoners. They were considered "wards" of the ILD. "The ILD took it upon itself," said Elaine, "to see that the children had a little something each month – it wasn't much because some of the families were rather large." In some cases, ILD supporters would take children into their own homes while the children's parents were in jail. That was hard with money so tight during the depression, but they did it nonetheless.

In December 1933, Grace Lumpkin wrote in the *Labor Defender:*

> *Listen!*
> *Can you hear them?*
> *Can you hear the cries of the unemployed millions?*
> *Workers are in prison for demanding their right to jobs . . .*
> *There will not be any Christmas trees for our prisoners and their families. There will be nothing for them but misery . . .*
> *Unless . . .*
> *Unless we listen to them, to the voices from prison.*
> *Unless we send them our pennies, our dimes, and dollars—for them, and their families . . .*

Summer Milk Drive

Each year, the ILD held a "Summer Milk Drive" to raise milk money for the children of labor prisoners. "The monthly milk check sent them provides the only extra nourishment these deprived little ones have," an appeal said. One of the most disgraceful features of the Depression was the dumping of milk and burning of oranges to keep prices up. "In some areas," said Elaine, "they would give milk to the children instead of dumping it, but there was no school in summer" – so no milk. Nor was the aid only for children of U.S. political prisoners.

International Red Aid

There were children of Spanish refugees and children of political prisoners in Japan, about whom hardly anyone was aware; their parents opposed Japan's aggression against China. "So there were . . . men and women in jail in Japan, and attempts were made to see that they got some help." Some of these anti-war Japanese "wasting away in jail," Elaine said, remained imprisoned until released by the U.S. Occupation Army in 1945, but "unless you were connected with the International Red Aid, you wouldn't have known. . . . We would get bulletins . . . as to what was happening internationally." Merchant seamen coming into the San Francisco port sometimes reported directly to the ILD on repression against trade unionists, Communists and anti-fascists in Japan, Germany and in Latin American countries. Sometimes messages would be written on small scraps of paper, smuggled out of countries ruled by oppressive regimes and brought to the ILD in San Francisco by merchant seamen. The carriers of these reports were a special breed – "Men," Elaine said, "who had been tested through struggle."

Mainly, however, the source of international news was the *Labor Defender.* With International Red Aid affiliates in 31 capitalist and 33 colonial countries, and an international team of writers, reporters and activists who got the news to the *Defender,* it was without doubt the nation's most reliable source of accurate news on the struggles in those countries. "Around the World with ILD" and "On the IRA Front" were regular features of the magazine and did much to arouse people in the U.S. to action. American workers had a responsibility, in "looking after the interests of prisoners, of protecting them from the brutal prison regime and of giving them material assistance." The ILD's affiliation with IRA was a result of U.S. workers and human rights activists understanding that "terror was not confined to the shores of the U.S.A."

By late 1931 the IRA had reported that 34 of its national sections had been forced to work underground, with five more in transition to illegality due to growing repression. Only 25 legal organizations of the IRA were left. However, whether legal or not, the IRA spoke for millions; it had nearly nine million members, individually and through affiliated organizations. It had 61 publications throughout the world with a circulation of six and a half million, plus millions more of pamphlets and an ongoing circulation of leaflets and posters. Even under conditions of terrorism, IRA affiliates increased their activities in defense of political and labor prisoners.

Fascist Terror

The *Labor Defender* during 1933 and 1934 told of the dire conditions under which trade unionists and anti-fascists worked and struggled against fascism and repression in countries of Europe, Asia, South America and the Caribbean. Across the U.S. northern border, the Canadian Communist Party operated "underground" and A.E. Smith, head of the IRA affiliate, the Canadian Labor Defense League, faced trial under Canada's national criminal syndicalism law. Brave reporters and activists got the news out, often risking their lives. Reports originated in Italy, Germany, Spain, Austria, Greece, Yugoslavia, Poland, Hungary, Romania, Finland, Czechoslovakia, Bulgaria, Latvia, Serbia, Lithuania, China, Japan, India, the Philippine Islands, Cuba and other Caribbean countries, Mexico, Panama, Nicaragua, Honduras, El Salvador, Argentina, Brazil, Uruguay, Bolivia, Venezuela, and Peru.

The *Defender* carried on-going detailed reports month after month on life and death struggles in places where "terror against workers and farmers and intellectuals raged . . . " It agitated for solidarity actions. The ILD raised special funds to aid victims of fascism and flooded consuls of oppressive regimes with protest letters and resolutions; its affiliates and members picketed, marched, and held conferences to rally and organize more effective, bigger actions. Never before had U.S. workers extended the hand and heart of solidarity on such a scale to their brothers and sisters in other lands; never before had they received such support in their own fight against U.S. repression.

One little-known aspect of that period was the young Soviet government's refusal to accept the return of Russians whom the United States wanted to deport for revolutionary or labor activity. Since such refugees could be deported only to the country of their birth and then only if that country would accept them, these political refugees – mostly from Czarist days and mostly radicals – were able to stay in the U.S. and continue their contributions to the struggle. This was one aspect; the other was the Soviets' acceptance from the United States, and many nations of political refugees whose countries of origin were fascist or repressive and to whom such deportation meant imprisonment or death. The Soviet government allowed such refugees, ordered deported by the U.S. Immigration Department, to be voluntarily deported to the Soviet Union. The ILD helped carry out this policy, mainly by raising money for the fares.

Internationalism was commemorated on holidays with special activities. In the United States, May Day brought large pilgrimages to labor martyrs' graves, special sales of flowers and sashes to raise money for the prison relief fund, and ILD-organized parade contingents. The annual March 18 anniversary of the Paris Commune was celebrated similarly, and often included the organization of large delegations to visit prisoners; this was especially true in California, whose prisons held one-third of the country's long-term labor and political prisoners. In 1936 Elaine helped to organize the largest delegation in history to San Quentin and Tehachapi's Women's Prison; it was led by ILD national secretary Anna Damon.

Elaine Carries on Bail Work

In California, the Cannery and Agricultural Workers Industrial Union was being beheaded of some of its most capable leadership. The great strike wave in the agricultural fields waned, but workers did not capitulate and upsurges of defiant actions continued. In San Jose, ILD attorneys, charging police brutality, won acquittal of 13 cherry-picker strikers. Lawrence Emery, last of the 1930 Imperial Valley prisoners, was released from San Quentin.

Elaine carried on her bail work. The Associated Farmers intensified its collection of names and pictures of "dangerous radicals" in the fields, disseminating them to trouble spots, coordinating with local governments and vigilante groups. A police "mug shot" of Elaine was among them.

Elaine and Karl were by that time living in a fourth floor attic flat at the corner of O'Farrell and Laguna Streets. The toilet was on one floor and the bath on another, but they took what they could get as few landlords would rent to mixed couples. Elaine maintained her pert appearance in Court always wearing a hat and gloves and, even with money scarce, coordinating her outfits. "For a couple of years my basic coat was a green coat. I would try to have dresses and . . . (accessories) blend in." Newspaper photos confirm her ladylike appearance. She continued to use the name "Elaine Black," a name, said Walter Stack, "that was synonymous with the ILD. The outstanding thing about her in my mind was her complete absorption with the movement. She devoted her life to labor defense. She was the only woman on the 1934 Longshore Strike Committee."

9.

Trouble on the Waterfront

Maritime Workers Hit the Bricks

Trouble had long been brewing on the San Francisco waterfront. Stevedores' grievances were articulated in a mimeographed newsletter, the *Waterfront Worker,* issued "by a group of longshoremen for longshoremen," as early as December 1932. Vol. 1, No. 1 announced in a column "Christmas for the Shipowners" that . . . "It has been decreed that wages will be 75 cents an hour – a 10-cent wage cut . . . " The *Waterfront Worker* became, through the years, a place where longshoremen agitated, shared news, aired opinions and gripes, and told who the scabs were during strikes and job actions. The splendid little paper helped pave the way for the struggle that lay ahead, and in the second issue, from his cell in San Quentin, Tom Mooney sent greetings and "best wishes for a strong, militant and fighting industrial union" of waterfront workers.

Women, too, wrote to the *Waterfront Worker:* Said one in the March 22, 1934, issue:

> I am the wife of a longshoreman . . . I am going to fight with him in the coming struggle. This is not only the fight of our husbands but the fight of every woman whose man works on the waterfront, be it husband, father or son . . . I stand 100 percent in favor of the coming strike, which is our only way out of our uncertainty and to a great extent our misery . . . we women have been silent long enough . . .

On May 9, 1934, under leadership of the International Longshoremen's Association (ILA), 12,000 men from all ports up and down the Pacific Coast hit the bricks. Joined soon by eight other maritime unions, including the small TUUL Maritime Workers Industrial Union, 35,000 workers took on the shipowners, demanding, above all, union hiring halls to replace the "shape-up," in which foremen chose workers a day at a time. Soon the name of a young

Australian dockworker, Harry Bridges, would become anathema not only to the power structure of San Francisco, but even out in the valleys, to the Associated Farmers. Bridges was chairman of the ILA rank and file strike committee.

On May 14, in San Pedro the Red Squad shot and killed Dick Parker, a 20-year-old striker, and wounded 50 others in an attack on pickets. Tom Knudsen, an old timer on the Pedro waterfront, was wounded in the same attack and died a few days later. The ILD called for the workers to hold their own murder trial and 500 men and women responded, strikers giving eyewitness accounts of the murders. Three ILD attorneys acted as prosecutors. "The murder was laid at the feet of the shipowners and their henchmen, the local government and the police, the Red Squad and AFL officials... although this was a so-called 'mock' trial it gave the workers of San Pedro a taste of what working class justice will one day mean," said the *Western Worker.*

Longshoremen in San Francisco tied up almost 100 ships, and shipowners denounced the strike as a Communist plot. The Frisco waterfront was orderly as, day after day, hundreds of strikers picketed the "front," marching behind the American flag.

Then on May 28, the waterfront became a scene of carnage as police – without warning – attacked the picketline. The strikers fought back with the only weapons they had – fists and bricks – against tear gas, clubs and guns. Reported the San Francisco *Chronicle,* "Under command of Lieutenant Joseph Mignola, a squad of police armed with sawed-off shotguns fired into the ranks of a group of strikers who were attempting to cover their advance on Pier 18 under a barrage of bricks and cobblestones." Longshoreman Alfonso Metzger was shot in the back. Then, in usual police fashion, he was arrested and charged with criminal assault. "The alibi of the police thugs," said the *Western Worker,* "is that he was picking up a rock to throw at Lieutenant Mignola... the courtroom during the trial was crowded to the doors with longshoremen. This frameup is one of the rawest the bosses have ever tried to put over and the presence of this militant audience was an embarrassment to the prosecutors."

With ILD attorneys busy on other cases, Elaine represented Metzger. He had two trials – one on a felony charge and the second on a misdemeanor when the first charge was reduced. They both ended in hung juries and charges were dismissed. After Elaine's death, Metzger wrote from Albuquerque, New Mexico, "She was my first attorney when I was in trouble in 1934 . . . I am going to miss Elaine. Well, we all got to go."

Bloodied Heads

Two days later was Memorial Day, designated by Left youth groups as National Youth Day.[1] The Young Communist League was probably the most prominent of the organizations participating in the San Francisco rally which chose as its main theme youth's solidarity with the longshore strikers. Some 250 young men and women gathered at the Embarcadero. However, the situation looked dangerou . There were a lot of police on the docks; later it was learned that 500 police were within a mile of the meeting place. The young people decided to cancel. As a young man began to announce this, the police attacked.

There were "massive arrests and bloodied heads down on the waterfront . . . and a number that were seriously injured," Elaine said. Sixty-five young men and women were downed by heavy police clubbings. A longshoreman witness had seen "violence and brutality in many forms all over the world, but I've never seen anything like that attack upon those kids . . . it was nothing but murder." Many longshoremen couldn't stand it and jumped into the fray, trying to protect the young people.

The following day, the San Francisco *News* headlined: "Police Blame Communists for Waterfront Rioting, Union Charges Brutality."

> More than a score were recovering today from injuries suffered when violence flared . . . police blamed the rioting on Communists and officials of the International Longshoremen's Association charged police with making an unprovoked attack, and engaging in unwarranted clubbing of women and children. One man, Frank Fisher, a former stevedore, was believed dying and 23 others were injured so seriously as to require hospital treatment.
>
> According to a statement at striking longshoremen's headquarters, six stevedores saw a policeman shoot a 17-year-old boy and club a 12-year-old girl . . . nearly 300 men and women were in the crowd when policemen with clubs flailing, rode onto sidewalks, kicking them down with blows on the head, trampling them down and throwing tear gas bombs.
>
> Many of the injured were innocent bystanders caught in the swirling rock-hurling mob. Some rioters attempted to pull policemen from their horses. Women scratched and screamed and tried to help

> the men who had been beaten down. For more than an hour after the riot started, policemen were active dispelling crowds in the adjoining area.... Longshoremen claimed police entered the cafeteria-style eating hall maintained by strikers at 84 Embarcadero and clubbed many of the stevedores.

The *Western Worker* reported that when "Billy Newman got up to speak, sitting on Jack Allen's shoulders, all he got out were the words 'Comrades and fellow workers, we have come here today in order to'... Then the police made one concentrated rush... A calvacade of mounted police waded in, swinging clubs in every direction, at men, women and children indiscriminately."

The strikers sent a formal protest to Lt. Governor Frank Merriam: "Local 38-79 of the International Longshoremen's Association vigorously protests the insane brutality of the San Francisco police in clubbing children and aged women into insensibility and in clubbing peaceful picketers and innocent bystanders. We recognize this unprovoked attack as an attempt to intimidate the longshoremen ... As acting governor of this state, we hold you personally responsible for future violence on the San Francisco waterfront."[2]

The ILD called a mass meeting the following night at which wounded youths with bandaged heads described the carnage to a packed California Hall audience. Speakers were from maritime and other unions, the ILD, Communist Party and community organizations. Henry Schrimpf, delegated by the ILA to attend the protest, told the rally, "I've seen all kinds of fighting. I was in the World War... never in my life have I seen such beastly brutality as the San Francisco police used in their insane ferocious attack..." An ILD investigation revealed that police had been ordered to beat women "only on the soft parts of the body" and quoted a police officer as saying that the strikers "got away with something today. Next time you'll be cases for the morgue." A Grand Jury investigation was demanded, the ILD charging the police with assault and battery with intent to kill, attempted murder and rioting.

Two days later the first strike rally was held at Civic Center in front of City Hall. In silence – and headed up by women and children – several thousand people marched eight abreast from the Embarcadero, where the youth had been brutalized. Elaine spoke for the ILD, offering the dockworkers legal support and pledging to help with strike relief. "The loudspeaker system was sabotaged... I was told afterward that mine was the only voice that projected to the whole crowd . . . I have this loud voice that would shatter anybody's ears . . . "

Elaine became a marked woman; both police and judges became familiar with her face, her voice, her defense of strikers' rights, and her disdain for the courts. "ILD Organizer is Going to Jail for Going to a Worker's Trial," said a *Western Worker* headline: "Arrested for the 'crime' of attending a court of capitalist 'justice' Elaine Black, District Organizer for the ILD . . . [is] now freed on bail awaiting trial on charges of 'vagrancy.' " Elaine was one of four arrested in the courtroom. Earlier in the week she had witnessed a "slugging" and arrest on the waterfront and, in court, demanded that the arresting officer reveal the charge against the arrested striker "so that she could place bail." "Arrest her too – she's a good vagrant," ordered the Red Squad chief. "When Black's case came up, Judge Dunne, angered by the fact that Black had previously exposed him on the waterfront as a fascist in his attempt to intimidate seamen from joining the striking Marine Workers Industrial Union, declared, 'Put her bail at a thousand dollars. She said I'm a Fascist.' "[3]

The Women's Auxiliary

Women's Auxiliary No. 3879 of the ILA came into existence on June 5, chartered by ILA president Joseph P. Ryan. The women decided at that first meeting to "get the facts of the strike before the public," and respond to the "need for financial and moral support to see that the strikers and their families were fed, clothed and housed." The auxiliary membership was to be "strictly wives of longshoremen," and "the plan for the Auxiliary was to solicit cash and food contributions from neighborhood stores and markets, contacting women's organizations for support, visiting families of strikers when necessary in order to find out what these families need." Hazel Mallen was elected chairperson.[4]

On June 17 an agreement signed between the conservative Ryan and the Waterfront Employers Association was rejected by the longshoremen as a "sell-out." The strike tightened. On June 19, for the first time in 45 years, not a single ship entered the port of San Francisco.

Elaine carried copies of the Bill of Rights in her purse and could quote it from memory. Rallies were held where strikers were informed of their legal rights in case of arrest. "We issued a little flyer that sold for one cent that said what to do when under arrest . . . Also we told the ILA Defense Committee they should not be surprised if there were attempts at frameups of their leaders . . . that Mooney and Billings [were] still doing time on a frameup . . . " The flier said:

> First and foremost: Remember at all times that the police, deputies, judges and prosecutors are not your friends, or they would not have arrested you. They are acting as agents of the boss class. Do not listen to any of their promises or agreements. At no time tell them anything; or carry on any conversation whatsoever with them, since part of their frame-up method is to get you into an innocent conversation to pump you. Remember, anything you say to them, no matter how simple, may be elaborated and used against you or your friends in court.

On June 19 Elaine spoke at the Women's Auxiliary on "how to answer questions put to us by police if arrested and advised us to give a different name and to decline to state where born."* The foreign-born were advised never to provide immigration officials with "free information," including address, place of employment, country of origin, date of arrival or status of citizenship.

"Forward to a General Strike!"

Elaine also reported that a "Dr. Chambers would examine all strikers' children who were sick." The auxiliary decided to participate in strike picketing; picket captains were Mrs. Johns for the morning shift and Mrs. Jurchan for the afternoon shift; shortly, however, the auxiliary pickets were removed at the request of the ILA strike committee.

With sentiment building among the strikers as well as other unions for a general strike to support the dockers, the women issued a leaflet: "FORWARD TO A GENERAL STRIKE!" When the Women's Auxiliary marched smartly into Civic Auditorium for a big strike rally, 20,000 people who packed the hall cheered until the rafters rang.

The Auxiliary Relief Committee solicited donations to help their striking husbands, sons and brothers and their families. They received both money and material aid, including 50 pairs of soles and heels from Joe's Shoe Repair Shop on Fillmore Street, and "deer meat for

---

*Auxiliary minutes

distribution to needy families." Mrs. Nelson volunteered to darn socks of strikers and, during the strike period, Yellow Cab drivers gave $1,000 per week for 15 weeks.

With so many arrests, Elaine spent more time "down at the Hall of Justice with large sums of money on me" than at the ILD office. "Many a time we had to walk from the ILD headquarters... Sixth and Market... clear down to the Hall of Justice on Kearney and Washington because there wasn't money in the general fund. Yet we had $1,000 or $2,000 in our purse. But it was holy. That was the bail fund... you couldn't take a dime out... you did not allow carfare out of that bail fund."

The "Red Angel"

Elaine became known as the "Red Angel." Carrying $2,000 cash, she went to the Hall of Justice to bail out two seamen but was stopped by members of the Red Squad. "Where are you going?" "I'm going upstairs to post bail." "No, you're not, you are coming with us." They arrested Elaine on a vagrancy charge.

"Oh, so finally they got the Red Angel," said one of the booking officers. And a few days later, when some maritime workers were brought in and booked, he told them, "Oh, don't worry. The Red Angel will be here. She'll get to you." The *Western Worker* picked up the phrase. So did the strikers.

After being held for almost 24 hours, the charge was dropped and Elaine was released, but during the strike she was picked up three more times on the $1,000 "vag" charge. The origin of the $1,000 "vag" law was as an earlier-instituted system of police shake-down to blackmail underworld types to come across with money or go to jail. It was also used against prostitutes and pimps.

Longshoreman and long-time friend Archie Brown said:

> "It wasn't by accident that she was called the "Red Angel." Elaine was always there when strikers and sympathizers got busted. Some way or another she scrounged up the bail and soon was included onto the strike committee because she showed how to organize and fight against strike-breaking, how to maintain and increase morale, how to spread unity with the rest of labor and how to reach other sections of the people in order to support the right to organize, strike and picket. In the process she taught everyone the necessity of building the ILD, the organization that mobilized hundreds of thou-

sands for many people's causes. Elaine told everyone that she learned her skills and understanding through being a Communist.

"It was people like Elaine who kept organizing and showing how to meet the shipowners' and employers' vigilante terror that was let loose during the strike. Gangs destroyed the Maritime Workers Industrial Union headquarters on Jackson Street, the book store on Grove Street, the Communist Party headquarters at 121 Haight Street, the Finnish Workers' Halls on Beaver Street in San Francisco and Tenth Street in Berkeley, besides raiding a number of workers' homes. The police attack and the killing of Nick Bordoise and Howard Sperry on July 5 resulted in the great general strike."

Elaine was there. Amidst the turmoil and tension, the threats and scare headlines, she thrived on the militancy and courage she saw all around her. And if sometimes the heartache was difficult to bear, that was part of the struggle too.

Bloody Thursday

The stage was set for conflict on Tuesday, July 3, with the shipowners' declaration of war. "The port is open," said the shipowners, said the Industrial Association, said the police, said the Chamber of Commerce. When shipping companies, with police help, tried to open the port with scabs, strikers stopped the trucks from getting through. Police attacked, firing guns, hurling gas bombs, and bloodying heads. The battle raged for hours. Twenty-five men, including nine policemen, were hospitalized. To avoid arrest, most of the wounded strikers were taken to private homes. Those in jail tended their wounds as best they could.

Wednesday, July 4, was a holiday. Both sides took stock of their positions.

On Thursday, July 5, shipowners again tried to move trucks through the strikers' ranks. Early that morning, Karl took Elaine to ILA strike headquarters at 113 Steuart Street where she was to meet with "Dutch" Deitrich, chairman of the ILA defense committee. "I left her there and went to join the big crowd of workers, strikers' families with many children, and many high school students. All had come to the waterfront in support of the strike... At exactly 8 o'clock, the ferry whistle blew, police began attacking the crowd with tear gas, and trigger-happy police using live ammunition shot at us indiscriminately as we ran for cover behind buildings. Others kept running up Market street. If you didn't run fast enough, you were beaten down by night sticks.

"While I was running up Market street, my mind was occupied with the fate of Elaine, because the police were rushing toward the strike headquarters, throwing tear gas and shooting live bullets."

ILA headquarters was just around the corner from Mission and Steuart. Elaine's meeting was to plan what to do about further police attacks and how to help those in jail. What did the strikers need from the ILD and what about the seamen who "had just gotten off the boat and found themselves in the clutches of the law?"

On the waterfront, strikers fought to keep their lines solid and the scab trucks from moving. Scores were being wounded, some critically.

When Elaine's meeting ended, she headed down the stairs. She smelled tear gas and heard a shot but thought it was a tear gas canister being fired. Outside, she started walking. A striker yelled, "Elaine, what are you doing here? They're shooting. Those are live bullets!" He grabbed her, thrust her into his car, and drove her to the ILD office.

Class War

Class war raged in the streets that day. By afternoon, the battle concentrated on Rincon Hill and near longshore headquarters on Steuart where several strikers were shot, and then into the downtown area where strikers and shoppers alike were beaten and injured. "Blood ran in the streets . . . " the newspapers reported; "Blood floods gutters . . . "

Later that afternoon, Elaine got a call to go to the morgue to identify a body. "I couldn't go because I had an appointment at five o'clock . . . I said that if there was still no identification, I would come down . . . There was nobody in the office . . . there were things happening on the front – arrests – and I wanted to be there to mobilize people to go down and bail them out."

Then Henry Schmidt, member of the strike committee, phoned. It was essential that Elaine come immediately to the morgue as the unidentified corpse, found between Steuart and Spear Streets, wore an ILD dress button* and she might know him. Howard Sperry, a longshoreman and active union member had been killed, too, at

*A "dress" model of a regular membership button.

Steuart and Mission; He was quickly identified. Schmidt told Elaine that he and "Dutch" Deitrich would meet her at the Hall of Justice and they would go together to the basement morgue.

"When they took the sheet off it was the man . . . I had the appointment with. I said, 'No, it can't be – it can't be.' I was supposed to meet him at five o'clock." It was Nick Coundeorakis – better known as Nick Bordoise – an active ILD member, a Communist. Bordoise helped out in the strike kitchen. He also sold the *Labor Defender* on the docks. His planned meeting with Elaine was to report on the day's events and determine who had been arrested and would need bail. Elaine never forgot the trauma and shock of that visit to the morgue. "I had seen people with gunshot wounds, broken limbs and with split heads, but I had never really seen a cadaver . . . someone who had been murdered in the line of action . . . to find him with a bullet in his back. There was no other mark of violence on him; he was shot in the back."

Elaine broke down. "It can't be him, it can't be him." Bordoise was a member of the Greek branch of the ILD and belonged to the Cooks Union. The murder site was lined with flowers. Inscriptions were written in white paint: POLICE MURDERS. SHOT IN THE BACK.

"Bloody Thursday" prompted Governor Frank Merriam to order 2,000 National Guardsmen into San Francisco.

Funeral Procession

All that next Sunday, at the Longshore hall, thousands filed silently past the coffins of longshoreman Howard Sperry and cook Nick Bordoise. Into the long night, thousands more came. The funeral procession was the next day, July 9. The strikers took over the streets. On the whole length of Market Street, 40,000 marched and not a policeman was to be seen.

Mike Quin wrote in a poem, "These are the Class War Dead:"

> *"Stop in your tracks, you passer by;*
> *Uncover your doubting head.*
> *The working men are on their way*
> *To bury their murdered dead . . . "*[5]

And curious passers-by did remove their hats at the orders of marchers and parade monitors. Elaine would have preferred to walk behind the caskets in that "awesome march," but Harry Bridges asked her to ride with Julia Bordoise, Bordoise's wife, Mother Mooney and Anna Mooney.* Elaine was one of the speakers at the Cypress Lawn Cemetery where Bordoise was buried: "This must never happen again. We have to close our ranks . . . " It was, wrote Mike Quin, a "Red funeral."[6] The next day Howard Sperry, a World War I veteran, was buried at the Presidio National Cemetary.

"I couldn't control my tears," Elaine recalled. An acquaintance expressed surprise: "My, you're crying!" "A comrade fell in the struggle," Elaine responded. "I don't know why, but some people think if you are active you don't have feelings and you don't show emotions; you know, this inscrutable mask that you're supposed to wear. But I have never worn a mask. If you have feelings – and sometimes I express them too much – the hatred I have for some people shows . . . " So, of course, did the love.

"First of all, Elaine Black Yoneda was a friend of mine," ILWU Secretary-Treasurer Curtis McClain said at Elaine's memorial. "As fierce a fighter as she was, she was a warm, humorous and gentle woman. My personal sorrow at losing her is immense, softened only by the satisfaction of knowing that hers was a life lived to its fullest, with intensity, fervor and love. . . . Elaine, of course, played a tremendous role in the history of our union. We first met her as the sparkplug of the ILD, the only woman on the 1934 strike committee. Over the years, she was intimately involved in the whole struggle to project the strength of the ILWU out into the community, on behalf of civil rights, peace, and social justice . . . She never let up. And, in her memory, and in the memory of all those who have gone before her, neither will we."

On July 12, 3,700 San Francisco and Oakland teamsters struck in solidarity with the maritime workers, and the next day 12 more unions representing 32,000 workers were out, as union after union took up the call for a general strike. The strike committee called for a general strike the following Monday. The San Francisco Labor Council opposed the strike, but decided to participate on the strike committee in order to exercise some measure of control over events. On July 16, the general strike was on, participated in by 160 unions representing 127,000 workers. Mayor Rossi put 5,000 special riot police on strike duty.

---

*Tom Mooney's younger sister.

10

Reign of Terror

General Strike

On July 16 the city was paralyzed and nothing moved. Three thousand more troops were moved in, but still nothing moved. Then came "the reign of terror led by the Red Squad, the Intelligence Bureau, deputized American Legionnaires and all the violent forces of the day," Elaine said. At least 500 men were deputized to preserve "law and order." The following day and continuing for several days, the "reign of terror" became an orgy of violence as police and vigilantes ran amok in the streets, attacking and smashing labor and leftwing headquarters, not only in San Francisco but up and down the Pacific Coast.

At ILD headquarters, David Merrihue and Jack Bishop boarded up the windows. Office equipment and records had been moved out after an earlier vigilante sweep. There was a knock on the door. Joe Wilson, San Francisco ILD organizer, described what happened:

> Bishop was savagely attacked, knocked unconscious and dragged to the car of one of the squads. The degenerate wreckers had returned. They started in doing a more thorough job of wrecking the place when Merrihue swept down the stairs with a cavalry sword in one hand and a bayonet in the other. Believe it or not, he ran them out the door so fast they tripped over each other!

Elaine organized delegations to the mayor's office to protest the deputizing of vigilantes, the cracking of heads, breaking up of headquarters, and the mass arrests by the Red Squad.

On the 17th, Elaine was at Communist Party headquarters when she got a phone call about a raid on the Unemployed Council office and another at the Workers Ex-Servicemens League[1] lot on Howard Street. People were being arrested by the dozens. Could she do something? Elaine said no, not until those arrested were booked.

She went to the Hall of Justice. Hundreds of people were crowded into the jail – no blankets, no showers, and rotten food. People were being held "in sort of kangaroo courts." Some were being sentenced then and there; many had heeded the advice of the ILD to plead not guilty and demand jury trials.

Thirty-two strike sympathizers – mostly young – were swept up and jailed on $1,000 vagrancy charges. Police subjected them to special harsh treatment as real or suspected "reds." The ILD took charge of these cases but, Elaine said, "We didn't have $32,000 [bail] to put up so they would have to stay in jail. But they were strong and solid."

Frances Perkins Walks a Tight Line

During the first days of the strike, Secretary of Labor Frances Perkins – a New Deal liberal and the first woman ever to be a member of a presidential cabinet – congratulated the strikers on their orderliness. It was, she said, "a tribute to the workers." And when Roger Lapham, president of the American Hawaiian Steamship Company, asked for government intervention because a Communist revolution was going on in San Francisco, she scoffed. "How dare you say such a thing. If you talk that way you are likely to put false ideas in the heads of the strikers."[2] She had also – to the consternation of the Industrial Association and the Waterfront Employers' Union – refused to recommend that the strikers return to work under an agreement between the employers and Joseph Ryan.

A former sociologist before President Roosevelt appointed her as his secretary of labor, Perkins' role was generally seen by the strikers as positive. Assistant Secretary of Labor Edward F. McGrady, however, was something else. He sought to make deals – turned down by the rank and file – and red-baited the strike. Whatever credibility he may have had upon arrival in San Francisco went quickly down the drain. "Strikebreaker Extraordinary" was one apt description.[3]

The problem that developed with Secretary Perkins during the strike was predictable. In those days the Immigration and Naturalization Service was a division of the Labor Department under Perkins' authority. As foreign-born strikers and strike sympathizers were rounded up and held for deportation, Perkins was accused of "obeying the orders of the American bosses . . . "[4] The feeling was bitter.

"Frances Perkins . . . has given active assistance to employers' efforts to destroy workers' organizations, by weeding out active aliens."[5]

Perkins was a stickler for following the letter of the law – as she interpreted it – and wired [now] Governor Merriam:

> The San Francisco [INS] district director has been keeping in close contact with the situation. The commissioner of Immigration and Naturalization at Washington has again wired today to the district director at San Francisco to act with promptness in any case in which there is evidence presented to or discovered by him indicating that an alien is deportable . . .

"I assure you," she told the governor, "that the Department of Labor will cooperate with California officials to the full extent authorized by law."

Courtroom Circus

The courts were a circus. Ready to pounce on hapless victims while patrolling the courtrooms of Municipal Judges George J. Steiger and Sylvain Lazarus were Immigration Department officials and Army Intelligence agents, "ready to take over all cases which come within their jurisdiction," the *Examiner* reported. "Both courts were scenes of confusion, hot arguments and swift action, with crowds of spectators leaping to their feet and cheering the judges as they denounced the radical element that has crept into the industrial troubles." Judge Steiger, whose hatred of "reds" was notorious, had Elaine removed from his courtroom.

Judge Lazarus, while of a more humanitarian bent than Steiger, recommended action to "ship these people back home so decent Americans can earn a living." District Attorney Matthew Brady said that deportation was the most effective weapon against "foreign radicals," while Governor Merriam recommended the deportation "of every alien agitator and revolutionist in the state . . . "

Seaman Otto Richter was arrested during the strike and ordered deported to Nazi Germany. He had entered the United States to escape persecution by the Hitler regime. The *Labor Defender* described him as "one of Miss Perkins' agents' first victims in their drive against foreign born workers." The ILD and the CPFB held a joint conference; "Miss Perkins' threats must be answered by a strong nationwide campaign against deportations and for the right of asylum of all foreign born workers and political refugees," the ILD said. Among others held for deportation were Ecuador-born Maximo Penaherrara, Chilean-born José Sepulvda, Ove Anderson and Kristian Nielson, both born in Denmark. These four had lived in the United States for periods ranging from six to 32 years.

None of this was enough, however, for American Legionnaires obsessed by a fever against the foreign-born, the strike, and real and imagined Communists. Even before the general strike, the Legion had designated an Anti-Red Week, and organized a "Citizens Committee" to carry it out, collecting names and addresses, and spying on the "Reds." The Legion held its state convention in San Francisco where Perkins came under "the most open and determined [attack] made on a member of the Administration since Roosevelt took office."[6] A telegram to McGrady was read to the convention wherein Perkins carefully explained that the reason some Russian aliens, although in custody, could not be deported was that Russia would not accept them. She spelled out that "every possible step has been taken to effectuate deportation by the immigration and naturalization service which under the present administration has become increasingly efficient and alert." Subject to deportation, she said, was "any alien who has entered the United States unlawfully . . . any alien who advocated disbelief in or opposition to all organized government or who advocates . . . the overthrow by force and violence of the Government of the United States."

Strike statistics compiled by the ILA Defense Committee, showed that many foreign-born seamen were arrested. Their home countries were Chile, Peru, Ecuador, Nicaragua, Panama, Mexico, Denmark, Sweden, Germany and Russia.

The ILD's attitude toward Perkins was formed as early as March 1933, when it protested her refusal to allow ILD attorneys to appear for persons held for deportation. In November 1934, when a delegation visited the Labor Department in Washington D.C. to protest Perkins' interpretation of deportation laws, Immigration Commissioner Daniel W. MacCormack told the group that the next year would see Congress pass even more restrictive legislation. The foreign born, he said, should avoid joining organizations that take part in strikes.[7]

Elaine had "a number of meetings around immigration cases when she [Perkins] was out here on the West Coast." Elaine termed one such meeting a "confrontation," where she protested "what was happening with immigration; that people who were fighting for their rights should not be intimidated by immigration officials . . . she [Perkins] listened. She didn't say get the devil out . . . I said the law says they can join a union on the one hand; on the other hand if they join a union and the bosses think they are radical, then that's ground for deportation . . . "

History reflects the overall positive role that Secretary Perkins played in the New Deal; however it also shows that even when she did have room to maneuver, she could and did interpret immigration law rigidly. In most of her duties, she was a mediator and conciliator and tended – in those early days of the New Deal – to verbally spank both management and labor as if they were naughty children. In the beginning of the general strike, when some administration officials urged drastic action, Perkins protested: " . . . I thought it unwise to begin the Roosevelt administration by shooting it out with working people who were only exercising their rights, under our Constitution and laws, to organize and demand collective bargaining."[8]

Perkins's estimate of Harry Bridges was rather precious. "He was a small, thin, somewhat haggard man in a much-worn overcoat, the collar turned up and pinned around his throat, and with a cap in his hand. He was polite, deferential, hardly finding the voice to make demands for the striking longshoremen. His suggestions seemed practical and reasonable. I recall putting down in my mind that he was a typical British worker." Before he "became an effective leader in the longshoremen's strike, Bridges was an unimpressive fellow," she said.[9]

"No Tampering by Communism"

Mayor Rossi congratulated the city's vigilantes:

> San Francisco was founded by liberty loving people and its traditions are sacred to us. We will tolerate no tampering by communism or any other interference with constituted authority . . . In justice, I must express my gratitude and that of the people of San Francisco to the many citizens who have been called upon and who have rendered their valuable services . . . Every Communist agitator will be run out of San Francisco. This is going to be a continuing policy.

In Seattle Mayor Smith announced: "We were just organizing a squad to rout Communists from the city when the riot crisis came . . . the police have lists of 250 Communists and we shall hunt for them and send them out of town. We shall raid Communist headquarters." City officials in Oakland, Portland and San Pedro followed suit and homes as well as halls were invaded. However, defiant leaflets continued to be churned out on hidden mimeograph machines.

"San Fascisto, California"

The *Labor Defender* issued a West Coast Special edition, using a title suggested by the New York *World Telegram:* "SAN FASCISTO, CALIFORNIA." It said:

> The General Strike was called a violent smashing of constitutional authority. It was labeled "terror." But who is responsible for the terror on the West Coast? Who killed Nick Bordoise? Who murdered Sperry? Who smashed furniture, tore up literature, destroyed meeting places . . . Who is violating the right to freedom of assemblage, freedom of the press, the right to belong to a political party of one's own choice?

The ILD called for nationwide support "in defense of the victims of West Coast terror."

Joe Wilson said the police "arrested every militant they could discover." They smashed the IWW headquarters, halls belonging to various language groups and at night, "the gangs again descended for the third time and this time they completely wrecked 121 Haight Street [Communist Party headquarters] and the Fillmore Hall. All along the police were raiding and jailing workers.

"This was the situation when we arrived early Wednesday morning," Wilson said. "We made contact with the West Coast organizer of the Marine Workers Industrial Union and went to his apartment late Thursday." That was on July 19.

Elaine Arrested

Elaine was the only woman in the group of four who met to plan strategy at Harry Jackson's apartment at 1026 McAllister Street; the others were Wilson and John Rogers. Elaine suggested they investigate the possibility of taking out a federal injunction to stop the raids. "How could we fight the reign of terror that was going on?"

HELD AS LEADERS—Accused of being "brains" of Communist activities, four demanded jury trials and were held in lieu of $1,000 bail. L to R, Harry Prevost, Joseph Wilson, John Rogers, Elaine Black. [S.F. *Examiner,* 7-21-34.]

"We mapped out a campaign together," Wilson said, "and were just leaving when the Red Squad smashed in. They did not have a warrant, but we did not resist as it would have been suicide. After an hour of questioning we were taken to the city jail and booked as vags with a bail of $1,000 cash." "Vagrancy," according to the Penal Code, meant the defendant "did wilfully and unlawfully not seek employment or labor when employment was offered to him, he having the physical ability to work and being without visible means of living; and . . . that the defendant did roam from place to place without any lawful business."

The men were put in the felony tank and Elaine in the women's tank. "They wanted to keep us from the 400 workers arrested . . . The jails were so damn full that the jailers couldn't find a place to spit."

The 32 ILD cases were still in jail. The young people voted that the four arrested strike leaders were needed outside and should be bailed out; they would stay in jail. Bail money was raised and Elaine and the three men were released. Usually joint arrests meant joint trials. However, the court split Elaine off; she would stand trial by herself. ILD Attorney George R. Andersen would defend the men.

On the following Sunday, at a protest meeting at Jefferson Park, Elaine was arrested again: another $1,000 "vag" charge – disturbing the peace and rioting. Elaine went back to jail. In the meantime, Louise Todd, Communist Party leader and campaign manager for Communist candidates, and party organizer Ida Rothstein were arrested in a raid on 1729 McAllister Street, and charged with vagrancy. Elaine told the ILD, "Get them out first." As the youngest of the three, she said, "I could take it . . . I wasn't too uptight about it, especially since there were 32 men on the other side who had been there a whole week and hadn't even seen the light of day." Ida and Louise would have to stay in jail, however, until bail was raised.

"Kentucky Mae"

That night, a woman known as "Kentucky Mae" was brought in "roaring drunk," and put into the main tank with Elaine, Louise, Ida, and a cell-full of women, most of whom were charged with prostitution. Drunk women were usually kept separate until they sobered up, but not "Kentucky Mae." She began screaming: "I want to get me a commie – my boyfriend and I were headed for the waterfront to get those damn commies!" The woman "was a mess," Elaine said. She befriended "Kentucky Mae," offered her a comb and helped comb her hair. Later, the matron attempted to provoke "Kentucky Mae" into attacking Elaine. The drunk woman refused to believe that Elaine could be one of those awful "commies." But "it could have been a bloody mess . . . "

On the following Saturday, Elaine joined the men in a hunger strike. She heard them shouting from the other side of the jail for soap, showers, and better food. When Elaine received a message – from an agent, she later figured – telling her the strike was off, she ate lunch. It hit the press like a bombshell. Elaine Black had "scabbed on comrades." It was quickly back on the hunger strike together with Margaret Coleman, member of the YCL who had been brought in for distributing anti-war fliers. "The first two days were terrible. We didn't even drink water." The men sent word that the hunger strike did not include water. The story that Elaine had scabbed even reached the press as far away as New York. "But that was how people began to know there was a hunger strike on and that there were 32 men in jail, and why they were there," she said.

In mid-week, Elaine and Margaret were taken to the matrons' lunch room. The scene was bizarre. There was a table set for two, complete with tablecloth, salad, rolls, butterballs in fancy shapes, and even raw steaks sitting on two dinner plates. "They asked us how we wanted our meat!" The two women, whose only sustenance had been one-half cup of water three times a day, were at first speechless, then angry. Just then a trustee doing mail delivery yelled out Elaine's name; he had stacks of mail, messages of solidarity from all over. They came "from Columbia University, from Berkeley, from the State of Washington, stacks and stacks. Telegrams and letters." A telegram from Columbia asked Elaine to convey the students' solidarity with the hunger strikers. Elaine was relieved. This was solid proof that word had gotten out and the purpose of the hunger strike was served. That was the important thing.

"Your Lousy Communist Ideas"

Elaine turned to her jailers: "We don't need your food. This [mail] is our food. This is what will sustain us . . . they were very mad, especially the matron." It was the same matron who had tried to goad "Kentucky Mae" into beating Elaine. One letter, however, was signed by a "100 percent American mother of a boy you ruined with your lousy communist ideas." The writer was "tickled pink" that Elaine was "in the hoosegow."

She worried about the hunger strike's effect on Margaret, who had a health problem and was losing too much weight. Margaret valiantly stuck with it, however. To keep up their spirits, Elaine and Margaret sang songs until stopped by the matron.

Another trick was attempted. A police lieutenant visited Elaine in her cell, claiming he had been a socialist back in 1904 and a member of the Teamsters Union, and was "very concerned" about Elaine and Margaret. "Can't I sneak you in a thermos of chicken soup?" he asked. "Nobody would know." The two women rejected his offer and Elaine bawled him out for the poor diet being proferred to the male prisoners. She told him that if he were true to his beliefs, he would see to it that the men got fresh vegetables and milk and were allowed to shower. "You would see to it that they got blankets in this cold jail." Actually, as acting chief jailor, he did order fresh vegetables "so he did have some compassion." He paid for it with a demotion in rank.

By August 11, there were 27 still on hunger strike; it was their seventh day without food. Dr. Franklin Bissell, Jr. of Berkeley described in a United Press report as "official physician" for the ILD, examined the prisoners, pronounced them fit, and was thereupon arrested. Police charged him with failure to "have his medical certificate registered" in San Francisco. Invited to have lunch with Police Lieutenant James Boland, the doctor refused. "It may take some time for my friends to raise the ridiculously high bail," Dr. Bissell said. "I may be here several days and I don't intend to eat anything until I get out."[10]

That same day, Elaine's mother and Joyce came up from Los Angeles. Mollie visited with Elaine while Joyce, too young to visit, waited. An officer taunted seven-year-old Joyce, "You've got a jailbird for a mother." Joyce's response was quick: "She's no jailbird. She's a worker. She's working for you. You're a worker too if you don't know it." Later, the officer told Elaine, "You've got a feisty daughter there."

Elaine argued with her mother against being bailed out even though she had to prepare for her jury trial the following Monday. The $4,000 bail required for Elaine's release "could take out four others instead of just me." Her bail was reduced to $2,200 and was posted in spite of her objections. "I don't want to go and leave my comrades." On the eighth day, the men called the hunger strike off; the sick were bailed out first. Said Elaine, who had lost 15 pounds, "This sacrifice was not in vain, all demands except reduction in bail [for the men] were won, including milk!"

Elaine got ready for trial. She would be tried alone and would defend herself. In the meantime, the *Examiner* was accusing Elaine, along with Harry Jackson, John Rogers and Joseph Wilson with being "the brains" of Communist organizing on the Pacific Coast.

The Trial

"There was such an overflow of people that my trial was held in City Hall." For the first time Elaine did not have counsel to turn to for advice, as she defended herself and did jury selection. Main evidence against her, as well as the other McAllister Street defendants in their trial, was provided by an Inspector Steel of the Police Department's "Communist Detail" who had joined the Communist Party as a spy under the alias of "Theodore Lindiner."

The American Legion paraded in Civic Center the day Elaine's trial began in Judge Alden Ames' court. "Legion Asks Death Penalty for Reds," one headline announced. The papers "were full of what they were going to do to the 'reds,' " Elaine said. "They were going to put them in Alcatraz and throw the keys away . . . they would . . . [dump] them in the mid-Pacific. There was a lot of vigilante terror. Facing that, I had to conduct the trial."

Elaine took control of her trial. She agreed to salute the flag only under the proviso that it stood for "the same things today that it did in 1776 – workers' rights." One of the charges against her was distribution of the ILD leaflet "What To Do When Under Arrest," the prosecution charging that it was a "subversive piece of literature." Another charge was "that I had made certain remarks about judges. Yes, I had said that we had two types of judges in our judiciary system here in San Francisco. We had the type of judge who was an open fascist and who gave us our castor oil straight. Then we had those who gave it with orange juice but were still part of the establishment."

Actually, Elaine conceded later, "Certain things in the leaflet . . . may have been a little inflammatory because we took on the judiciary and the police department and pointed out that they were actually at the behest of the employers and big business, and not for the little man or the preservation of the rights of the workers." The leaflet identified as "agents of the boss-class," police, judges and district attorneys.

"During all labor activities," it said, "such as strikes and demonstrations, the worker who takes a militant part in them is constantly faced with arrest. This leaflet is issued for the benefit of any and all workers who may be subjected to this kind of boss oppression."

However, said Elaine, all that "was just advice." The ILD, she told the jury, "would not defend workers who believed in individual terror." It defended Communists "because it is the Communists who are persecuted."

Eyewitness Report

"An Eyewitness" described the trial in vivid detail in the *Labor Defender:*

> "Incompetent, irrelevant and immaterial!" shouted the prosecuting attorney, backed by a picked jury, the judge, police, Industrial Association, Chambers of Commerce and government officials, when Elaine Black, District Organizer of the ILD, took self-defense in her trial in San Francisco, and pointed out the role of the ILD in the class struggle, its leadership in defense of workers' rights.
>
> Charged with vagrancy, Elaine Black was clearly tried not because she was even suspected of being a vagrant, everybody in the court had known her and her activity in Frisco for years, but only because of her political opinions. Only because her ceaseless activity on behalf of the working class, only because she dared to commit the crime of telling workers what their rights are, how to fight for them, and how to defend themselves in their struggles.
>
> Even in court Elaine Black was not accused of being a vagrant, but of working for an "illegal" organization. When she asked to hear the law, code, statute, or authority, which declared the ILD to be unlawful, the prosecution against thundered, "Incompetent, irrelevant and immaterial."
>
> In the final summary of her defense, Elaine Black explained to the jury the functions of the ILD, its leadership in defense of the masses in exercising their rights to organize and better their conditions, and she pointed out that she was being prosecuted, not because she was a vagrant, but because the ruling class does not want labor to organize, does not want them to exercise their constitutional rights, does not want them to gain the solidarity that will win their struggles, but wants to crush them into further misery by means of all the capitalist weapons of courts, press and police violence against unarmed workers. She explained the meaning of workers self-defense—self-defense by means of organization, against the armed forces of the bosses; self-defense in court against the judges, prosecutors and juries, who are all paid tools of the bosses.
>
> Then the prosecuting attorney summed up his case against her, no mention of the vagrancy charge. Only a play on the petty preju-

> dices and stupidity of the jury. After a series of vicious lies in regard to the ILD, he referred to Elaine Black's statement in regard to saluting the American flag. She had stated that she saluted it only in view of what it should and will stand for, but she did not salute the flag of fascism.
>
> Said the prosecuting attorney to the jury, "And you, ladies and gentlemen of the jury—is there one of you who would hesitate one minute before saluting the American flag? Comrade Black says [he continually referred to the defendant as "comrade," whereupon she, knowing that he was a member of the American Legion, called him "buddy"] that prisoners are forced to eat vile hash and beans in prison. Comrade Black doesn't admit that the prisoners eat halibut on Fridays. But Comrade Black is an atheist so what does she know about halibut?" And so the prosecution summed up its case—without reference to law, or to the charge, or to the defense.
>
> Fifteen minutes later, the jury had reached its verdict of "Guilty." It was perfectly clear that they had reached their verdict before the trial had begun. Charged with vagrancy, tried because of the so-called illegality of the ILD and not knowing about halibut, convicted on vagrancy. No lawyer could have got an acquittal for Elaine Black because her case was a frame-up and the jury was "picked"; she was sentenced to six months and her case is being appealed, but Elaine Black brought out the working class issues and gave a not-easily forgotten education to every juror and every listener in the courtroom.

The press noted that Elaine was the "first woman to be so punished [jail and fine] for radical activity." The joint trial of Louise Todd and Ida Rothstein was proceeding in Judge Theresa Meikle's court at the same time as Elaine's trial. They were defended by Gallagher and won acquittal. "Now I'll be free to go back to my campaign work," Todd said.

"Radical Girl Sentenced"

"Radical Girl Sentenced." "Communist Girl Sec'y Gets 6 Months." "Miss Black Protests Verdict," announced the headlines. The case went to appeal and Elaine got out of jail on bond, declaring, "I was not convicted of vagrancy. I was convicted because of my political beliefs."

Elaine was characterized by Charlotte Christiansen, who worked with her in the 1930s, as "the embodiment of defiance against injustice... she never allowed herself to be sidetracked into petty

CONVICTED—Elaine Black (center), Communist, is shown in court with two friends. She was convicted yesterday of vagrancy. She acted as her own lawyer. [S.F. *Examiner,* 8-15-34.]

politics. Neither did she ever lose her zest for life. I remember well her quick smile and her quick step."

Elaine's conviction, like that of the three men arrested, was overturned on appeal filed by Andersen. The decision, returned on January 22 the following year, was signed by Presiding Judge Walter Perry Johnson, and Judges James G. Conlan and C. J. Goodal. It noted that the police raid on Jackson's apartment was conducted without either search or arrest warrants and that all defendants were "immediately placed under arrest in furtherance of a plan of 'rounding up all known radicals.' " The arresting officer had personally arrested about forty radicals during the raids. While the leaflet on legal rights "exhibits an animus against peace officers, jailers and the judiciary, there is really nothing inflammatory in the instructions," the decision said, and "mere radicalism in the sense of advocacy of sweeping changes in laws or in the system of government, with a view of remedying by peaceful means what are believed to be social or economic evils, is not a crime."

The defendants, while charged with vagrancy, were "really convicted of communism," the judges said, "notwithstanding the fact that under the law of California, communism as a political faith is not made a crime." The "Communists have a status in this state equal before the law to that of the Socialists, the Democrats and the Republicans. At the recent elections the names of the Communist candidates, along with the names of candidates of the other officially recognized parties, were printed on the ballots at the expense of the State. Such being the situation, fellowship in the Communist party cannot of itself be treated as a crime."

General Strike Ends

The general strike had ended "while we were still in jail," Elaine explained. "It had collapsed in a sellout by certain people in the leadership of various unions . . . " That is, on July 19, the Labor Council advised all unions that were engaged in sympathy strikes to return to work, thus aborting the strike. However, the strike continued in Maritime and did not end until the longshoremen voted to accept arbitration; on July 27 the longshoremen voted 6,378 to 1,471 to return to work. After negotiations between unions and employers as well as between the various unions themselves, the seamen and other maritime workers also voted to return to work and the maritime strikes ended on July 31.

Never in the course of the ups and downs of the strike or the sometimes difficult inter-union relations was there a breakup of solidarity on the waterfront. The maritime workers – and the whole union movement – had shut the town down; labor knew its power. The atmosphere, said writer Tillie Olsen, was "as if the emotions of thousands of people were . . . those of one human being, deciding they had to act."[11]

Now, the merchants who had posted hand-written signs in their store windows, "Closed til the boys win," could take them down and reopen for business. This was an unprecedented and historic victory, and there was a new triumphant spirit among San Francisco's working people. "We stood our ground through the strike, were attacked and abused by Capital, Police, and the bayonets of the military forces," said a striker. "We saw our fellow workers blood run on the sidewalks . . . then we returned to our jobs United."[12]

Said a longshoreman's wife: "Before the strike my husband was always complaining about conditions on the waterfront, how hard he was working and how much the bosses were hollering . . . Since returning to work after the strike he is a changed man completely. He seems different and happier and even finds time to pay a little attention to his wife . . . thanks to the strike, a change for the better has come for the men on the front and a change has taken place in our home life."[13]

And said another: "The [women's] auxiliary was born . . . for the purpose of furthering the interests of our husbands in their tasks of winning better conditions for themselves and consequently their families . . . and in our future struggle ahead you cannot help your husband in any greater way than by getting into the ranks of the Women's Auxiliary and working side by side with him. Remember, his fight is your fight!"[14]

When the great strike had been played out to its conclusion, the longshoremen had won a hiring hall with a union dispatcher, a shorter work day and week, and time-and-a-half for overtime. The waterfront, the city of San Francisco, all of its working people, and their trade unions would never be the same again. San Francisco was a union town.

In the fresh winds of victory, the city's working people were solid, and longshore leader Harry Bridges had earned the hatred of San Francisco's employers. Fifty years later, Bridges summed up the significance of the strike [see notes].[15]

Labor Defense in the Strike

Elaine wrote later in an unpublished account:

> Labor defense was an important part of the great maritime strike of 1934. The shipowners, the police and many other agencies tried to break the strike by wholesale arrests. There were almost one thousand workers arrested in San Francisco alone during the three-month strike. So we see that labor defense was not only important but absolutely necessary to defend the right to strike for better working conditions and pay . . . and the ILD helped to organize that defense.
>
> What happened to those arrested? Did they go to prison? They did not. The thousands of workers on strike and the tens of thousands who supported them, organized a mass defense that defeated every attempted frameup.

Approximately 620 cases were immediately dismissed with some 300 more freed during trials or upon appeal; only 41 were convicted, serving very brief jail sentences.

The successful ending of the strike stopped the remaining attempted labor frameups.

ILD attorneys Leo Gallagher and George Andersen were "in the forefront of that great fight to defend the rights of workers ... the police arrested me four times on seven charges, but the ILD got me out, just as it did hundreds of other workers... The experiences gained in the great defense campaigns of 1934 proves to us that frameups... can be defeated, and that the defense of those whom the big employers are trying to railroad to prison, is the defense of democratic and civil rights of all the people."

ILD attorneys often worked without pay. They "didn't get their just due... it was a labor of love for most of them," Elaine said. Attorney for the ILA during the strike was Leo Collins who had "never before this affair represented or done work for a labor organization," according to the ILA Defense Committee report. Collins "stated that the Industrial Association vigorously prosecuted ILA men but were more bent on getting the 'reds.'" Collins' policy was "to secure the release of the men. He did not attempt to make an issue of the strike."

The strike brought Edith Jenkins to help the ILD that summer. Descendent of an old San Francisco family, she "had just gotten involved with the politics of the Left, starting with the 1934 General Strike. The waterfront strike had been an electrifying experience for many middle-class people like me, and we were very much involved with the issues of the strike. Since the ILD had been the organization that had defended so many of the workers who had been arrested... as well as defending other workers' efforts to organize throughout the West, it was an organization I felt I wanted to give my services to.

"So I volunteered to work at the ILD for that summer. Two energetic and extraordinarily capable women, Ida Roth and Elaine Black, were in charge. We knew that the phone was tapped – I believe it was by the San Francisco police – and the tapping machines were very crude, so that you could hear the police station come in on the wire. Elaine and Ida would speak in Yiddish when they communicated with each other by phone. Elaine was distinguished not only for her excellent work, but also for her warmth and humor."

For Elaine, a source of great pride throughout the strike was people's honesty in dealing with the bail fund. In only one case was the ILD left holding the bag. There was "so much bail put up, about one hundred thousand dollars in that one period," Elaine figured, "and the only thing we lost was two hundred and sixty dollars that was confiscated because two seamen didn't show up in court . . . " Elaine always had a feeling they didn't appear because they couldn't get through the ring of National Guardsmen who surrounded the National Maritime Union headquarters, not letting members in or out.

Upshot of the ILD's work, said Anna Damon, was that it "really rooted itself among the masses in California . . . " In carrying out the ILD's militant policies with spirit and imagination, the indefatigable Elaine proved herself to be not only fearless, but a brilliant tactician.

PART TWO

11.

Class War Escalates

Pause Before the Storm

Numerous headquarters and offices ransacked and destroyed by vigilantes on both sides of the San Francisco Bay were put back in order. Life on the Left went on. The *Western Worker* was back in business; its editorial office and printing press had been smashed. The *Worker* had been a special target, not only because it was the Communist Party newspaper, but because its special "Baby Western" edition carried official strike news and bulletins.

For awhile Elaine and Karl resumed a quieter, more normal life. Each day had been worrisome for Karl as he sweated out whether Elaine was safe or in jail. He had taken an active role in the strike, convincing Japanese farm workers and other migrant laborers not to scab on the strikers. In combatting employers' attempts to recruit farm workers as strikebreakers on the docks, Karl organized them instead to collect vegetables and fruit for the strike kitchens. In this he worked with the ILD, the Cannery and Agricultural Workers Industrial Union (CAWIU), and the Communist Party. There were times when he and Elaine didn't themselves have enough money for food and were fed at friends' houses. He worked for a time as dishwasher at the St. Francis Yacht Club, from which he would sometimes "rescue" such food items as steak and squab.

During the primary election campaign, Karl was also busy running for State Assembly in the 22nd district on the Communist Party ticket, the first Asian ever to compete for a state office.

Criminal Syndicalism

Elaine continued to run bail for arrested strikers in the valley. There were many cases, but the one that overshadowed all others and became the cause celebre of the whole California labor movement was the Sacramento Criminal Syndicalism case.

On July 20, while the San Francisco maritime strike was at its peak, 22 men and women farm labor organizers were arrested in a brutal vigilante raid on CAWIU union headquarters. Attackers used rubber hoses and blackjacks and carried sawed-off shotguns. The big ranchers considered it an opportune time to destroy the militant union. The charge brought against the unionists was criminal syndicalism, and "organizing of picketing" was one of the counts. Eighteen of the 22 were eventually to go to trial, but not until later that year.

"ENTIRE STATE FIGHTS RED PERIL," proclaimed the Hearst press.

> Throughout the whole of California, an aroused citizenry continued its spontaneous drive against Communism yesterday. San Francisco municipal courtrooms resembled immigration "melting pots" as a motley crew of assorted Communist agitators, representing almost every race and color, appeared to answer charges of strike violence.
>
> In Sacramento, Caroline Decker and Pat Chambers, said to be responsible for most of the State's agricultural labor disturbances, were arrested and charged with criminal syndicalism. In nearly every Northern California city, police were rounding up agitators suspected of seizing upon the general labor unrest to spread subversive propaganda.[1]

The vigilantes were on the move throughout the valley. In a raid on a Salinas labor camp on September 21, Mrs. Marguerite Vitacion, a Filipino field worker, was burned to death.

"Welfare Lady" Told Off

The ILD had its hands full. In Sacramento, Elaine appeared in court for a man charged with disturbing the peace and harassment of a welfare worker. ILD attorneys were involved in other litigation, and there were so many cases that bail money was all tied up. "I told the judge he could proceed and I would appear as a friend of the court and do my best to protect this man's rights . . . even prepare for an appeal if need be." The judge allowed it. The welfare worker "had called . . . [the man] a bum" and ordered him to leave her office. "He had come back several times asking for temporary relief, asking for work . . . he was going to sit there until he got some relief."

The man "had no place else to go . . . [not even] a flophouse." Elaine said to the woman, "You were the only person in the area to whom he could appeal. You were the welfare lady." She was pursuasive and eloquent. The judge interrupted. Elaine had assured him that she was not an attorney but he suspected otherwise. Just what law school had she gone to? Elaine responded:

> I went to the courts. That has been my only legal training—watching, and being a defendant, and seeing the violations . . . Men and women are doing long terms right now under Criminal Syndicalism because they organized, because they were unemployed, because they turned on somebody's heat so a child wouldn't die from pneumonia. That has been my school. No formal training. In fact, I don't even have a high school diploma.

The jury found the man not guilty; Elaine had won another case.

"You sort of learned by ear," Elaine said. "You did what you could, and hoped . . . I wasn't just fighting for the other guy. I was fighting for myself too. It was my rights I was trying to preserve . . . I wanted this country to be . . . a haven for people regardless of their race and their monetary status."

While women were prominent in ILD leadership, Elaine considered it regrettable that there were no women ILD lawyers on the West Coast. "Whenever we heard of a woman attorney, we tried to find out what her persuasion was . . . Was she ILD material? The lack of women lawyers was unfortunate because I think that sometimes a little bit more warmth emanates from a woman."

Elaine did not consider herself a scholar, nor did she read Marxist writings in great depth. She concentrated on reading material "that had to do with the fights to maintain rights to organize . . . Not that I wanted to be a lawyer, but that was my field." And while each court case was different, there were certain basics: "Basically . . . you fought for your rights, basically you asked for a jury trial, and [you] don't give any more information to the police than you legally have to give." Elaine did recognize her ability to "sort of absorb" an overall case or situation and she was proud that she was able to quote the Bill of Rights word for word.

"Mother Mooney, We'll Finish Your fight!"

Tom Mooney's mother, Mary, died of a heart attack on September 2, 1934. She was 86 years old. The previous day she had gone to San Quentin to see the son she loved so dearly. In Mooney's small cell, the only photograph on the wall was that of Mother Mooney. There wasn't anywhere she wouldn't go to fight for her son. An old lady, not well, an international tour had taken her in 1932 from San Francisco to Moscow where she attended an International Red Aid Congress, then to Rotterdam, Amsterdam, The Hague, Paris, Hamburg, Berlin, London and Dublin. On December 30 that year she was at the Executive Mansion in Albany, New York, where she spoke with President-Elect Franklin Delano Roosevelt. "I wish you would do your utmost," she told him, "to help my boy, who has been in prison, although he is innocent, for almost 17 years. My boy is a good boy."

"Let the funeral of my mother," said Mooney, "be the funeral of a brave soldier in the class struggle who died in action. Let every speaker at my mother's grave, let every tribute to her heroic life, bring out that she was a part of the struggle of the workers."[2]

Thousands of people demanded that Mooney be allowed to attend his mother's funeral, but this was refused by state officials. With members of Mooney's family and Harry Bridges, Elaine traveled with the funeral cortege that on September 8, drove Mary Mooney's mortal remains to the gates of San Quentin in the hope that her son would be allowed one last look at his mother's face. This, too, was refused and the hearse returned to San Francisco.

At a packed Civic Auditorium, 15,000 mourners heard an embittered Leo Gallagher refer to the non-religious service: "For 18 years Mother Mooney has seen the churches stand silently by while her innocent son languished behind the walls of San Quentin. How often have the churches and their leaders been appealed to, to come to the aid of Tom Mooney, and how often have these leaders in cowardly silence turned not a finger?"

Mother Mooney, he said, "realized that only in a united front of struggle is there a possibility of a successful end to the bitter exploitation of the working class. She therefore joined with the Scottsboro mothers in appealing for the freedom of the Scottsboro boys as well as the freedom of her own son."

"Farewell, Mother Mooney," Mike Quin wrote in the September 17 *Western Worker.*

". . . She did not pray to the sky above
Or kneel at plaster shrines,
Or hope for aid from parasites
Who own the mills and mines.

She looked to the strength of the working class,
In its march to victory,
To rip the bars from the cold stone walls
AND SET TOM MOONEY FREE.

. . . Not your tears, but your fists and your pledges;
Not kneeling but standing upright;
Bid farewell to a valiant comrade.
Mother Mooney, WE'LL FINISH YOUR FIGHT!"

Not long before Mother Mooney's death, Elaine rode in a car with her in the "Bloody Thursday" funeral procession. "As we rode up Market Street," Elaine remembered, "Mother Mooney turned to me and said, 'Elaine, when I go, I would like to have the workers pay respect to me and my son, but I want to be buried near my son if he's still in San Quentin.' " In accordance with her wishes, Mother Mooney was buried near the prison in Mt. Tamalpais Cemetery in Marin County.

Defiant Election Rallies

Many Communists ran for state offices in 1934 and, as the November general election drew near, rallies were held in city parks. Mini Carson was a candidate for Congress as well as the Communist Party's election campaign manager. When she mounted a bench to speak in Jefferson Square, the police charged and dragged her to the paddy wagon. The police had decreed that "the Communist Party must not be allowed to hold election rallies anywhere in the city."[3] Six more speakers were arrested as one after another they mounted the park bench. Charles White, Helen Kline, Lillian Lewis, Mark Thornton, George Gould and George Stafford were all taken away to jail. The ILD provided bail.

The Communist Party announced: "The campaign for the defense of free speech and assembly and the fight of a legal political party to conduct the election campaign without police interference will go forward in Jefferson Square again on Sunday, Oct. 14 at 1 p.m. when Karl Hama, Communist candidate for State Assembly, 22nd District, will speak on behalf of his candidacy. A representative of the ILD will explain the reasons for the current police suppression of election campaign activities."[4]

"HAMA, THREE OTHERS JAILED IN FREE SPEECH FIGHT" headlined the

Oct. 18 *Western Worker.* But, it said, the party would return on the following Sunday. And it did. The largest crowd yet assembled and "in face of the threatening police, sang 'The Internationale!' "

A Momentous Year—1934!

Leo Gallagher returned home from his European tour in behalf of Dimitrov and the German antifascist movement. He brought a message from Berlin:

> We, the Red Aid Workers of Germany, and with us millions of militant anti-fascists, know that you, through your mass protests . . . under the leadership of the International Labor Defense, have most decisively prevented the murdering of our comrades Dimitrov, Torgler, Popoff and Taneff,* which Hitler and Goering wished desperately to accomplish . . .
>
> We know that you have contributed penny by penny, to the support of the 200,000 political prisoners, of the relatives of more than 3,000 murdered workers, the wives and children of more than 240,000 fugitives . . .
>
> The terrors of the concentration camps . . . take on from day to day more horrible forms. Imprisoned comrades, Social Democrats, unaffiliated workers, Jews and Christians, are literally martyred to death . . .

From Moscow, where he was given asylum, Dimitrov said that the ILD could be proud not only for its "struggle against reaction in the United States, but . . . against the campaigns of terror in fascist countries . . ."

On his return, Gallagher left immediately for Canada where he participated in the sedition-criminal syndicalism trial of A.E. Smith, national secretary of the Canadian Labor Defense League. A fight to force Canadian Immigration to admit Gallagher into Canada was successful. Smith was acquitted.

National Scottsboro Week

In the U.S. November 26 to December 2 was set as National Scottsboro week while the ILD in Cuba set November 27 as a national day of protest. United Front Scottsboro Conferences were held in many

*Reichstag Fire Defendants

Elaine with Angelo Herndon (left), Nov. 20, 1934, when Herndon stopped in San Francisco on his national tour.

U.S. cities. A delegation of prominent liberals, Black and white, went to Washington, D.C. to demand that President Roosevelt intervene. Alabama sharecropper leader Ralph Gray was killed at a Scottsboro protest meeting. Urged by some church leaders to repudiate the ILD in exchange for life sentences, the Scottsboro defendants refused.

Congress Against War and Fascism

In the Scottsboro case, there was hardly a corner of the earth where the fight for the youths' freedom was unknown. In August, the Scottsboro mothers appealed to the International Women's Congress Against War and Fascism, meeting in Paris, for support. Ella

Reeve "Mother" Bloor led the U.S. delegation of 40 women, two of whom were ILD members, to the Paris congress. The Congress call included a special message to U.S. women:

> American Women! Ten and a half million of you work in America's factories and mills. You weave the cloth, make the clothes, make the shoes that America wears. You work in the metal plants that turn out bullets and shells, in the chemical and dye plants that will at a moment's notice produce the deadly materials for chemical warfare. You teach the youth of the country. Millions of you are housewives and domestic workers. You have a great responsibility.
>
> Will you use this power to aid in preparing another war? Will you let the industrial and financial magnates, the profiteers of the last war, throw the world into another war? Will you weave the cloth for uniforms, make shoes for the army, make bullets with which your men will be sent to kill sons, husbands and sweethearts of other women like yourselves? Or will you join in this fight which is your fight?
>
> Women of America! United we are an invincible barrier against war and fascism.[5]

International Red Aid played a prominent role in the Congress, urging the creation of women's committees "to adopt the families of murdered and imprisoned anti-fascists . . . " From Germany, where German Red Aid was illegal, the delegate said, "I can assure you that we are not frightened . . . On the contrary, during these trying times our activity has increased."

Sacramento Trial Gets Underway

In December the Sacramento criminal syndicalism trial opened. Gallagher was defense attorney. Elaine helped to organize a mass meeting in San Francisco on December 21 "For the Defense of the Sacramento Prisoners." It was jointly sponsored by the ILD, the AFL Rank and File Committee, the Democratic Open Forum, the Conference for Labor's Civil Rights and the Epic League of San Francisco. The meeting unanimously decided to hold a state-wide united front conference the following February to work for repeal of the Criminal Syndicalism Act.

Merry Christmas

As it did every year, the ILD sent Christmas greetings to U.S. political prisoners and their families:

> *Greetings, that are not empty wishes, greetings that are a pledge of support all year round, greetings that are a pledge of solidarity with you who are behind bars for your loyalty to the working class and with your wives and children outside.*
>
> *We shall continue the fight for your freedom until victory is ours, and until that day we shall continue to do all in our power to provide regular relief to you and your families—not as charity but as solidarity.*

J.B. McNamara, San Quentin No. 25314, had a Christmas message for the ILD: "... My undying confidence is in the workers; and why not? They create and produce all the material things of life."

12.

Facing 1935 . . .

S.O.S. for United Action

By 1935 the ILD was 10 years old. The trade unions faced a resurgence of repressive legislation, militant foreign-born workers confronted increasingly severe deportation laws, a plan was in the works for a Federal Criminal Sedition Law. The ILD held President Roosevelt and the New Deal responsible and believed that there was a threat of fascism in the United States.

Especially, said the ILD, "The fight for protection of the foreign-born, for the right of political asylum in America, is the fight for the democratic rights of the native-born, the fight to save the lives of our own fighters against fascism . . . Facing 1935, this is our task."

In California, the Criminal Syndicalism Repeal Campaign went into high gear and in January, the ILD printed 50,000 copies of "An S.O.S. for United Action" signed by the 18 defendants:

> We, 18 men and women now on trial . . . face 6 to 84 years imprisonment each for our labor activities, a total of 1512 prison years . . . Most of us have been prominent in agricultural strikes—strikes which gave exploited field and cannery workers 25 to 100 percent wage increases . . .
>
> We have already spent 6 months in jail . . .
>
> The line-up of forces in the trial explains all. It is finance-capital versus labor. The prosecution is backed by the Chambers of Commerce, the banks, the Power Trust, the Industrial Association, the Associated Farmers, Inc., Big Business, the American Legion. The defense is organized labor and all the issues of humanity for which it stands . . .

In Northern California, a United Front Conference for the Defense of the Sacramento 18 and the Repeal of the Criminal Syndicalism Law was held February 10 at Carpenters Hall, 112 Valencia Street, San Francisco. The 110 delegates represented 90 organizations, including 18 AFL unions. In Southern California, 101 organizations were involved. Statewide, these ranged from Democratic clubs to the Communist Party, from women's clubs to the California section of the Veterans of Foreign Wars.

The ILD initiated a campaign to obtain 240,000 valid signatures to get a Criminal Syndicalism Act repeal measure on the ballot. Simultaneously a campaign was started to get a repeal measure through the State Legislature. There were meetings, rallies, and conferences up and down the state.

Elaine participated in numerous speaking tours in the repeal campaign, which continued into 1936. That was the year that the California State Federation of Labor voted at its state convention to support both the repeal campaign and the demand to release the Sacramento defendants. Bills to repeal were introduced in the State Assembly in 1936 and 1937, failing both times.

"Don't Let Them Take Him"

On St. Patrick's Day, 1935 the ILD scheduled a repeal rally in San Francisco's Mission Dolores Park. Elaine, scheduled to be one of the speakers, dressed in green in honor of the day. Leo Gallagher had come in from the Sacramento trial. Some ministers were also present. Rally organizers weren't looking for trouble. A young man named Edward Johnson began to address the crowd. "All of a sudden," Elaine said, "the police swooped down . . . and grabbed this man off the bench." As he was dragged off, Elaine jumped up onto the bench. She shouted for people not to let the police take Johnson in by himself. "They will kill him!" She entreated the crowd: "They're in a murderous mood – they'll kill him. Go with him!" Elaine's concern was due to the arrests the week before of two men who had been taken in singly for distributing leaflets. They were badly beaten by police and "were a bloody mess when we bailed them out."

Free Speech Fight

Elaine was grabbed off the bench and arrested along with Johnson. "They took us across the street to a church and put us up against a wall. A [police] car drove up and they started to put Johnson in by himself. I raised my voice, 'Don't let them take him by alone . . . If they get him alone in that car, they'll beat his brains out!' " Elaine pulled out the Bill of Rights that she carried in her purse and began reading it aloud. She shouted, "Is this Nazi Germany?"

Leo Gallagher and a couple of ministers hurried over. Gallagher and one of the ministers were promptly arrested. The minister was soon released, but not Gallagher. Spectators protested and were arrested in turn. Ten in all were taken into police custody: Paula Morton, Elaine and eight men. Johnson was taken alone and in the privacy of Mission Station was savagely beaten. The charges against the ten were inciting to riot and disturbing the peace. Maximum sentence for "riot" was one year in jail.

On March 23, at an evening street meeting at Fillmore and Ellis streets, there were more arrests. Eight were taken into custody as police broke up the meeting; four women jumped out of the paddy wagon while the cops were arresting and gathering up the men. Della Dale, however, did not escape and was brutalized both in the patrol wagon and at the police station. She described the scene at the station:

> . . . One of them took my arm and twisted it . . . they fastened my arms together with the handcuffs across my back and threw me down on the floor . . . kicked me and knocked me down again . . . one officer came up and began beating my head up and down against the floor . . . [then] banged my head up and down against the bench until I could not remember anything . . . Pretty soon I realized I was lying there in a pool of blood . . . I got up . . . trying to walk . . . a policeman came over and threw me down again, and I stayed there until they took me to the hospital."

The ILD issued a leaflet: "EVERY OPEN AIR MEETING AND ELECTION RALLY OF WORKERS ON STREET CORNERS AND IN PARKS IN SAN FRANCISCO IS BEING ATTACKED BY POLICE. FELLOW WORKERS, PACK THE COURTROOMS."

The following Friday, representatives of the ILD, the Conference for Labor Civil Rights, Communist Party, and American League Against War and Fascism met with Mayor Angelo Rossi and Chief of Police William Quinn to protest police attacks on park and street meetings. "The street meetings which were broken up by the police will continue to be held," Rossi and Quinn were informed. Another meeting was announced and on March 28, the *Western Worker* reported that "Mayor Rossi's blue-coated, women-beating thugs were forced to allow more than 300 workers to attend . . . " Protesters' children flew kites with "Free Tom Mooney" and "Fight for Free Speech" slogans.

The Red Squad resisted the people's right to free speech in city parks for a long time; Dolores Park was the last holdout. Denial of free speech there, as in Columbus and Jefferson parks, was ultimately to fall under the pressure of the free speech fights.

People exercising their right to free speech were arrested time after time, Elaine said. There was a constant campaign to win and maintain free speech rights through street corner meetings, meetings in parks, meetings in halls. There were "innumerable arrests year after year." It didn't matter what the meeting was about or whether it "was called by the International Labor Defense or the Communist Party or an election campaign, or some workers on strike . . . there [was] arrest after arrest and there would be protest after protest."

It was through these "constant meetings and constant arrests" that free speech rights were won. And they were won on the legal front too – cases won in court and cases thrown out. Sometimes, Elaine said, it took "two years of fighting to be able to conclude a speech . . . then [if] the person wasn't arrested . . . you knew you had won . . . "

Railroading in Sacramento

On April 1, after a 4-month trial, the jury in the Sacramento case rendered its verdict. While Gallagher's brilliant defense resulted in acquittal of ten of the defendants, the jury was persuaded that while not guilty of a single act of violence or sabotage, eight of the defendants had "conspired" to commit such acts. Prosecutor Neil McAllister had introduced almost 200 pieces of literature to woo the jury to the view that the defendants "advocate the overthrow of the government of the United States by force and violence. By force and violence! . . . "

It had been a "mad spectacle," according to the *Western Worker*. When Gallagher attempted to read from prosecution-introduced literature, Judge Dal Lemmon charged him with introducing "extraneous propaganda" and disallowed it.

Said Gallagher: "When the prosecution was reading from these pamphlets, the court placed no restrictions on them and all the objections of the defense were almost always overruled. Now when we try to read from the same pamphlets, you assume the role of prosecutor and make all the objections for them. They [the prosecution] sit back there like three dumb oxen and none of them have opened their mouths . . . "

McAllister "rose in ponderous wrath. His neck turned red and he challenged Gallagher to meet him in the hall..." The writings were his main evidence, yet when the defense attempted to use them to refute McAllister's claims, McAllister said the message of the pamphlets was "a camouflage for the real aims of the Communist Party."

Judge Lemmon finally allowed the defendants to read some of the material. However, "scores of exhibits have been stricken out rather than allow the defense to read parts of them," Gallagher noted.

Gallagher "also protested an editorial in the *Sacramento Union* which urged the court to race through proceedings and bring the trial to a hasty conclusion. He pointed out that not only the freedom of these defendants but that of hundreds of other workers is menaced if the present railroading succeeds. 'Literally thousands of acts of vigilante lawlessness have occurred in the past year,' said Gallagher. 'Yet there has not been one instance of arrest or prosecution. Instead of that, thousands of dollars have been spent to prosecute these defendants against whom there is no evidence whatsoever.' "

Defendant Pat Chambers told the jury: "No strike leader will incite violence. Calling a strike is a great responsibility... Go to the agricultural fields and see for yourselves how miserable the conditions of life are there. You will see children with the terrible imprint of hunger on their faces... I swore above all that these children would not go hungry. I have seen so much misery, starvation, brutality, I am glad I took part to a small extent in the struggle against them, and against the banks that caused them."

But McAllister appealed to fear and hysteria:

> There is only one way it [force and violence] can be stopped... and that is you, ladies and gentlemen of the jury. If you don't an aroused public will stop it, and the vigilantes will stop it. You'll have bloodshed, another Pixley and another Harlan, Kentucky...
>
> They attempted to justify this revolution by what? By the majority. A majority has no more right to overthrow this government than has a minority... Think of the covered wagons. Think of the Donner party... [the defendants] propose to... overthrow the government. From Moscow! They are paid by Moscow!... The eyes of the nation are on you, asking you, begging you, pleading with you to stamp out this insurrection... [1]

"Their Fight is Our Fight!"

Sentenced to terms of one to 14 years were Chambers, Caroline Decker, Nora Conklin, Jack Crane, Albert Hagoudry, Lorine Norman, Norman Mini and Martin Wilson. Wilson was the local ILD representative. While not a lawyer, he – like Elaine – sometimes defended workers in court, winning acquittals and hung juries.

Wilson put words to the tune "While the Roll is Called up Yonder:"

. . . You have rolled in wealth and comfort
from the workers' misery.
You have fattened off the sweat of
Labor's toil.
But now a day is coming when the
workers will be free
And they're organized to take back
all your spoil.
All the jails, and guns, and tear-gas
Cannot stop the march to freedom,
Nor defeat the working class.
So we say "To Hell with all your C.S. Laws."[2]

From the Sacramento County jail, where the three women waited to be transported to Tehachapi State Prison – California's "Model Prison for Women," Lorine Norman wrote to the *Labor Defender:* "During the months I have been in jail [I] have been surprised to find that many of the girls in here know something about Scottsboro, Pixley, Mooney and other struggles . . . I am proud to be a Communist, an ILD member and that I carried the Red Flag representing the solidarity of the workers and farmers on the last . . . May Day, for all of which I was convicted of CS." Norman, whose married name was Lorine Kinz, was pregnant at the time of her arrest; she was released on bail later that year and saw her baby die in birth.

From Tehachapi, Decker wrote:

It is difficult to explain how a labor prisoner feels about the International Labor Defense. No matter how strong the conviction of the prisoner; no matter how well he understands the forces that placed him in prison; no matter how strong he is in spirit, he is made that much stronger to straighten his shoulders and raise his head against persecution by knowing that for him and with him out there stands the ILD and its many friends.

The ILD is usually, for a labor prisoner, the living, active bond between the case he went to prison for and himself. The individual members and friends of the ILD may forever remain unknown to us as individuals, but let them know that they are each a part of the collective strength of an organization whose work commands respect and admiration because it is an important part of the struggle to wipe out injustice and to make this a happier world to live in.

It is easier, of course, for those of us who have no children—no dependents on the outside. Working class children are too precious to neglect. It is in the fight to secure their lives in plenty and happiness that many of us go to prison . . . And it is the care of the children and families of ILD prisoners that is the noblest work of the ILD.

The Sacramento prisoners were still in prison when the Trade Union Unity League (TUUL) leadership, recognizing a new stage of struggle and need for unity in the trade union movement, began the process of disbanding, urging members to join appropriate AFL unions. The stricken CAWIU, dealt a death blow by the Sacramento trial, was among the first to do so. From prison, Chambers and Decker, young militant CAWIU leaders, called upon agricultural and cannery workers:

Instead of allowing ourselves to be divided, we should all unite to fight for our common demands. If we remain divided, the employers will continue to use one group against the other. Therefore, the District Committee of the CAWIU urges all workers, organized and unorganized, to join the AFL.

By October the movement against the Criminal Syndicalism Act had intensified and both Northern and Southern California ILDs held conferences centered around winning the release of the Sacramento prisoners and others who faced trial on CS charges. "THEIR FIGHT IS OUR FIGHT" was the slogan. Anita Whitney chaired the San Francisco meeting; among speakers was Tanna Alex of the Utopian Society who represented the United Labor Campaign. Two years after their conviction, the Sacramento Criminal Syndicalism cases were reversed on appeal and the prisoners were released.

Gallagher Disbarment Sought

The first trial of the St. Patrick's Day Mission Dolores Park case took place on May 7 before Judge Lazarus. The jury dismissed charges against six of the ten defendants, but deadlocked 9 to 3 for conviction of four: Elaine, Gallagher, Paula Morton, and Edward Johnson. Now there would be a retrial and it was obvious to Elaine that the "heat was on" to disbar the ILD's chief counsel. Here was "a man who had studied and taught corporate law [and] had become an advocate and firebrand for workers' rights. He was something to behold . . . "

Gallagher's nine-year tenure at Southwestern University had terminated in 1932 when he was dismissed for labor activities. One of his first Left movement defense cases had been as attorney for six YCL members who had jumped onto the track during the 1932 Los Angeles Olympic Games wearing "Free Tom Mooney" signs. He was attorney for J.B. McNamara, worked in the Mooney defense, and participated in hundreds of big and small labor and political cases. Elaine was not only convinced that "they were trying to give him the ax," but that one pretext would be his association with "lewd and dissolute people," meaning herself and Karl who lived together in defiance of the anti-miscegenation laws. She had overheard snide references to this during the previous trial and felt sure that "at one point or another they are going to bring it up." Elaine and Karl began to make plans to get married. They had several months leeway, however, before the new trial.

Elaine and Leo Gallagher in court where they are being tried with 15 others on charges of inciting to riot at a meeting in Jefferson Square. Gallagher is both defendant and counsel at the jury trial. [S.F. *Call Bulletin*, 5/8/35.]

13.

Organize!

Overview

Roosevelt's New Deal paved the way for one million unorganized workers to join established AFL unions. Company unionism grew, too, however. The AFL continued to reject industrial unionism, maintaining craft unions and refusing to organize on an industry-wide basis. Out of the struggle that ensued, the Committee for Industrial Organization (CIO) would be born in November of 1935.

There were 14 million foreign-born workers in the labor force, more than 60 percent of them in heavy industry. Forty-seven deportation and other anti-foreign born measures were introduced in the Congress. The ILD set a new members goal of 5,000; the recruitment of employed industrial workers was a priority. One-third of ILD members were Black; however, Anna Damon pointed to the lack of "a united membership of Negro and white," with an "entirely Negro membership" in the South and a "very small" Black membership in the West. She urged more attention, also, to the recruitment of women, especially Black women.

In Birmingham, Alabama, the KKK issued fliers:

> "NEGROES BEWARE. DO NOT ATTEND COMMUNIST MEETINGS. THE KU KLUX KLAN IS WATCHING YOU . . . " A defiant ILD responded: "KKK! THE WORKERS ARE WATCHING YOU!!"

The Case of James Workman

By February 1935, Mother Lode Local 48 of the Mine, Mill and Smelter Workers Union had been on strike in Amador County for four months in a bitter dispute, mostly over hazardous working conditions in the gold mines. In the October 1935 *Labor Defender*, Elaine told the story:

...[Edward] Vandeleur (one of the betrayers of the San Francisco General Strike), President of the State Federation of Labor and the San Francisco Labor Council, was in charge of the strike and defense.

In February a reign of terror led by the sheriff and vigilante groups broke loose in Amador County. Several members of the local were framed on charges of possessing "concealable weapons," "rioting," etc. The ILD sent protests and an offer of aid in defending the workers arrested for strike activity. The workers at first tabled the communication. Their minds had been poisoned by labor fakers.

Over 30 workers had been arrested and only five who were the most militant were not bailed out. Among them was James Workman who was held for $500 cash bail. The ILD offered to bail him out and he accepted. At the preliminary hearing the bail was suddenly raised to $2,000 cash, without protest from the attorney retained by the AFL. Workman went back to jail. Vandeleur's press agent, a Miss Logan, told a committee from the National Students' League, who went to offer assistance on the picket line, "It will do Workman and the others no harm to stay in jail and cool their heels!" (Workman has T.B. and continually spits blood. The jail is a hell hole with no sanitary provisions, light or air, only one small window in the entire basement).

After visiting Workman a second time and bailing him out again, he asked that an ILD attorney be associated in his case. The AFL refused. Workman then decided to have the ILD alone defend him. After this, one of the AFL attorneys agreed to be associated with George Andersen (assigned to the case by the ILD). In the meantime Alfo Canales, who was arrested with Workman, was sentenced to 1 to 5 years in San Quentin, for having the same weapon that Workman is also charged with concealing. The Workman trial lasted 10 days, brought out the true nature of the frameup against the strikers, but ended with Workman's conviction. A new trial has been won for him over the desperate protest of the prosecution.

A branch of 43 members, mainly miners and their wives has been formed in the gold mine country. It is called the Canales-Workman Branch (ILD). The greater majority of the miners—about 95—and their wives, who subsequently have been arrested on the picket lines have asked for ILD defense. Canales is now out on bail furnished by the ILD, after spending five months in the Jackson jail and one month in San Quentin. He has requested that an ILD attorney be associated in his appeal or that the ILD take it over completely.

Elaine Smells a Rat

Workman's bail was raised to $2,000 – he was taken back to jail. Elaine went to get him out. Carrying the cash bail, she rode to Jackson with Joe White, one of the first Black longshoremen on the San Francisco waterfront. Their car was part of a May 12 – Mothers' Day – caravan of cars and trucks carrying food and clothing to the hard-up miners' families. This was organized by AFL Central Labor Councils of Alameda, San Francisco and other northern California counties. With 500 cars as a goal, San Francisco longshoremen had called for "a big enthusiastic caravan to build workers' unity between the maritime workers and the inland workers" by combining a "Sunday outing with building working class solidarity."[1] A rally was to be held at strike headquarters in Jackson. As they neared the town the long caravan was directed off the main highway by its Highway Patrol escort, and held there, ostensibly to wait for cars from Sacramento to join them. "I smell a rat," Elaine told White. "They're keeping us here because they're getting ready for something . . . "

Finally the caravan was released and arrived in Jackson. Instead of an expected crowd at strike headquarters, however, only two men were there. They said the caravan was expected up at the Argonaut Mine. Elaine had planned to bail Workman out of jail and bring him to the rally where he would be one of the speakers. While the big caravan headed for the mine, Elaine went to the jail to get Workman out. The sheriff, however, was nowhere to be seen; Elaine needed him for the paperwork. She would find him at the mine, the jailer told her. She and Joe caught up with the caravan, their car falling in at the rear.

They proceeded to the mine at the top of a hill. Some strikers' families were there but not as many as were expected. Then it happened: "There were these deputized men coming up with pickhandles and everything else." The road was blocked. It was a trap. "Men and boys [vigilantes] got out of cars armed with rifles, clubs, pick handles, blackjacks." White was able to turn his car around; he stepped on the gas and escaped the trap. He and Elaine saw the sheriff and his men drive the strikers down the hill "right into the arms of the vigilantes." Most cars couldn't turn around and the main body of the caravan was attacked. Many strikers and supporters were injured. A "spirited show of solidarity" was broken up.

A stevedore wrote in the May 20 *Waterfront Worker:*

I arrived in Jackson with the caravan of good will which consisted of wives, children and workers from various trade unions of the Bay Region. Also a truckload of food and money from the Ladies' Auxiliary Local 38-79. Brothers, what I witnessed in Jackson will never be forgotten. We all know the foul tactics of the police, but to see an AFL representative point out militant AFL members to the police is the lowest thing I have ever seen. I was arrested with several other brothers . . . We were thrown into a dirty filthy jail with hardly any ventilation, Brothers, wives and mothers, and we found two young miners—just kids. Their only crime was to dare to fight for the right to organize for American principles. One of the kids is under a $3000 bail. His name is J. Workman and O! what a pity. The poor boy is tubercular. His dry cough can be heard a block away.

The $2,000 cash bail money Elaine was carrying that day "belonged to a lot of workers. I wasn't about to have it confiscated." She and Joe White agreed they couldn't wait around to see what happened; they had to get out of there. They drove back to the Bay Area. On the way, she picked up a newspaper. The day wasn't over but already the press was asserting that Elaine had "instigated a stevedore riot in Jackson [and] escaped in an expensive car driven by a Negro chauffeur."

An *Associated Press* report provided additional details of the Jackson events:

Gun-bearing citizens led by sheriff's offices routed pickets at the gates of two famous gold mines here today, and then completed the destruction of a strikers' camp which, in the meantime, had been set ablaze during the night by vigilantes. The sheriff's army then went into action again. Stoves, chairs, tables, boxes, everything that had been collected by the pickets were thrown into the blazing rooms of strike headquarters.

The next day Elaine was in a San Francisco courtroom defending herself in one of her trials. A newspaper report asserted that she was being sought for the Jackson "riot." She told the jury: "If they're looking for me, why aren't they here?"

Elaine did return to Jackson and did post bail for Workman. A subsequent investigation of the "riot" conducted by the San Francisco Central Labor Council revealed, Elaine said, that "it was someone from the State Federation who had arranged that side play . . . There was quite a hassle. Jack Shelley, who later became congressman and mayor, helped expose Scharrenberg* and Vandeleur. If certain strikes in the state didn't suit them, they . . . [were willing] to see the workers lose out." Elaine was given the floor at the Labor Council investigation to "expose that ploy . . . and I spoke there and got more support for the gold strikers. But they didn't send any more caravans." On May 30, a longshoreman's wife reported, a delegation of wives returned to Jackson "to take a few things to the miners . . . we went to a miner's house, whose wife had a baby, just eight days old. The woman is under-nourished, the child is also . . . What chance have the miners unless we get behind them? This isn't just a miners' strike, but that of all labor."[2]

The Mine, Mill and Smelter Workers Union would before long become one of the earliest CIO unions, and in September 1935, the *Waterfront Worker* would report that "the year old strike of the heroic Jackson miners was settled on 9-16 as far as the fight with four major companies . . . the demands were made and ratified for a year's working agreement, recognition of the union and grievance committees; wages ranging from $4 to $5 per day. This climaxes one of the State's most heroic labor battles."

The "Modesto Boys" Case

Another notorious labor frameup of the mid-1930s involved the "Modesto Boys," oil tanker seamen involved in what labor reporter Mike Quin termed a "hopeless and inadvisable strike"[3] called by Scharrenberg, whose antipathy to the newly-formed militant Maritime Federation of the Pacific was well known. Seamen on Standard Oil tankers worked under some of the worst, most rotten conditions of all maritime workers and the '34 strike had not resolved them. These seamen bided their time, preparing "for a really effective move at a later date." That was the situation when Standard Oil executives and Scharrenberg, their "willing ally," saw their chance to destroy the Maritime Federation.[4]

It didn't work, but in the process, eight men were framed and sent to prison. These were the "Modesto Boys." A pamphlet published at the time by the Joint Marine-Modesto Defense Committee

---

*Paul Scharrenberg, secretary-treasurer of the Sailors' Union of the Pacific

exposed the plot. On April 20, 1935, Standard Oil Company guards and the Stanislaus County sheriff stopped two cars outside of Patterson, a tiny rural community near Modesto. Eleven men were hauled out, the cars searched. Dynamite, time fuses, and detonating caps were found. Two of the men – later found to be company spies – disappeared. Nine were arrested and charged with conspiracy to blow up some Standard Oil gas stations as well as the Del Puerto Hotel at Patterson; it was housing Standard Oil strikebreakers. The arrested men said they were in the area to check out the hotel and assess public opinion, local residents being "far removed from contact with unions and the problems of union labor and thoroughly saturated with Standard Oil propaganda." If feasible, the strikers planned to establish a picketline at the hotel.

The defense effort was headed up by the Modesto Defense Committee and the Maritime Federation of the Pacific, with the help of numerous trade union organizations; the following year, at its 1935 national convention, the American Federation of Labor endorsed the defense. Before that only the Mooney-Billings and McNamara cases had received national AFL endorsement. The ILD's role was central to the course of the Modesto case.

While found innocent of conspiring to blow up the hotel, a jury found the defendants guilty of possession of the dynamite with which to accomplish the act; that is, they had the dynamite, the jury said, but no use for it! Pending appeal, seven of the men were sentenced to five years in San Quentin and one to Folsom. They were John Rodgers, John Burrows, Henry Silva, Victor Johnson, Robert Fitzgerald, John Souza, Patsy Ciambrelli and Reuel Stanfield. Alphons Buyle was ill and not tried.

The frameup was exposed a year and a half later when James Scrudder confessed that he and Hal Marchant, the two spies, had planted the dynamite and snitched to the police. ILD attorney Grover Johnson was instrumental in documenting the evidence of the frameup. Victor Johnson credited the ILD with playing a valuable role in securing the confession, thus bringing "before the public irrefutable evidence of the subversive methods used by employers against trade unions and militant workers."

So crass was this frameup that the State Legislature conducted an investigation. A majority report issued on April 14, 1937, said that the title of the case should have been "The People of the State of California and the Standard Oil Company of California versus the Defendants." The investigation clearly exposed the relationships between Standard Oil, the San Francisco police and the prosecution, and recommended full pardons for seven of the eight men in prison. By that time, two of them were out on bail and sentences for two more had been reduced to two years. Scharrenberg was eventually expelled from the Sailors' Union of the Pacific.

Elaine remembered organizing monthly visits to San Quentin to see the "Modesto Boys." Stanfield, not freed until 1938, wrote to the ILD: "I feel that every worker in the world ought to know of the work your organization has done in behalf of the Modesto case and organized labor. I wish that every one of them knew how you people stood shoulder to shoulder with us – never thinking of self glory, only trying to free us . . . my trust is in the workers."

Lumber Strike

There was to be no rest for Elaine and the ILD. Lumber workers in Eureka, Humboldt County, 300 miles north of San Francisco, appealed for help. Their union was Sawmill and Lumber Workers Local 2563, AFL. Said Albert "Mickie" Lima:

> "I first met Elaine in 1935. We were organizing the lumber workers in the Redwood district into an industrial union. In the middle of the year we were maneuvered into a premature strike.
>
> "The Redwood Association organized 1,000 vigilantes who were all deputized by the County Sheriff. They also imported twenty gun thugs to beat up on union members. In June they attacked our picketline, resulting in three union members being murdered and a dozen brothers and sisters badly wounded. Following this murderous attack they used the vigilantes, the Sheriff's office and the police department to arrest the strike leadership. They put us in jail and threw away the key. No one was allowed to visit us—no family or friends, and no attorney in the area would agree to represent us. No bail or charges were set, and the Redwood Association proceeded to break our strike."

In early 1935, wages for lumber workers were 35 cents an hour, the workweek was 60 hours. Strikers demanded union recognition, higher pay, and a shorter workweek.

Elaine vividly remembered the strike and the "cold-blooded massacre of the unarmed pickets." The San Francisco ILD immediately sent attorneys Gallagher and Andersen to assess the situation and see what they could do for the strikers. "The lumber barons had a history of trying to beat down unionization," Elaine said. "Decent [people] . . . were aroused by the arrests, the conditions in the jail, and the high bail . . . " The first annual memorial service for the murdered strikers was held in 1936 and "they were still trying to raise funds for the families and to pay funeral expenses."

Lima related how Elaine and Gallagher once maneuvered their way through vigilante lines to get into Eureka. "A well-to-do woman friend loaned Elaine her very handsome sedan and another friend posed as a chauffeur. When the car was stopped on the highway roadblock, Elaine and Leo waxed indignant, demanded the names of the vigilantes and threatened to contact their 'good friend,' the governor of California, if they were not allowed to proceed. The vigilantes let the car through."

Elaine and Gallagher forced the County to bring charges and set bail. The ILD made a public appeal for bail funds and got everybody out. Some strike sympathizers who put up their homes as bond found their names listed in the local press. The Humboldt *Times* and Humboldt *Standard* viciously attacked the strikers.

Elaine was the main speaker at a Eureka Labor Temple protest and memorial meeting for the murdered strikers. More than 500 overflowed the hall, and many more stayed in their cars because of a heavy rain. From the pockets and pocketbooks of hard-up workers and their families, Elaine took up a collection of $120, a phenomenal amount in view of the prevailing hunger and need.

In a long legal process involving three trials, Gallagher won hung juries and the county finally was forced to drop all charges.

"Die Quietly in Bed"

Young James Workman, still on trial in Jackson, was incensed by the cold-blooded massacre of striking lumber workers. He sent a telegram to the mill owners up North: "There are only two courses open to you. Either you may realize in time that your mill owners and their kind are doomed to defeat, and come over to the side of the people – or you may continue in the present course, hoping that you may have the good luck to die quietly in bed before your brutalities finally arouse the people to revolutionary action."

The union thanked the ILD and District Secretary Elaine Black for their "splendid spirit of helpfulness and aid . . . "[5] While the lumber strike was lost, it laid the basis for eventual success organizing the lumber workers.

Eureka resident Noel Harris met Elaine for the first time during the 1935 lumber strike. "As a left-wing high school student I became acquainted with Elaine Black and greatly admired her warmth, courage and ability." He and Ina Harris said, "She fought the good fight for six decades. Her many contributions live on."

Lima said: "Elaine set an example for all of us in the people's struggles . . . " Meanwhile, on the waterfront, July 8 was the first anniversary of "Bloody Thursday," and a longshoreman wrote a tribute:

> They did not die in the gaudy uniforms of an emperor's regiment. They fell in the worn, sweat-soaked working clothes of union men.
>
> They did not fall on distant battlefields, but on the dirty sidewalk of the Embarcadero, and their red blood flowed in shining pools on the pavement of San Francisco.
>
> They did not go down before the guns of a gallant enemy. They were unarmed workers shot in the backs by the San Francisco police. For this was not the greedy, plundering war of nation with nation, cheered on by heroic ballyhoo and the beating of drums. This was the class struggle—the struggle of the working men against the rich—the struggle of those who do all and own nothing against those who own all and do nothing . . .
>
> Sperry and Bordoise . . . died for decent wages for their fellow workers and a better life for all.[6]

Tar and Feathers in Santa Rosa

Violence and sadism against workers and union organizers in the harvest fields in 1935 was epidemic. The Associated Farmers helped to organize the California Cavaliers whose purpose was to "stamp out all un-American activity among farm labor," and on June 10, crosses were burned on the hills outside of San Jose as a warning to fruit pickers. Then, in the apple orchards of Santa Rosa and Sebastopol on August 1, pickers and packinghouse workers voted to strike. Their meeting hall was attacked by 250 vigilantes.

On August 5, local Works Progress Administration officials were warned to drop "all Communists, Reds and radicals from WPA payrolls or face the wrath" of 300 vigilantes.

On August 23, vigilantes kidnapped five men and dragged them through the streets of Santa Rosa. Solomon Nitzberg, a local rancher, and Jack Green, a sign painter, were tarred and feathered and beaten unmercifully for refusing the mob's demand that they kiss the flag. Nitzberg's home was ruined by massive rifle fire. The orgy of mob violence went down as "the wildest scene in the history of Sonoma County."

Elaine said, "The case aroused tremendous interest . . . The men who were tarred and feathered were not strikers. They were . . . supporting the strikers . . . One was a Communist Party organizer, one was the union organizer and others were members of unions that supported the apple pickers . . . I tried to have the apple pickers who had been arrested on the picket line bailed out and to have attorneys there." The San Francisco *Examiner* hailed the "tar and feather party . . . as a direct answer to the red strike fomenters." In Santa Rosa, there was exultation in high places. According to an unsigned report in the local *Press-Democrat:*

> . . . plans were started for rounding up several known Communist leaders . . . We must have looked like a band of highwaymen, masked and carrying rifles . . . Fists swung through the air. Both men dropped to the floor semiconscious . . . Clippers were produced and hair hacked from their heads. Shirts were ripped from their backs. Buckets of tar paint were hurled over them . . . From two men, they had been transformed into fantastic, ghost-like creatures . . . the vigilantes are just as determined that there will be other such nights as long as Communists continued attempts at radical agitation in Sonoma County.

It was widely acknowledged that the mob was led by local bankers and businessmen. The San Francisco *News* reported that the vigilantes "paraded (Green and Nitzberg) through the streets of Santa Rosa, shouting and singing."

14

Matrimony At Last

That "Piece of Paper"

As the year wore on, time overflowing with the needs of the movement, it clearly became necessary for Elaine and Karl to tie the knot of matrimony. As the time for retrial of the Dolores Park free speech case approached, Elaine became increasingly fearful of a threat to disbar Gallagher. Disbarment of the brilliant lawyer would deprive California workers and the Left-progressive movement of their most valuable defense lawyer.

It was a concern to many. A *Western Worker* column warned that "Gallagher's long record of self-sacrifice and loyalty to the working class has made him one of the principal stumbling blocks to employers in their attempts to use the courts against labor . . . Authorities are seeking to obtain a conviction of Gallagher in order to provide grounds for disbarring him from practice."

"I had butterflies in my stomach," Elaine said, that the prosecution would "throw up the fact" that she and Karl were living together. "Cohabitating and mixed marriage were illegal in this state." The question of legality didn't matter to Elaine and Karl; "That piece of paper [marriage license] isn't going to do anything for Karl and me." But they must think of Gallagher.

Anita Whitney lent them money to go to New Mexico to get married, but the Mine, Mill and Smelter Workers were on strike there and the ILD had offered its help. "The local papers had reported that the Black woman was on her way there to do her dirty work like she did in other places," Elaine recalled. "We went to Washington [state] where we had friends." Even on the train Elaine didn't dare to sit with Karl. "We were to cross state lines, and under the Mann Act they might charge him with transporting me for immoral purposes. He sat in one coach and I sat in another. We ate in the dining room together . . . "

In Seattle, they got a license at City Hall, and found a progressive

Methodist minister who married them on November 5. In San Francisco, Gallagher's attempts to get the trial postponed failed; a telegram from Ida Rothstein congratulated the newlyweds but told them to get back home immediately.

Edward Johnson, in the meantime, had to be institutionalized. One of the four remaining Dolores Park defendants, he had been beaten too many times and had "gone violent," Elaine said. Three defendants were left.

The Dolores Park Trial

Gallagher, Elaine, and Paula Morton went on trial on November 9. As usual, Elaine acted as her own attorney. The courtroom was packed. As was expected, Judge Lazarus made Gallagher his central target, attacking the lawyer as "mean, impertinent and ignorant. I don't know how you were ever admitted to the bar," he said. Shortly after, as a point of law was being argued, Judge Lazarus told Gallagher, "No use bringing in the law. I boast that I never open a law book."

When the prosecution claimed that Johnson had always been a violent person, Elaine was sharp: ". . . it was *your* clubs and *your* beatings."

Reverend Dillon Wesley Throckmorton and Reverend Harry Johnson Lane, both of whom were present at the Dolores Park meeting, testified that at no time had the rally been disorderly or riotous, firmly contradicting prosecutor Gillin's contention that "a howling, menacing, dangerous mob threatened the peace and happiness of citizens of San Francisco, and that one of the ringleaders leading this mob to violence against the police was none other than Leo Gallagher."

When Assistant District Attorney Leslie Gillen accused Rev. Throckmorton of speaking at a Communist meeting, Throckmorton acknowledged that he often spoke on the same platform as Communists and would continue to do so as Communists were people interested in improving the welfare of the people. The specific meeting referred to, he said, was a United Front protest of the tarring and feathering of workers in Santa Rosa.

And then it came – what Elaine had feared: the prosecutor began the fatal sentence. "Elaine, what I know about your personal life . . . " Elaine sprang to her feet and pounded the table. If he knew anything "that had to do with the charge of rioting . . . tell it to the jury."

Otherwise, it was immaterial. He didn't pursue it and Elaine recalled wondering "if I really would have had the stamina to pound that table . . . if we didn't have that legal [marriage] document . . . it was just a few days old."

Elaine became violently ill the night before the defense was scheduled to make its summations to the jury. She "didn't know what it was and we decided maybe I could get into Mt. Zion Hospital . . . the son of the head of the Medical Department was on duty and saw Karl and me – he probably recognized me . . . his first question was, 'When did you have gonorrhea or syphilis last?' " An ILD member – a German refugee who was a nurse – had accompanied Elaine to the hospital and followed the doctor into the hall where she heard him put in a phone call to the County Hospital. He said, "I'm sending you the Black woman – suspected VD." Elaine's nurse friend "came running back to me and said, 'You're not going – come on home, Elaine!' "

A woman doctor friend and ILD member arranged for Elaine to enter Franklin Hospital where she immediately ordered a Wasserman test for VD and urged Elaine to pursue a lawsuit against the Mt. Zion Hospital doctor. Elaine, however, saw the danger. "I can't afford the headlines now," she said. "I'm in the middle of a trial and Leo is involved . . . that's why I went to Seattle last week."

A very ill Elaine was hospitalized and had surgery for acute appendicitis. She remained in the hospital for three weeks; the trial was postponed until December 9. For once a newspaper headline was accurate: "Elaine Black Very Sick." She returned to the courtroom, shaky and weak, but firmly told the jury in her summation that it must find them not guilty – to do otherwise "would be a violation of our Constitutional rights to petition, to protest, to speak." On December 11, the jury came in with a vote of nine for acquittal to three against, the exact opposite of the first trial jury vote. The nine jurors pressed around the defendants, especially Gallagher, congratulating him and shaking hands.

ILD Survey

Nationwide, an ILD survey estimated to cover only 35 to 40 percent of the total, found that labor and other people's struggles in 1935 resulted in 5,277 arrests, 3,143 of which occurred during strikes and union organizing drives; unemployed demonstrations resulted in 842 arrests and anti-fascist activity in 716 arrests. Also, based on incomplete figures, there were vigilante kidnappings of 26 persons, 16 police raids, 13 vigilante raids with much destruction of property, and, in the South, widespread terrorism against Black and white sharecroppers. There were 24 recorded lynchings, all in the South, most connected with sharecropper struggles, all except one of Black people.

In Lowndes county, Alabama, Black sharecropper Willie Witcher, shot down on August 19 by Sheriff Woodruff, told the sheriff: "You can kill me but you can never scare me."

And in the Alabama County of Jackson, town of Scottsboro, history was made when a Black man named Creed Conyers sat on the grand jury. The U.S. Supreme Court had for the second time been forced by massive public pressure and excellent legal work to reverse the Scottsboro death sentences on the basis of exclusion of Blacks from the grand jury. A two-thirds vote was needed from the 18 Jackson County grand jurors to re-indict all nine Scottsboro youths; and it was done. This blocked a third appeal to the Supreme Court. The ILD called for an intensified effort to save the lives of the Scottsboro Nine.

There were 39 persons on the ILD's list of long-term political prisoners – persons persecuted for labor action, political belief or for reasons of race and nationality; 29 of these – which included the nine Scottsboro youths – were Black and four were women.

Angelo Herndon Appeal

Angelo Herndon lost his U.S. Supreme Court appeal to set aside his conviction on charges of "insurrection," an ancient pre-Civil War statute designed to forbid agitation for freedom from slavery. The court refused to take jurisdiction and his sentence of 18 to 20 years on the chain gang was upheld. The following year, the court again refused.

Herndon wrote in the *Western Worker:*

> Friends, this is only the beginning of the Herndon fight . . . We can make the Supreme Court change its mind! We who have followed the leadership of the ILD have done so much, and it is only a token of our strength! When I was sick in the hell-hole of Fulton Tower Prison, the ILD and its hundreds of thousands of supporters and sympathizers took up the challenge of the Georgia officials, and raised $15,000 in bail that I might be free for a time at least. But we

> must have speed, speed! . . . Workers! You saved Tom Mooney from the noose! You can save me from the chain-gang and smash the lyncher's slave law.

A national petition campaign for Herndon's freedom was initiated by the ILD and other organizations. Before the year was out, the Socialist Party, headed by Norman Thomas, had joined the signature drive. This support, however, was predicated on the ILD providing the SP with petitions which separated its campaign from any joint campaign "with the ILD or any other Communist organization." While refuting the "serious misconceptions as to the character, role and work" of the ILD, National Secretary Anna Damon supplied the Socialist Party with the requested 5,000 petitions carrying the name only of the Socialist Party and the Young People's Socialist League.

Herndon's "real offense," said Thomas, "was that he was a Negro and a Communist or Communist sympathizer and therefore easy prey for a notoriety-seeking prosecutor. There is no justice in Georgia, and not much in America, if he is to be compelled to serve 20 years in the hell of a Georgia chain-gang . . . His cause is our cause."

Damon welcomed the Socialist's cooperation. "We know how vital it is at this moment, to save the life of Angelo Herndon." The "United Front for Herndon" obtained hundreds of thousands of signatures. The campaign spread to almost every state in the union as well as many foreign countries. Public officials, trade union leaders, intellectuals, and other prominent individuals demanded his release.

Not until April 26, 1937, would the U.S. Supreme court rule 5-4 that the Georgia slave insurrection statute was unconstitutional.

Mass Arrests

In San Francisco, Elaine and staff were in constant meetings. In mass arrests the ILD did not have sufficient funds to bail out all those arrested, so first they bailed out the sick, those who were badly beaten up, and those with families to support. Priorities in taking people out were determined by the ILD executive board in consultation with the organization involved. Organizations planning demonstrations would apprise the ILD so that it could be prepared as well as possible for the subsequent arrests. Communists often defended themselves in court.

"Sometimes I would take issue with a planned demonstration," Elaine said, "... [as] it's too close to another demonstration – will we have the forces there? Will we be able to provide a proper defense? ... if there were mass arrests, who among the defendants would defend themselves? If non-Communists wanted to defend themselves we would have to discuss the plan with the attorneys and explain some of the pitfalls." Also, many of the protests were spontaneous; "... You would hear about a neighbor being tossed out on the street and you would be there."

The ILD also organized "workers' juries." Observers attended trials to determine if defendants got a fair trial "or whether their rights were in fact being further violated by the court." And they would publicize their findings. Elaine was a strong believer in "packing the courtroom to show that we had friends; that saved a good many men and women from long terms in prison. We gave out thousands of leaflets asking people to be in the courtrooms. The press took note. The prosecutors and some of the judges might make remarks about courtrooms packed with riffraff. But in those days, most women came to court wearing gloves and hats."

Shipscalers Murder Case

In December 1935, the ILD became involved in the Ship Scalers Union case. The union had been out on strike a year longer than the other maritime unions in the 1934 strike. These men, mostly immigrants from Central and South America, had the lowest of all wage rates and did the dirtiest work, chipping paint and crawling into the hot ships' holds to scrape soot. Divisions as to whether or not to go back to work had resulted in a big fight in the union hall. In an attempt to avoid the fighting, a member jumped out of a window and died from the fall. Allegations were made that he was thrown from the window. Archie Brown tells the story:

> "Together with three Latino leaders of the strike—Francisco Jiminez, Julius Canales and Natalio Villi—I was arrested on a charge of murder. No bail was permitted and we sat in jail for 80 days as the noose was drawn tighter.
>
> "The ILD, their great peoples' lawyers Leo Gallagher and George Andersen, as well as Elaine, went to work. The ILD organized not

> only nationwide but worldwide protest for us Scalers. The trial judge invited our attorneys and myself (I was defending myself) into his chambers and after showing us drawers full of letters and telegrams, he complained: "They keep demanding a fair trial—aren't you getting a fair trial?" From then on, I knew the value of protest, marches, rallies, letters. Don't let anyone tell you that your protest doesn't count—it could save someone from going to jail or even death."

On December 26, 1935, the headline of the *Western Worker* was jubilant: "ILD WINS FREEDOM OF SCALERS." Gallagher and Andersen had forced the prosecution to reveal a statement the man had made in Spanish before he died, that he had indeed gone out of the window of his own volition. The jury was out only seven minutes.

"Elaine celebrated the victory with us but kept right on going," Brown said. "There were other matters calling for her attention. Her life had many sides – she made many contributions to the cause of the workers and her Party. We can only hope to emulate her. There are new times at hand, new struggles are here or aborning. The new times and struggles will create the necessary organizations and call forth new Elaines to meet the situation. We won't ever forget Elaine."

Henri Barbusse

Henri Barbusse, world famous French novelist and Communist, was a contributing editor to the *Labor Defender*. His articles were powerful calls to action, bringing passion and eloquence to rally international support for the defense of victims of fascist terror in Germany and Italy and for the defense of political prisoners in the United States. He died in Moscow in 1935. "He lent his brilliant pen, his flaming words, his unquenchable vigor to every major defense battle of the laboring masses," said the *Labor Defender*. "He helped mobilize millions for the defense of Sacco and Vanzetti, Tom Mooney, the Scottsboro Boys, Angelo Herndon, Gramsci, Thaelmann, Dimitroff – with all the elegance at his command." To build a powerful organization for the defense of the working class, he said:

> Do not leave out a single organization, a single group of workers, trade unionists, pacifists—who by virtue of their principles should

be with us—and who must if they can—fight in our ranks. Do not wait until they come to you. Stretch out your hands—open wide your arms . . .

As early as June 1928, Barbusse had directed a special appeal to the people of the United States to support the victims of Benito Mussolini's fascist terror in Italy. "Only one thing can make them reply, one thing alone can force them to halt and retreat," he said. "And that thing is the great avenging voice of the outraged public opinion of mankind. It is with the hope of strengthening our outcry with that of all honest men throughout the world, that I am now making this appeal to the American public." Across the United States, to honor his memory, ILD branches took the name of Henri Barbusse.

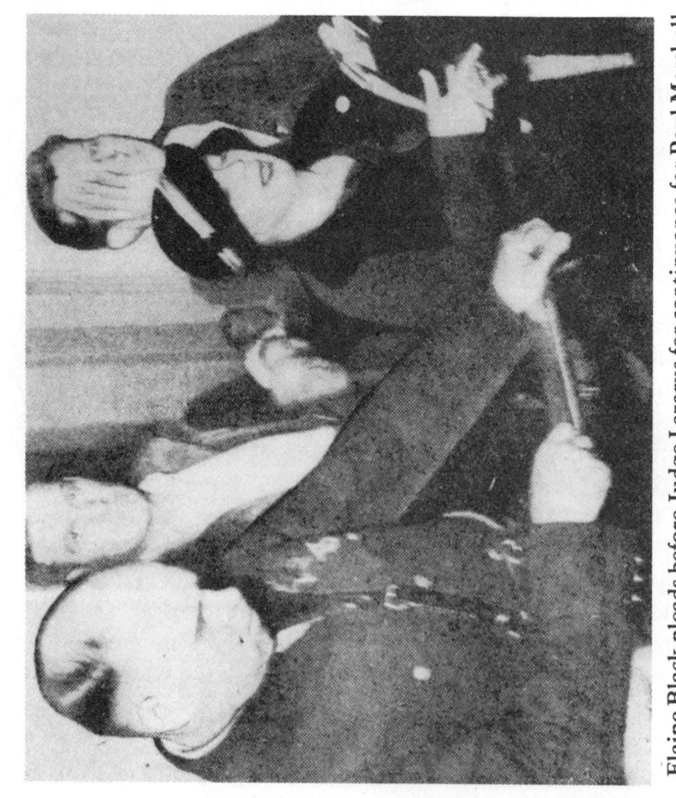

Elaine Black pleads before Judge Lazarus for continuance for Paul Marshall (right) and Oscar Moelloskog, arrested when police broke up a Communist meeting on Embarcadero. [S.F. *Call Bulletin*, 18/2/35.]

15.
The "Tiger Girl" Emerges

Salinas Lettuce Strike

In Salinas during the bitter 1936 lettuce packers strike – one of California's most violent agricultural strikes – the police labeled Elaine the "Tiger Girl." At stake in the strike for the ranchers was a $12 million lettuce crop; for the workers it was their union, Fruit and Vegetable Workers Union No. 18211. An AFL affiliate, Local 18211 was composed mostly of white workers, many of whom were former "Dust Bowl" farmers from Texas and Oklahoma.

The drought that forced them off their land was the most severe in U.S. history; it affected 24 states – 75 percent of the nation's land area. In addition, the New Deal program of "food destruction and crop reduction" translated not only to a "third class diet" for the majority of Americans, as acknowledged in a November 29, 1935, speech by President Roosevelt, but to actual starvation and near-starvation for millions. "If the nation lived on a first-class diet," the President told his Atlanta, Georgia audience, "we would have to put more acres than we have ever cultivated into the production of an additional supply of things for Americans to eat."[1]

Wives of "Dust Bowl" farmers worked in the sheds and fields as well as in local stores and restaurants. "Wherever they are, they unionize the shop," said Donald Henderson, president of the National Committee to Aid Agricultural Workers.[2] The lettuce pickers, doing stoop labor in the fields, were mostly Filipinos and Mexicans.

The Associated Farmers, well-entrenched now into the power structure of state and local police agencies, was ready for blood and determined to wipe out the shed workers' union. Buttressed by the American Legion, Chamber of Commerce, and paramilitary vigilante groups, the local sheriff declared a state of emergency. He ordered, under threat of arrest, all males in Salinas between the ages of 18 and 45 to be deputized and ready to move against the strikers at a moment's notice. Some 2,500 got ready; they armed themselves with rifles, grenades, brickbats, and pickaxe handles. They patrolled the streets, itching for trouble.

The growers led off by instituting a lockout against the shed workers, their aim the destruction of the existing wage agreement won by the workers two years before and up now for renegotiation. The shed workers walked out. They demanded union recognition and a "union preference" clause, overtime and holiday pay, the right to refuse to scab, and equal pay and conditions for women workers.

They organized a good strike, setting up two soup kitchens capable of feeding up to 1,500 members three meals a day. "That ought to show we're ready to fight this thing out to a finish," said George Kircher, chair of the union organizational committee. "Preferential hiring," tagged by the employers as a "pretty nickname" for the closed shop, soon became the key issue, the union charging the employers with "intending to eliminate union workers [who] invested their wages in homes in Salinas" and should be granted some guarantee against replacement by "new inexperienced workers with no stake in the community."

Colonel Sanborn

The Filipino field workers, members of the Filipino Labor Union, "came out in sympathy and also had their own demands," Elaine said. The Associated Farmers sent in an Army Reserve colonel who actually took over the running of the city and county from the elected officials. "This led to a wide reign of terror against the AFL workers." When the shed workers appealed for ILD help, Elaine left immediately for Salinas.

Henry R. Sanborn, a colonel in the Army Reserve, was a rabid Communist hater and union baiter. Editor and publisher of *The American Citizen,* a red-baiting sheet published in San Rafael, he exhorted a meeting of the Salinas "citizen army" of vigilantes to "drive the radicals out of town." An "expose" of Elaine in his newspaper included a front and side view mug shot of Elaine, and said:

> Elaine Black, alias Bochman, Ross, Hamma, etc. is one of the most ardent and militant of the Communist agitators on the Coast—of either sex—and has a long police record of arrests for disturbing the peace, vagrancy, failing to move on, seditious utterances, inciting riot, unlawful assemblage, resisting an officer, etc. as well as an

unenviable record as an organizer and disturber . . . [is member of] a flying squad of agitators. In her brushes with the police, by demanding jury trials, arranging postponements, writs of habeas corpus, taking appeals and militantly "insisting upon her rights," she has been convicted by juries on a couple of occasions and once drew a six month's sentence in the county jail.

By the time Elaine arrived in Salinas, "some of the misleaders in the AFL" decided to have nothing to do with the ILD. There was a lot of red-baiting. However, Ray Branham, husband of one of the arrested women, Louella "Happy" Branham, didn't care if the ILD "is red Russian or purple Russian, or the man in the moon . . . if they are going to get Louella out of jail . . . " He told the union leaders, "Don't tell me now that I can't get Louella out because you've changed your mind. Our Executive Board voted to call these people in, and I am sticking by the Executive Board decision!"

Elaine went with Branham to bail his wife out. "And when I walked into the courthouse, there was one great big six-footer of a deputy sheriff, and he said, 'Who are you?' And I said, 'Elaine Black,' and he let out a holler, 'Elaine Black is here!' Then all of a sudden a large number of deputies appeared, all with guns drawn. I don't know what they expected."

"Tiger Girl"

The San Francisco *Call Bulletin,* the "All Bull," Elaine called it – hinted rather broadly at what they must have expected in a September 18 story from Salinas. "The city was flooded with inflammatory propaganda today, with Elaine Black, young 'tiger girl,' firebrand of California Communists, making flying visits to camps along the highways." Ella Winter was an ardent supporter of the farmworkers, mostly raising money, and the same story charged her with being a "veteran Communist and widow of Lincoln Steffens, the author, [who] had established secret headquarters in a butcher shop here for the distribution of red propaganda."

Miss Black checked out of a downtown hotel here last night as police and highway patrolmen sought her. The federal investigators, it was learned, have amassed detailed information that communists under orders from New York and Moscow are planning to make Salinas an example of what communist terrorism can do. Their campaign is

A lynch rope for Elaine during Salinas lettuce strike, 9/16/36

part of an extensive plot connected with the San Francisco waterfront trouble. The agents have uncovered information that the reds plan, in an emergency, to cut all telephone and telegraph lines leading into Salinas.

At the jail, Elaine – though admittedly frightened – didn't tell the big deputy, when he asked, that she had the bail money with her for "Happy" Branham. "I had an intense feeling that if I had said 'yes,' something might happen to me on the way out." She told him she left it at union headquarters.

The court had increased the bail, but finally Elaine did place it and got "Happy" out of jail. On the several trips she made to Salinas, there was always harassment. The newspaper hysteria did not let up either. Colonel Sanborn issued a statement over the names of both the sheriff and chief of police that threatened the strikers for "failure to sign up for duty under the sheriff's proclamation of a state of emergency. I want you boys," he told the vigilante deputies, "to tell every man on the street it is his sworn duty to report here at once."

A Noose for Elaine

Elaine stayed in auto courts when her work took her to Salinas. "They were sort of cabins, very rough, and you put your car in between." She took the train from San Francisco when she was invited to speak to the Filipino Labor Union. Leaving the train, she was immediately surrounded by about 20 Filipino men who had come to protect her because "the vigilantes were running rampant and said they would kill any radical who arrived on the scene. They took me to an auto court . . . the next morning outside the door there was a lynch rope hanging with a note saying, 'Elaine, you are next.' "

That didn't, however, scare off either Elaine or her protectors. She continued to bring bail money to Salinas and fight for fair trials. The *Call Bulletin* was inspired to announce that "special investigators had learned that Elaine Black, young 'tiger woman' of California communism, was returning to Salinas tonight with money to furnish bail for the arrested strike pickets."

"Everyone . . . [was tagged] a Communist," Elaine said. "Anyone who had anything decent to say about the strikers, about their right to strike and to get better conditions was a Communist." In spite of the red-baiting and terror, the ILD never "copped a plea" – pleading guilty to a lesser charge to get a lesser sentence. "If anyone ever copped a plea, it was on their own," Elaine said, " . . . in fact, we withdrew support."

Louella "Happy" Branham stuck with the ILD and shared the platform with Elaine on a statewide speaking tour to rally support for the Salinas strikers. An ILD leaflet advertising a September 20 noon rally at San Francisco's Jefferson Park described Louella as the "Girl Striker arrested on the picketline and bailed out by the ILD." It urged the public: "Show your support for these workers! Protest the gassing of babies and of men and women strikers and their supporters. Protest the bombing of the Salinas Central Labor Council by the Highway Patrol."

Louella went on to work on subsequent cases too. "She had never been in any organization except the Shed Workers . . . she was really quite something to behold. She had been exposed to trade unionism and now she was able, in the civil rights fight, to take hold and become part of it, not only in her own defense but for the defense of others," Elaine said. They became fast friends.

The courage of the Salinas strikers endured as the jails filled. Grammar schools and movie theaters closed; high school students were forced to cut ax handles into clubs to use against strikers – in some cases, their own fathers. Some residents, frightened by the hysteria aroused in the press and the patrolling of their city by armed trigger-happy vigilantes, left town. "It was a campaign of terror – attempted kidnappings, murder, everything else," Elaine said.

There were times, particularly at dusk, when Elaine became aware that she was being protected by strikers "surrounding me . . . I also became aware that there were [other] men in the background with green armbands, the vigilantes."

LaFollette Investigation

Senator Robert LaFollette's Senate Civil Liberties Committee was a subcommittee of the Senate Committee on Education and Labor. A Senate resolution authorized it to hold hearings throughout the country on interference with the rights of labor and violations of free speech and assembly. Hearings on the Salinas situation exposed the "horrendous frameups" against field and shed workers. For example, it was revealed that the California Highway Patrol purchased huge amounts of gas bombs, long range shells and gas riot guns for use against striking agricultural workers – the purchase equally distributed between Los Angeles and Sacramento, with all of the Sacramento arms shipped to Salinas.

Ignatius McCarthy, tear gas expert for the San Francisco police during the 1934 general strike, flew a planeload of gas equipment into the Salinas-Watsonville lettuce strike area. According to the September 24 San Francisco *News,* he demonstrated use of nauseating yellow gas in Watsonville to Highway Patrol officers, police, deputies and deputized civilians for gas attacks on Salinas strikers.

But in spite of all the notoriety accorded her by the press – the accusations that Elaine's visits to Salinas were to "stir up trouble," she was never asked or subpoened to testify at the hearings. She regretted the omission.

The ILD strongly supported the LaFollette Committee; the evidence the committee collected shocked and outraged the nation. It documented the murder and kidnapping, the spying and terror campaigns. Then, said Elaine, with the La Follette hearings underway, "The AFL State Federation of Labor held a convention in September of 1936 and said that the effort to break the Salinas strike did more to crystallize and unite the California labor movement than any other event since the maritime strike of 1934."

Here was "violation of the most basic civil rights, the right to organize and better your conditions, the right to have unions and make demands . . . the State Federation of Labor sent a telegram to Roosevelt protesting the actions of the sheriff in Salinas who was assuming a power equal to the wartime power of the President, by drafting all male citizens . . . to act as strikebreakers and guards in Monterey County," Elaine said.

The AFL convention urged railroad workers not to handle "hot" lettuce picked by strikebreakers, and threatened a recall movement against California Governor Frank Merriam if he didn't restrain the State Highway Patrol. It also instructed its attorneys to provide all aid possible to Filipino field workers in the strike zone. All of this happened, Elaine noted, just as the "CIO was about to burst forth."

The Right to Organize

A Federal mediator flew to Salinas from Washington, D.C. but an arbitration attempt failed. The violence continued with police and Highway Patrolmen escorting strikebreakers, while State police gassed strikers. The American Civil Liberties Union charged that the Highway Patrol was in fact "an effective strike-breaking agency." Through use of motion pictures, Northern California ACLU director Ernest Besig documented the Patrol's strike-breaking activities, and scored the "reckless abuse of power by the Highway Patrol, local police and deputized vigilantes who have united to prevent peaceful picketing . . ."

The San Francisco *News* on September 17 photographed a large Salinas mob: "Special deputies armed with clubs march along a

Salinas street to clear it of striking lettuce worker pickets." Aware of the mob, the 3,000 strikers stayed in their homes that day to avoid slaughter in the streets. As the Salinas Central Labor Council met to consider a general strike, 24 carloads of heavily-armed deputies and 16 truckloads of state police convoyed scab lettuce from the fields, and a strikebreaker was shot by mistake by a trigger-happy guard.

In Watsonville, as 500 strikers picketed up and down the highway alongside lettuce fields and packing sheds, deputies barricaded strike-breakers in the sheds, constructing a 14-foot galvanized iron fence around them, plus an additional outer five foot barbed wire fence. Armed with rifles, shotguns, revolvers, tear gas capsules and dysentery and nauseating gas, they provided a constant presence of terrorism in the fields as well as in the sheds. The growers also erected two 20-foot guard towers equipped with machine guns and flood-lighted the area at night.

Elaine found Salinas "as frightening" as anything she had ever encountered. The National Labor Relations Board assailed the "inexcusable police brutality, in many instances bordering on sadism," and the LaFollette Committee report concluded:

> The right to organize is the most important of the civil liberties before the nation, because denying the workers the right to organize invariably means denying them the fundamental civil rights which are the basis of our democratic system.

A Bitter Loss

The strike was lost, the union destroyed by what a union attorney termed the "provisional dictatorship" that had been established in Salinas. This regime, set up with such preparation and care was too vast, carried too much power in high places, and had too many guns and clubs for 3,000 shed workers and 500 field workers. Responsibility for the loss, however, also had to be charged, wrote Canadian professor Stuart Jamieson, in a 1945 report on *Labor Unionism in American Agriculture,* to "the union's failure to organize the unskilled and semi-skilled nonwhite field workers employed in harvesting crops owned or controlled by grower-shippers." The defeat, he said, "demonstrated the weaknesses of an organization restricted to white workers employed in processing industries only."

Elaine a "Tiger woman?" Yes, said her friend, Bob Rohatch. "Elaine Black Yoneda was a real warm person who fought like a tiger for the rights of the working people and for peace throughout the universe. We will miss Elaine's fighting spirit and smile. Farewell Elaine. There will always be room in our hearts for Elaine, who not only spoke but led the fight for decency for all human beings."

Elaine "didn't resent being called 'Tiger Woman.' If a tiger is one who stalks his prey, I was stalking the enemy to free those who had been unjustly imprisoned."

King-Ramsay-Connor Case

Frameups of militant labor leaders are as old as labor history. The 1936 case of Earl King, leader of the Pacific Coast Marine Firemen's, Oilers, Watertenders and Wipers Association, and of E.G. Ramsay and Frank J. Connor, both rank and file members, was as rank a frameup as any that had ever gone before. The three were sentenced to 20 years each in San Quentin for complicity in the murder on March 22 of George Alberts, chief engineer of the S.S. Point Lobos; conviction was based on the testimony of one shaky police informer.

The murder has never been solved but what is clear is that King was a man marked by both employers and criminal elements still trying to maintain some control on the San Francisco waterfront. In 1939, he was offered his freedom in return for testifying against Harry Bridges; "We know you are not guilty," he was told. King refused to perjure himself, saying, "Nobody is going to take (my self respect) . . . away from me."

A King-Ramsay-Connor Defense Committee was set up by the Marine Firemen's Union and received the support of almost 100 Bay Area union locals as well as Central Labor Councils up and down the coast. The California State Federation of Labor also endorsed the defense. The ILD worked with the defense and helped with attorneys. But increasingly defense committees independent of the ILD were organized as workers shook off the crippling influence of and control of the AFL bureaucracy. Unions were building their own defense funds. This was bound to happen as the CIO came onto the scene, electrifying and mobilizing the trade union sentiment of millions, and setting off a new employer anti-union crusade.

The Frisco Waterfront Again

In San Francisco, by October 1936, the shipowners had amassed a $200 million fund to fight the maritime unions. The unions decided not to bargain as separate units but to present a solid united front to the shipowners. A main objective of the employers was the elimination of the union hiring hall. The workers were determined to keep and expand all the gains won in 1934. The hiring hall was not negotiable. Bargaining broke down completely and on midnight, October 29, the strike was on, with ships and docks all up and down the Pacific Coast empty and silent.

For the next 99 days, nothing attempted by the employers worked. Not the threat by the Associated Farmers of a march on San Francisco by 10,000 farmers to "Open the Port," not the distribution on the waterfront of Colonel Sanborn's *American Citizen* calling for vigilante action against the "Muscovian attack" by "foreign agitators," not employer attempts to divide the workers through separate negotiations for sailors and firemen. The strike was solid, disciplined – undefeatable. It ended that way on February 4, 1937. By then, the waterfront employers and shipping line executives had targeted longshore leader Harry Bridges as "the alien Australian" and decided he had to go – back to Australia, that is.

Tom Mooney with Anna Damon, left, and Elaine, San Francisco, 1936

16.

People On The Move

ILD Digs In

The years 1936-1937 were rife with change, contradiction, mass actions, and reactions, both at home and internationally. "Defense and aid to the people of Spain, Germany, Cuba, and Brazil, suffering under fascist and imperialist attacks, have occupied the attention of growing millions in the United States in the last year," the ILD noted.[1] In Cuba, trade unions had been outlawed by the Batista dictatorship and both the AFL and CIO protested. The ILD campaigned actively for the release from a Cuban prison of labor leader Cesar Vilar, and helped organize picketing at Cuban consulates.

One-third of the nation's long-term labor prisoners were in California prisons and 25.6 percent were in southern prisons or chain gangs. Labor and political prisoners' families, in more than half the national cases, relied for their main support on the monthly relief check sent by the ILD. And from San Quentin, a prisoner wrote that "the increase in our monthly allowance... not only represents to us the comforts which it affords but is a symbol of increasing brotherhood and unity... in this brotherhood rests our hope and our future."

National ILD Prisoners' Relief, headed by Rose Baron, could care only for the needs of long term prisoners, defined as those serving one year to life. State and local ILDs cared for hundreds of short-term prisoners.

Labor and political prisoners – denied in the U.S. as in England the status of political prisoner – often got harsher treatment than that accorded "common" criminals. The ILD initiated a campaign to establish the category of political prisoner and drew up a bill for introduction into local and state, as well as federal jurisdictions, spelling out the rights and privileges of political prisoners. During the 1936 election, the Northern California ILD organized a symposium at which candidates for state office addressed the issue. San

Francisco *Chronicle* columnist Chester Newell termed this "blatantly impertinent."

The ILD was unique – as well as impertinent – and it grew, both in formal trade union affiliations and individual memberships. It also established non-formal ties with religious, civil rights and fraternal organizations. More than 1,000 lawyers worked with the ILD, half of them with established ILD legal staffs. They defended thousands of trade unionists, unemployed demonstrators, civil rights activists, and African-American and other minority victims of racist persecution and terrorism.

Elaine, like all ILD workers, cooperated with many organizations that defended people's political, civil and labor rights. Among these were the Workers' Alliance, a militant organization that fought for the rights of the unemployed and people on relief; the American Committee for the Protection of the Foreign Born (ACPFB); the newly formed National Lawyers' Guild; the Michigan Conference for Protection of Civil Liberties comprising 311 Michigan organizations; the International Juridical Association (IJA); the NAACP; the ACLU; and the National Committee for Defense of Political Prisoners (composed mainly of well-known writers, artists and professionals).

Roosevelt Wins Second Term

Roosevelt won a 2nd term in November 1936 with the enthusiastic support of most working people and especially, the CIO, which was organizing millions into industrial unions. Many of the first CIO organizers were Communists. Elaine said, "They may not have been officials in the union[s], but certainly a good many of them served on executive boards and on strike committees." At the same time, the big business right-wing American Liberty League was established. "Join the CIO and Help Build a Soviet America" was the title of a pamphlet distributed by the National Association of Manufacturers.

On the people's side, Labor's Non-Partisan League was the strongest workers' political movement of the time. It convened a national convention in March 1937, with 600 delegates representing 3,500,000 organized workers. The National Negro Congress had been in existence for a year; it was helping to bring Black workers into the trade union movement. In the deep South, the Southern Conference for Human Welfare demanded jobs and civil rights. Everywhere the people were implementing gains won in the New Deal: the Social Security Act and the National Labor Relations Act (NLRA) which guaranteed workers the right to bargain collectively and the right to strike.

But there was still pervasive hunger in the land and the Works Progress Administration (WPA) and Civilian Conservation Corps (CCC) represented a pittance of what was needed; people needed jobs – millions of them. Especially hard hit were the foreign born. In New York City alone, between June 30 and August 20, 1937, 31,499 foreign born were dropped from WPA rolls; 10,327 of these were fired as a result of the emergency Appropriations Act giving preference to citizens.[2] Citizen or foreign born, the jobless starved together.

Political Work and Internationalism

The ILD got deeper into political work in 1937 with adoption, for the first time in its history, of a legislative program aimed at building state as well as national legislative activity. Aim was to build a "lobby of the people . . . [to] fight for or against legislation which is respectively beneficial or harmful to labor . . . "

The ILD membership book issued to Elaine for the years 1937-1938 reflected the worsening international situation, spelling out the duty of ILD members to provide "aid to the victims of fascism in all lands, the victims of imperialist violence in the struggles of the peoples of colonial and semi-colonial countries, and of national minorities."

On January 1, 1937, U.S. citizen Lawrence Simpson, a seaman, was returned to the United States after spending 18 months in Hitler's jails. He had been caught and imprisoned by the Gestapo for bringing anti-fascist literature into Nazi Germany. The ILD organized the campaign to free him and charged that the U.S. State Department did nothing to effectively protect Simpson's rights until forced by a "crescendo of pressure . . . " Simpson's "greatest consolation" throughout his long ordeal, he said, was knowing that the ILD was working to free him.

Other organizations, too, fought for asylum rights. Max Alfred Meister, escapee from a German concentration camp, came to the United States on July 8 as a stowaway. Ordered deported by a Board of Special Inquiry at Ellis Island, the American Committee for the Protection of the Foreign Born prevailed upon the board to parole Meister into the committee's custody.[3]

Imprisoned German working class leader and Communist Ernst Thaelmann described how it was in Nazi Germany:

> The militant workers become the ready game of fascist justice. Those thousands who find themselves behind the bars of fascist jails, are guilty of nothing but fighting for the freedom of their class, fighting against terror and oppression. Families lose their breadwinner, children lose fathers and sometimes their mothers.
>
> Millions of people, regardless of political or economic affiliation, owe these victims the duty of support in return for the sacrifices they have made. Do not forget them, brothers and sisters. Concentrate your efforts on supporting with all your strength, the International Labor Defense, the organization of solidarity.

A Polish Jew whom the INS ordered deported was saved by Oregon U.S. District Court Judge Claude McCulloch. In granting a writ of habeas corpus, the judge said, "I hold the Immigration Service in the highest regard, but the Service should, it seems to me, be sure of its ground and of the necessity for deportation of Jewish people in these days of renewed persecution of their race, and the Service shouldn't be unmindful of President Roosevelt's recent restatement of this nation's historic policy of sanctuary for the stricken and oppressed."[4]

In Spain, on September 3, 1937, Henry Eaton, an American "premature anti-fascist," was killed at Belchite, while fighting for the Spanish Republic with the Abraham Lincoln Brigade. Eaton was an ILD field organizer.

On the Home Front

On the home front, the great strike movement of those years eclipsed anything that had gone before in sheer numbers – and, if possible, in violence waged against it by employers desperate to maintain the open shop. Some of the most bloody strikes in U.S. history took place in basic industry: steel, auto, rubber, mining and electric. While no panacea, industrial organization did set the stage for the fight for equal union rights for Black workers and for women workers to put forward the principle of equal pay for equal work.

On the West Coast, the Pacific Coast district of the ILA – under Harry Bridges' leadership – seceded from the ILA and joined the CIO as the International Longshoremen's and Warehousemen's Union.

Agricultural workers were not covered by the National Labor Relations Act. By 1937, with the influx of desperate migrant labor from the drought-ridden Dust Bowl and the difficulty of organizing under new conditions, there was widespread starvation in the fields and valleys of California.

Representative Vito Marcantonio of New York became national ILD president in June 1937. Elected to Congress in November 1934, the young congressman was a fighter; his eloquent and biting tongue earned him the love of his constituency and the respect of his opposition. A lawyer since age 23, "Marc" defended labor activists and Communists, fought racism and anti-Semitism, was sometimes the sole voice raised in Congress for the rights of the foreign-born, the poor and oppressed. He fought valiantly but unsuccessfully in Congress for NLRA coverage for field workers.

The CIO United Cannery, Agricultural, Packing and Allied Workers of America (UCAPAWA) held its first convention that year, attempting to fill the void left by the trail of unions destroyed by the Associated Farmers and agribusiness.

Karl became a UCAPAWA organizer; he and Mary Imada, Hiroshima-born ILD activist and Communist Party member, organized more than 1,000 Japanese farm workers and women cannery workers in an area stretching from Terminal Island up to Stockton. "It was quite a force in those days," Elaine said.

The Fiery Marcantonio

Elaine was impressed with the fiery Vito Marcantonio when she attended the 1937 national ILD convention in Washington, D.C. She was Northern California District secretary; the convention elected her Pacific Coast vice-president. She remembered that President Roosevelt sent greetings and congratulated the ILD for its work on civil rights.

National ILD secretary Anna Damon documented the previous 15 months for the convention:

> . . . a period of great change in the American scene, particularly in the field of labor. Organized reaction "received a decided set-back from the American people in the last Presidential election. The LaFollette Committee . . . uncovered the system of espionage, coercion, intimidation, open terror, organized against the American labor movement . . . The Black Legion was unmasked and a great deal of its effectiveness as an anti-labor weapon broken down.

> American labor rallied to the banner of progressive trade unionism under the leadership of the Committee for Industrial Organization ... the forces of reaction have ... been knocked breathless by the blows they have received ... They have been forced to retreat ... while they gather their forces together again and consolidate themselves into new positions.

According to Damon, it was on "the West Coast and in the South, citidels of reaction, [that] the crystalization of the democratic force into an organized civil rights movement is most noticeable. The people of the United States, Negro and white, the progressive forces in every walk of life, are on the move."

The ILD, together with the ACFPB and the ACLU fought numerous deportation and "alien" registration drives. In the first session of the 74th Congress alone, more than 100 bills dealing with "aliens" and deportation were introduced. Earlier, Marcantonio had charged that the "alien" the reactionaries wanted to deport was the "one who organizes, who protests, who joins his fellow worker in trying to better their living conditions ... "

Elaine knew well the plight of Mexican field workers in California who constantly faced the threat of deportation. It was at "the end of the season when it was time to pay off ... that the swooping down by the Immigration Department seemed to happen. It didn't happen when the harvest was going full swing." For U.S. citizens of foreign birth targeted for deportation, Elaine provided legal advice and helped to organize protest meetings. In 1938, Marcantonio introduced a bill providing for asylum for political, racial or religious reasons; it died in committee. The need to fight deportation of political refugees from Nazi Germany and fascist Italy was clear to most; it was less generally recognized that this was also true for Japanese anti-fascists in the U.S., particularly after Japan declared war on China in July, 1937.

"My Comrades in Spain"

There was much activity on the Left in support of the Spanish Republic. In the beginning, Elaine said, " ... many of us didn't realize what was happening in Spain ... or grasp the full meaning ... " But Jim McNamara knew, she said, and gave the cause of Spanish freedom the only tangible help he could. From his cell in San Quentin, he wrote to the ILD to stop sending his $5.00 a month prison relief and send it instead to Spain. "My comrades in Spain need it more than I do." Elaine met people from all over the world but "I never met a man of the stature of J.B. McNamara." Known "as Uncle Jim by all the prisoners . . . he was such a warm, kind human being and he tried to help everyone . . . " The admiration was mutual, McNamara crediting the ILD with possessing the "feeling and devotion . . . to put life into a rock . . . I envy them as I sit on the sidelines and watch them work. Their support has fortified me to buck the strife and storm."

Protest at the German Consulate

Elaine's final arrest in that period was on January 29, 1937, in front of the German Consulate to protest Nazi Germany's intervention in Republican Spain. Hundreds marched against the Nazis, against the swastika flapping in the breeze. They carried anti-fascist banners and booed the swastika.

"I was not supposed to be on the line . . . George Andersen and I were to be the observers." They rented a hotel room across the street from the demonstration for a clear view. Elaine, as usual, had bail money with her. Suddenly the police attacked. Elaine watched the melee; suddenly she saw that police were heading for her elderly friend Anita Whitney. "They were coming from an angle and she seemed to be the target. I said to George Andersen, 'I can't take this any more.' " Elaine hurried down and crossed the street just as "they began attacking Anita and dragging her down the steps. So they dragged me too. We were charged with rioting and a whole lot of other things." Nine persons were arrested.

At the trial Elaine represented herself and won a hung jury. However, she was cited for contempt of court and sentenced to 20 hours jail time for refusing to give the court her home address. She explained, "Some of us who were defending ourselves refused to give our personal addresses . . . on the basis that our homes had been invaded and there had been attacks. In my case, I stuck to my guns . . . "

"So You Won't Talk, Eh?" said an *Examiner* headline.

"Here Comes Elaine!"

Elaine appealed the 20 hour sentence, doing her time "the hard way." Under the appeal procedure, she was in and out of jail as new appeals were filed and new bonds placed. When the bail was lifted, she would surrender herself at the jail. "I used to like corned beef and cabbage, and I knew that Tuesday was the day they had it in the county jail. I would always try to arrange that it would be a Tuesday when I would surrender... And I would make the matron put down whether it was an hour, or twenty seconds, so it would go down against the 20 hours." Bond would be posted and she would be released again. "In fact, I even went to a National Convention of the ILD in Washington D.C... Then I came back and did another two hours." Elaine lost the appeal; "I finally did the twenty hours."

Elaine's friend Charlotte Christiansen remembered that "Elaine thought on her feet and was damned good at it." She recalled the judge ruling that it was permissible for Elaine to serve her sentence in short stints because she had a small child. "The depression was on and Elaine wisely chose the lunch hour. 'Well, girls, it's time for lunch,' the matron would sing out to the women prisoners, 'Here comes Elaine!' " "Elaine," wrote Christiansen, "has taken her place in history among those rare individuals who want no special privilege for themselves and who demand justice for those who have not yet learned to fight ... "

17.

Back to the Mother Lode

Gold Strike!

In January 1938, a gold strike erupted in Nevada County. The strike front ranged over a wide area from Grass Valley in the west to Truckee, close to the Nevada state border, in the east. On January 20, picketing strikers, members of CIO Mine, Mill and Smelter Workers Local 283, were attacked by a mob of State Highway Patrol police, the sheriff's posse and members of the Mine Workers Protective League, a company union. Six strikers were arrested for "inciting to riot."

The union sent for the ILD. Elaine not only got there with bail money, but made herself useful – helping to deliver big milk cans of hot coffee to strikers on that long picket line. As the weeks became months, the ILD maintained a close check on the situation. The strike prevailed.

Then, on April 5, a picketline of 60 strikers in the county seat of Nevada City was stormed by 300 armed vigilantes. Twenty-four pickets were seriously hurt, 12 were hospitalized. The vigilante mob circled the hospital, shouting epithets and threats. To protect other patients, Dr. Richard Landis was compelled to send the miners elsewhere for medical care. The frustrated mob waited for the cover of night to wreck the miners' union hall.

Two days later, before daybreak, as 16 strikers attempted to retrieve union records from the destroyed hall, deputy sheriffs forced them out by firing tear gas shells into the wreckage. The strikers were arrested and thrown into jail. A howling mob gathered outside; they wanted a lynching. Sacramento *Union* reporter Edward Sterne was backed up against a wall and told to get out – "We don't want any strangers around here . . . " All out-of-town news personnel were threatened.

Nevada City Nugget editor H.M. Leete appealed outright for "lawlessness" to repeal the Wagner Act. It could be done, he said, "by the people taking the law into their own hands . . . Here in Nevada City we have shown the way for repeal. Mob action has pointed the way to end the CIO Communists and the crazy New Deal labor laws which support them."

The vigilantes listened and acted – again. On April 9, they drove 200 gold miners and their families out of Nevada City. The City Council passed and Mayor Benjamin Rail signed a resolution:

> We are determined that the radical Communist elements never shall gain a foothold here and since this purge of these undesirables we are glad to say that conditions here . . . are more peaceful and orderly than they have been for many months.

Sheriff Carl Tobiassen threatened that a "serious situation" could develop should the miners and their families return. The citizens, he said, "are pretty well riled." When "the vigilantes drove whole families out of their homes and into the cold," Elaine said, " . . . they made their way in whatever way they could to Sacramento." They called the ILD to say they were on their way. There were 200 of them, including 75 children. Elaine, George Andersen and Herb Resner met them in Sacramento.

Governor Throws Elaine Out

The miners – among whom were lifelong residents of Nevada City – camped on the State Capitol lawn. They made signs: "We are refugees from Nevada County where Law and Order has ceased to exist." "We have been driven from our homes in Nevada City."

Elaine went with a delegation to see Governor Merriam to demand food, tents and medical care. "Some of these women and children were quite ill . . . some of the men, too. A good many of them had rashes." It could have been from poor food – or no food, she said. The delegation demanded that the vigilantes be arrested. "Merriam had State Police take us bodily and throw us out of his office against the marble wall of the Capitol, and told us to get out of there." First Elaine, then Andersen and Resner "came flying out." Elaine was not certain, but thought she might be pregnant. She was hurt; Andersen and Resner rushed her to a hotel. She began to hemorrhage.

"The blow up against the wall caused me great distress and I was quite ill. But we did get them to put up tents at the fair grounds."

Elaine returned to San Francisco. "I stayed in bed . . . my activities for the rest of 1938 were quite limited."

Such terrorism against workers and those who defended them was too much to sweep under the rug. Governor Merriam was forced to appoint an investigating committee. Fiorenzo Musso, owner of Nevada City's New Deal Cafeteria had been driven out of town with the miners. He testified that on the night of April 7, a vigilante mob had entered his cafe and beat up customers. "They tore down a CIO sign and stamped on it," he said. "They tore down my calendar with pictures of President Roosevelt, George Washington and Abraham Lincoln."

The committee investigation was suppressed, Elaine said, but a report did conclude that "law and order had completely broken down in Nevada County." The strikers, of course, knew that already.

Elaine and Karl had for some time talked "off and on" about enlarging their family. Joyce had come to live with them in 1936 so another child would mean a family of four to support. They decided to have a baby but "nothing happened . . . Then we decided that we would wait until Karl got back from Alaska . . . he was going up there as a representative for the Alaska Cannery Workers Union . . . well, lo and behold, I got pregnant after we decided to wait."

It was a difficult pregnancy. "It may have been the blow."

"Why Don't You Take Up the Law?"

Elaine's court work continued. She made a plea for lower bail for young people arrested during the annual Youth Day demonstration. "Judge Theresa Meikle and Edith Wilson, who was from the District Attorney's office, called me in to . . . chambers after I had made this plea for lower bail. And they said, 'You know, Elaine, you are a born Portia. Why don't you take up law? If you want to, we can help get you into law school.' "

"I am not even a high school graduate."

"Oh, we could arrange that."

Elaine felt they were attempting to sidetrack her ILD activities and wasn't interested. Besides, she was too busy having a family. Several years earlier, University of California law professor Max Radin* had told Elaine she should consider studying law. He "felt

*Professor of Law, Boalt Law School, University of California from 1919 to 1948

that I had the poise to be an attorney. I didn't think so . . . and said no . . . [and] I felt it would take me away from an important period in the fight for workers' rights."

Auxiliaries Picket Scrap Iron

Like thousands of women opposed to Japan's expansionist war against China, Elaine gave up wearing silk stockings imported from Japan. Karl played a prominent role in organizing picket lines on the docks protesting the shipment of scrap iron to Japan; the Maritime Federation appointed him as picket captain. Longshoremen were able to keep tabs on such shipments; there was the time, for example, when the Western Pacific Railroad Company sold 280 carloads of scrap steel rails to be loaded onto old Alaska Packer ships and sent to Japan.[1]

The women's auxiliaries supported all of these actions; the women brought their children to the picketline. Joyce often picketed with Elaine. The Japanese branch of the ILD and progressive Japanese, as well as workers who had been or were still in the agricultural unions or worked in the canneries were all active in this campaign.

In September 1938, Karl "was pulled off of the picket line by the Red Squad," Elaine remembered. "They took him aboard this Japanese ship on which the scrap iron was being loaded . . . " The captain of the ship threatened Karl: "What do you think is going to happen to your mother in Hiroshima if you keep up these activities?" How did he know where Karl's mother lived? Collusion between the shipowners, the police and the Japanese government was clear.

In December a March from Chinatown to Pier 45 brought thousands to protest the loading of war materials onto a Greek ship bound for Japan. The longshoremen walked off the ship and for four days, the huge protest halted the loading. Local 10 received numerous messages of support; a telegram from the New York Japanese Peace Society expressed "our appreciation for refusal to handle ammunition shipment to Japanese militarists who are crushing our own people in Japan as well as committing history's greatest mass slaughter."

The Nazis Again

On October 2, 1938, several hundred protesters picketing a "German Day Fete" organized by the Nazi Bund at California Hall were charged by mounted police. Police clubbed heads and sharp horses' hooves bloodied legs. The picketline constituted, police said, an "unlawful disturbance of the peace" of San Francisco. Many were arrested but only four went to trial, their defense handled by the ILD. Frank Spector, secretary of the Communist Party, defended himself. The jury, in the first trial, deadlocked. In the second, the vote was 11 to 1 for acquittal and charges were dropped. In the November 1938 elections, San Francisco voters defeated an anti-picketing ordinance. It had been the city administration's third try.

When the Bund announced in February 1939 it would hold a second Nazi rally at the same hall, so extensive and swift was the response to a call for a mass protest that the Bund called off the meeting, and – as reported by the San Francisco ILD – a police captain had a change of heart: "The same police captain who ordered the arrests on October 2 insisted that the Nazis cancel their meeting, and at the same time gave permission for the organization of a street meeting in front of the hall – to an anti-fascist organization."

ILD People's Lobby

The ILD's "People's Lobby" continued its legislative work, stressing labor's role in preserving democratic rights. "We must stress the need," the Southern California ILD said, "for . . . bringing to the support of labor the small farmers and small merchants, of consumer groups and non-labor organizations . . . We must push for the unity of labor itself and organize a democratic front in state and national elections." New affiliations to the Southern California ILD District included 12 AFL and nine CIO unions.

The ILD, Leo Gallagher said, was the "Shield of the Working Class." In October 1938, in a letter to the Los Angeles Bar Association, Gallagher chided judges who "were not honest enough, or courageous enough to live up to their oath of office, to see that defendants were given their legal rights . . . by directing verdicts and dismissing complaints against defendants who had been arrested solely for attempting to exercise their rights under the Constitution . . . [which] . . . has been trampled under foot 10,000 times by so-called law enforcement officers."

18.

Mooney Freed!

Full and Unconditional Pardon

The campaign for Tom Mooney's freedom reached a peak in 1938. The California State Assembly had no power to grant a pardon; yet, year after year, resolutions were introduced calling for a full pardon. By a vote of 45 to 28, the first pardon resolution had been passed in 1937 when the Democrats had their first majority in the Assembly since Mooney's imprisonment 20 years before. The resolution failed in the State Senate by a vote of 34 to 5 with State Senator Culbert Olson arguing for it. In 1938, in an unprecedented action the Assembly, by a vote of 36 to 30, subpoenaed Mooney to appear before it to plead his own case.

On March 18, he was taken from his cell in San Quentin, and thence to Sacramento. His supporters even flew a sympathetic but sick senator from his hospital bed to Sacramento to vote for a new resolution. Again passing the Assembly 41 to 29, it failed in the Senate.

But the ball was rolling. Culbert Olson got labor's support in the 1938 race for governor in return for a pledge to free Mooney as his first official act. In Washington, D.C., 86 Congressmen and 25 Senators urged a federal investigation of the Mooney-Billings case; there was also a proposal to bring Mooney to Washington to speak before the Congress. Labor was solidly demanding his freedom. Fourteen days before the California election, the Dies Committee on Un-American Activities charged that all top Democratic nominees were Communists or Red sympathizers. The ploy didn't work. Olson became California's first Democratic Governor in the twentieth century, and Mooney was granted a pardon on January 7, 1939.

Among the audience in the packed Assembly chamber in Sacramento were members of the Abraham Lincoln Brigade, just returned from Spain. A seat had been reserved for Elaine but due to her difficult pregnancy, she could not attend. The ceremony was broadcast coast to coast, and in San Francisco Elaine and Joyce listened. Elaine remembered that Governor Olson asked if anyone could give a reason why Thomas Mooney should not be granted a full and unconditional pardon. "There was . . . a silence on the radio. I became hysterical," Elaine said. The ILD had received a threat against Mooney's life. Joyce shook her: "Mother, stop crying. He's going to be free. He's going to be free." Joyce knew Mooney from going with Elaine to visit him in San Quentin. Then came the Governor's pronouncement:

> I have made an extended study of the voluminous records of this case and am convinced that Thomas J. Mooney is wholly innocent of the crime of murder for which he was convicted and that his conviction was based wholly on perjured testimony presented by representatives of the State of California. In view of my convictions I deem it my duty to issue a pardon to Thomas J. Mooney.
>
> Now, therefore, I, Culbert L. Olson, Governor of the State of California, pursuant to the authority vested in me by the Constitution and Statutes of said State do hereby grant Thomas J. Mooney, San Quentin No. 31921, a full and unconditional pardon of the crime of murder in the first degree and do hereby restore said Thomas J. Mooney to all of his civil rights and privileges as a citizen. Tom Mooney, you are now a free man.

"Then, of course," said Elaine, "he was free" and Elaine and Joyce wept in joy.

Olson told the happy crowd that Warren K. Billings should be immediately recommended for a pardon. In an emotional response, Mooney pledged his full efforts toward freedom for Billings – "my co-sufferer, co-defendant, and co-worker . . . " The next morning, Mooney was driven to Folsom Prison, stopping enroute to plant a rose bush at Mother Mooney's grave. At Folsom he met with Billings and then with J.B. McNamara. Mooney vowed to fight for their freedom, and an exultant ILD, while marking "the notable victory" in Mooney's release, noted that the victory "is not complete, however, until Warren K. Billings, J.B. McNamara, Earl King, Ernest Ramsay, and Frank Connor are also freed."

"The next day, as the world knows," said Elaine, "Mooney came to San Francisco and there was this massive outpouring of humanity that walked with him up Market Street. Of course I was in no condition to march, but Karl drove me down to the waterfront so that I could see him come off the ferry . . . " Driven to City Hall for the official welcome, Elaine sat with all the dignitaries. A Methodist minister friend sitting next to her gave up his seat next to Elaine to Anita Whitney and the two staunch fighters for Mooney's freedom, one of them nine-months pregnant, shared their joy.

Nation Rejoices

In the nation's capital, Congressman Vito Marcantonio took the floor in the House of Representatives: "I rise simply for the purpose of noting in the Record that on Saturday, January 7, Tom Mooney, a great and honest man, was liberated and vindicated by the granting to him of an unconditional pardon by the Governor of California. This established legally and for all time what we have always known, that Tom Mooney was innocent and framed. I take this occasion to congratulate the present and ex-Members of Congress as well as the world, who have participated in this historic struggle to right this tremendous wrong. I also take this opportunity to state that every true believer in justice and democracy rejoices over the liberation of Tom Mooney, even though it comes exactly 22 years too late."

Two days later, on January 10, 1939, Dr. Frances Foster, friend and doctor, drove Elaine and Karl to St. Joseph's Hospital. Karl had decided that he wanted "our son to be named Thomas Culbert" and Dr. Foster had laughed as they argued back and forth on the way to the hospital. "I thought Karl was into the emotional impact of what was happening – Tom being free . . . "

Always prepared to bail somebody out of jail, Elaine had $1,500 in bail money with her. "A demonstration was planned and other [bail fund] trustees were going to be out of town." The money was entrusted to the hospital safe while Elaine gave birth to a son.

For four days, Elaine held off from naming the baby. Karl did not change his mind, however, and Elaine came to feel that "Thomas Culbert" was an "appropriate name" for the time. What would have happened had the baby been a girl, they didn't consider.

Mooney was the baby's godfather and Louise Todd was godmother. A bitter note to an otherwise happy time was the hospital superintendent's pronouncement to Dr. Foster that "half-breed births" were not welcome at St. Joseph's. The superintendent was a Catholic nun.

Warren K. Billings was not freed until the following October – not pardoned as Mooney was – but his sentence commuted to time served even though the frameup against him was exactly the same as against Mooney. Billings spent 23 years in prison, at that point exactly half of his life. Finally, on Dec. 22, 1961, he was pardoned by Governor Edmund G. "Pat" Brown.

Guilty of contempt for refusal to give home addresses, 4 Communists drew 12-hour jail terms. Hayden Perry (2nd from left), George Parker (3rd from right), Elaine Black and Mary Dana (center). [At far right is Anita Whitney]. From S.F. *Examiner*, 3/17/37.

19.

Bridges Victory

That Australian Again

Elaine got back into activity, taking infant Tommy on picket lines and representing the ILD at deportation proceedings against Harry Bridges on Angel Island. James Landis, dean of the Harvard Law School, was trial examiner. According to news reports, Bridges was asked if he knew Elaine and her husband Karl. Bridges acknowledged that Karl was a longshoreman, and as for Elaine, "I even danced with her."

"Certainly," Elaine said, "Bridges and the ILA . . . [and] then the ILWU, worked with the ILD on cases that pertained to longshoremen and others . . . [in the] fight for civil rights for workers . . . " Elaine's name was woven in and out of the hearing several times by government witnesses attempting to taint Bridges by association. An *Examiner* news account identified Elaine as "Elaine Black, admitted big shot of the Communist Party on the Pacific Coast."

Almost four months later, Landis found in favor of Bridges. In a long opinion, Landis said: "That Mr. Bridges' aims are energetically radical may be admitted but the proof fails to establish that the methods he seeks to employ to realize them are other than those that the framework of democratic and constitutional government permits."

Attempts to deport Bridges, and later, to revoke his citizenship would persist for more than 20 years. Never in history had such persecution by obsessed government and employer agents been focused so fanatically on one man. Walter B. Fisher, legislative representative of the Maritime Federation of the Pacific, told the 1939 national ILD conference that the forces attempting to destroy Harry Bridges must be taught "the real meaning and interpretation of civil rights." He called upon all unions to "defend civil rights for yourself, defend civil rights for your organization, defend civil rights for everyone else in the labor movement and then we will get civil rights from our legislators and Congress and the Senate of the United States."

Refugees

The July 1939 national ILD conference in Washington, D.C. noted a decrease in political and labor arrests, crediting mainly "the operations of the National Labor Relations Act and the whole New Deal policy of the administration . . . " Arrests decreased from 22,007 in 1937 to 7,615 in 1938 and 2,223 in the first six months of 1939. Yet, said the ILD, those figures did not reflect "a general index of civil rights. The balance sheet actually shows more on the debit than on the credit side." Those debits ranged from the growth of fascist and semi-fascist organizations to the fact that "vigilante mobs can still drive a whole community of gold miners and their families from their jobs and homes and 'exile' them from their native city" as happened in Nevada City, California in April 1938. Elaine was closely involved with this case.

Within the U.S. borders, "the presence and growth . . . of some 800 fascist and semi-fascist organizations" was accompanied, the ILD reported, by an "accompanying growth in hooliganism and dissemination of racial, religious, and political hatreds . . . "

International aid to the growing numbers of political refugees and victims of fascist oppression was among the subjects discussed at the 1939 conference, with Dr. Max Yergan, president of the National Negro Congress, terming this issue "one of the most serious problems in all history." In 1938 the ILD had established a Non-Sectarian Committee for Political Refugees to aid international anti-fascist political militants, "those whose lives are in greatest danger." The ILD credo, printed in its membership dues book, reflected the organization's stand for "democracy and progress, for preservation and enlarging of the constitutional, civil, and human rights of the basic population. It is against fascism in all its forms, and against reaction. It is against imperialist war." A special dues stamp was issued: "Give to build homes for the children, hospitals for the wounded of Spain." The ILD was affiliated nationally with both the American League Against War and Fascism and the ACPFB.

Snatched from the Gestapo

Anna Damon reported that although the Non-Sectarian Committee was new, "immediately after Hitler's march into Czechoslovakia on March 15, we were instrumental in literally snatching out of the hands of the Gestapo 200 political refugees who are now safe in Poland and England . . . " Damon urged a renewed nationwide campaign for the right of asylum in the United States for all political and religious refugees.

Resolutions passed at the National Conference endorsed campaigns for the freedom of the five remaining Scottsboro Boys; for King-Ramsay-Conner, J.B. McNamara, and Matthew Schmidt; Warren K. Billings and Jack Schneider in the U.S.; for Dr. Pedro Albizu Campos and seven other Puerto Rican prisoners in the Federal Penitentiary at Atlanta, Georgia; Ernst Thaelmann and all German anti-fascist prisoners; all victims of Nazi and fascist aggression in the jails and concentration camps of Italy, Germany, Japan, Poland, etc.; all political refugees from fascist terror regardless of race, creed or nationality; for 18 members of the Abe Lincoln Battalion held in Franco's Spanish prisons; and freedom for all labor and political prisoners in the Caribbean countries (Barbados, Jamaica, Trinidad and British Guiana).

Delegates also decided that prison relief work in the United States must be broadened to include more than material aid to prisoners, that investigations of prison conditions needed to be undertaken in order to alleviate the "inhuman conditions, the continued use of chain-gangs, third degree, other cruel and unusual punishments . . . "

And to the Mayor of Dunellen, Florida, the conference sent a wire protesting the torture-beating of two Black children.

Fascist Threat Grows

As the fascist threat spread over Europe, in the U.S. there was an alarming increase in anti-Semitism. There were, reported the ILD, "thousands of instances of anti-Semitic meetings, picket lines, demonstrations . . . " In Chicago, on February 23, 1939, the "Joint Committee of Patriotic Organizations" threatened to "clean the kikes out of Chicago . . . We'll make Hitler look like a cream puff." On February 26, in a New York City subway station, Irving Berger was stabbed when he protested anti-Semitic remarks, and 17-year old Irving Gitlitz was stabbed for going to the aid of 65-year old Hyman Mankus when he was being beaten up by thugs on an elevated train. In Baltimore, Maryland there was the penknife branding of 14-year old Melvin Bridge and in Los Angeles, the brutal beating and near-blinding of 58-year old Joseph Greenberg.

The "National Gentile League" was on the prowl, as were the Nazi Silver Shirts, Christian Front, Ku Klux Klan, and a myriad of other organizations dedicated to violence against Jews.

In the South the KKK was riding – lynching and shooting, burning fiery crosses and marching openly in the streets. The murder of labor organizers and strikers continued. In the nation's capital, Congressman Marcantonio warned that the "Ku Klux Klan is by no means dead... it is very active in many sections of the country where the American labor movement is attempting to organize workers, particularly in the South. AFL and CIO organizers who have felt the terror of the Klan can testify as to its virulent existence."

The ILD supported the Federal Anti-Lynching Bill, pressuring Congress, circulating petitions and providing assistance to the NAACP and the National Negro Congress, the organizations that led this campaign. It also worked with the Southern Conference for Human Welfare in the drive to abolish the poll tax which robbed at least 10 million potential voters in the South of their right to cast a ballot.

The ILD gave free help to foreign-born persons threatened with deportation. Attacks on the foreign-born were seen as opening the floodgates to restriction and prohibition of the civil and political rights of all Americans. In the House of Representatives, Congressman Marcantonio was at first the lone voice speaking out against cutting non-citizens from WPA rolls, yet he pursuaded 41 congressmen to join him in voting against the measure.

In California, violence against UCAPAWA strikers persisted. Attacks included arrests of apricot pickers in Patterson; the holding incommunicado of strikers in Marysville for "conspiracy to violate the Yuba County anti-picketing law," with strikers' children threatened with reform school if caught at strike headquarters. There were kidnappings and beatings of strikers, and arrests in Visalia, Hanford, Pixley, Madera and Chowchilla. There were shotgunning and terror campaigns against Filipino and white strikers in Pescadero and Stockton.

At a National Conference for Civil Liberties held October 13-14, 1939 in New York City, the ILD participated in spite of attempts by some to isolate the ILD from the distinguished committee sponsoring the conference. These included New Deal officials, artists and intellectuals, and labor, religious and academic figures. "Among the most outstanding features of the conference," said the ILD's *Equal Justice,* "were the speeches and statements of Attorney General [Frank] Murphy, Assistant Attorney General John Rogge and Alfred Bettman, who was with the Department of Justice during the World War; all three hammered away at one point: "The Constitution of the United States does not change in war or peace . . . It is nonsense to speak of suspending civil liberties in order to protect the Constitution."

"Especially in the light of the present situation and witch-hunt these words tell a big story – and should be remembered by all friends of justice and democracy," said *Equal Justice.*

Two years later, Karl and Elaine Yoneda, along with 120,000 Japanese-Americans, would have good reason to recall those words.

Starving Children

In California, by 1939 poor children's health had deteriorated to the point where half of the children in a rural district "showed definite signs of starvation. One child out of every four suffers from rickets, scurvy, or pellagra – all serious diseases resulting from lack of fruits and vegetables . . . "*

The relief budget provided only $42.03 a month for a family of four to cover food, housing and utilities. There was no provision for clothing, school supplies, personal needs, or transportation – including carfare to look for work. Money for these had to be taken from the small food budget. In California, 100,000 children were growing up on relief; nationally, 41 percent of persons on relief were 16 years old or younger.

Such reports upset California growers. In Stockton, Chamber of Commerce and Associated Farmer representatives set up a Citizens' Relief Committee to fire "all Communists from the State Relief Administration."

Yet, in spite of the continuous attacks, the terrorism and the red-baiting, working people could not be held down or shut up. ILD attorneys George Andersen and Herbert Resner won some of the Marysville UCAPAWA cases and appealed others, while the strike

*According to a medical health survey conducted by the State Relief Administration.

leaders still in jail organized themselves into "The Marysville Jail Congress for Industrial Organization Prisoners." They conducted such a militant, and noisy, hunger strike that their jailers were forced to treat them more decently, including recognizing their Grievance Committee.

The CIO, predicted to totter and die, was obviously here to stay. Said John L. Lewis at the 1939 CIO Convention, "The CIO has held its own and maintained its ranks through a long period of bitter unemployment and in face of the most vicious and concentrated attacks of its enemies." Indeed, not only the CIO but AFL unions, too, were invigorated by the people's struggles. Clearly the main task of the labor movement was to organize the unorganized.

Build A Better San Francisco

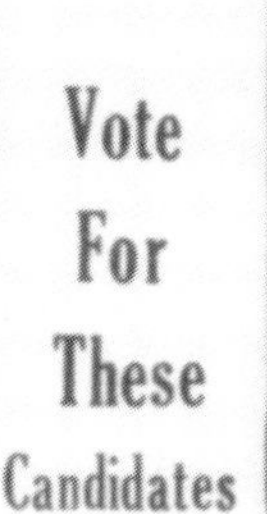

Oleta O'Connor Yates
For Assessor

Elaine Black
Board of Supervisors

Archie Brown
Board of Supervisors

Defeat Rossi!

- -

Name .... Address ....

Please send me Election Literature ....

Tell me more about Communist Party ....

1939 Election Campaign Flyer

20.

The Women's Slant

Elaine Runs for Office

Having once been admonished by a Municipal Court judge for being "just a Communist [who] has no standing in this court," Elaine found out what standing she had in the San Francisco community in November 1939, when she ran for Board of Supervisors, receiving a very respectable 20,506 votes. She was 33 years old. Almost 50 years later, on July 28, 1988, the Board of Supervisors' meeting would adjourn out of respect to her memory and "with a profound sense of civic and personal loss . . . conscious of the many fine qualities of heart and mind which distinguished and brought justifiable appreciation to Mrs. Yoneda in the community."

While the position of Supervisor was a nonpartisan post, Elaine's campaign was endorsed and widely publicized by the Communist Party. She was by then active in the ILWU Women's Auxiliary; her campaign reflected specifically the needs of women, with child care a major focus. For her, lack of child care meant that as the mother of a young baby she had to run most of her campaign from her home. Using the initials of her last name "BLACK," her program called for:

- B abies in Free Day Nurseries;
- L ow Cost Housing;
- A nti-Racist Discrimination;
- C ivil Rights Protected;
- K eep America out of Imperialist War.

Archie Brown also ran on the Communist ticket for a seat on the Board while Oleta O'Connor Yates ran for Assessor.

"S.F. Cops Remember Communist Candidate" reported the *People's World:*

> Elaine Black . . . veteran defender of civil liberties is well (but not gladly) known to the San Francisco police. Every time they pinch a

> worker for picketing or distributing leaflets, [Mayor] Rossi's bluecoats know they'll hear from Elaine. In fact, after a recent violation of civil rights by the police, an officer picked up the telephone, heard a woman's voice ask for the desk sergeant, and simply said, "It's that Black woman again."

Sue Barry in her October 10 *People's World* column – "The Women's Slant – urged "every working class mother in San Francisco" to support Elaine's program for a free city-wide nursery school program. "She knows that if you have to depend on a meager salary you can't give your child the many advantages it must have to develop into a well balanced adult – constant health supervision, play in pleasant surroundings, expert psychological treatment and day-long attention."

No Messy Kitchens, Please

That was a different time, reflecting a different attitude toward women's issues, or perhaps the Communist Party believed that an appeal to women voters had to reflect that women were indeed in the kitchen as well as in civic affairs. Elaine made several radio talks. In one, she said:

> Hello everyone. I think it is safe to say that if any housewife made as big a mess of her kitchen as some politicians have made of our public affairs, she wouldn't keep her husband five minutes. Then why, will you tell me, do these politicians manage to hang onto the public vote?
>
> Your civic government is as important to every family as the kitchen is to the housewife, or a job is to a man—something he cannot afford to neglect or get in a mess. We must make it a government of, by and for the people—not government by dishonest politicians indebted to corporations.

If the formulation sounds archaic, the content was challenging. Elaine called for jobs programs, free medical and dental care for all children, free garbage collection, development of city land for parks and recreation, making racial discrimination illegal, full academic freedom for teachers and students and support for President Roosevelt's peace policy.

Defend Bill of Rights

A week before the election, Elaine told a KSAN audience:

> . . . one plank in my platform becomes more important than any of the others—that is, the question of civil liberties, the protection of the Bill of Rights . . . because even as I am speaking, vigilantism is raging without restriction in the central part of our state against cotton pickers who are on strike for higher wages. Their leaders are beaten and jailed—their attorneys 'escorted' out of town . . . Governor Olson has sent his representatives into the area, but what are they doing to curb vigilantism? Nothing! His officers are standing idly by while strikers are beaten and jailed.
>
> Nationally we have that American-made Goering—Mr. Dies* —parading through the nation on a witch hunt for 'Reds,' bellowing forth that the nation must be saved, that the Communist Party must be outlawed. It is impossible to deal with the subject of civil liberties in the United States without establishing an attitude toward the Communist Party, as to whether Communists may also be entitled to the rights of citizenship guaranteed by the Constitution and the Bill of Rights, or whether they shall be excepted from these rights . . .
>
> In practice, there is not a fight for popular liberties which has failed to receive the loyal and self-sacrificing support of the Communists. And if the day should come when the cause of civil liberties has been abandoned by all other parties, I can assure you that the Communist Party will still stand and fight for the right and opportunity for the people, the great majority, to control their own destinies in every way . . . Let me warn you that the attacks now being made on the Communists and the Communist Party is but a forerunner of the attacks to be made later on the trade union movement, progressive organizations, on Democracy itself.

Cigar Workers Honor Elaine

Elaine's campaign took her before old friends as well as people who knew her only through what they had read in the local press. She appeared before League of Women Voters meeting at the St. Francis Hotel where "some of the women were surprised to see what I looked like. I don't know how they envisioned me." After all, deputy

*Congressman Martin Dies (D. Texas), chairman of the Special Committee on Un-American Activities, established in 1938, and succeeded in January 1945 by the House Committee on Un-American Activities

sheriffs in Salinas had expected the 4-foot 11-inch Elaine to be a "great big giant."

"I think women's organizations listened a little closer to what the women candidates had to say, regardless of what their party was," said Elaine. She also spoke before old allies: the Machinists Union, Cigar Workers, Ship Scalers, Cleaners and Dyers, Shed Workers, Filipino Workers Association. She was endorsed by ILWU Local 10 and the Alaska Cannery Workers, receiving standing ovations. Black church congregations were very welcoming. They knew of the ILD's work in the Scottsboro case and that "had it not been for the ILD, the Scottsboro Nine would have been long gone," Elaine said.

Among credits for her work during the stormy thirties was honorary membership conferred by the Cigar Workers Union as well as the Cleaners and Dyers, an AFL union. The Cigar Workers, in a September 1933 strike of North Beach cigarmakers for a living wage, had received picket line support from the TUUL and legal advice from the ILD. When police attacked and beat up scores of pickets, 73 were arrested. Elaine raised bail and helped with lawyers. They never forgot.

"Actually," Elaine said, " . . . it was a tribute to the ILD rather than to me personally." No doubt it was both but whichever, the petite fiery battler for workers' rights – the *"Red Angel,"* the *"Tiger Girl"* – was becoming a legend in her own time.

"We Stand on Our Record"

After the elections, Elaine no longer worked full time in the ILD office, although she continued to function as Pacific Coast ILD vice president, helping to raise funds and participating in ongoing cases. The ILD remained active in all parts of the country. However, an era was coming to a close. The ILD – reflecting a new reality – was changing its emphasis from courtroom and picketline confrontations to political action. It organized opposition to the Concentration Camp Bill (H.R. 3), first passed by the House of Representatives in May 1939. This provided for the imprisonment without trial or bail of foreign born non-citizens who could not, for whatever reason, be deported to the countries of their birth; it was to be reintroduced in 1941.

The ILD also opposed a wire-tapping bill, a Dies Committee-supported bill on Universal Labor and Military Conscription, and a House Resolution which urged the states to outlaw the Communist Party from participating in elections.

The annual Summer Milk Drive included an appeal to supply milk not only for the children of U.S. political and labor prisoners but for ILD foreign "wards," refugee children of Germany, Spain, China, Austria and Czechoslovakia. The milk appeal was signed by many prominent persons, including Archibald MacLeish, actor Raymond Massey, Rabbi Benjamin Plotkin, Vincent Sheean, Donald Ogden Stewart, Richard Wright, Dr. Max Yergan, Stella Adler, Ida E. Guggenheimer, Cong. John M. Coffee, William Gropper, Dr. Mary E. Woolley, Leland Stowe and Countee Cullen.

Said Vito Marcantonio: "The air is filled with cries for help – cries that appeal to the conscience of mankind . . . cries of the children – Spanish, Chinese, German – blond or dark, Jew or gentile, their hunger and misery is the same."

Subjected to a vicious red-baiting attack in 1939 by Congressman Martin Dies' Special Committee on Un-American Activities, the ILD persevered in its historic role of championing the rights of labor and defending democratic political and social rights. In a ringing challenge to the American people, Congressman Vito Marcantonio told the 1939 National ILD Conference:

> "I say that we are going to beat reaction in this country. But that can only be done by unity on the part of all progress-loving people. And we of the International Labor Defense find ourselves well equipped to do battle, to take our place in the front line trenches on behalf of American democracy. As President of this organization I am mighty proud of the Americanism of the International Labor Defense, and I am ready to match that Americanism against the un-American activities of Mr. Martin Dies or any other snooper or stooge of the fascists in the United States of America. We have nothing to hide.
>
> "Sure, they want investigations. Let them come and investigate us. We have nothing to hide. We have nothing to conceal.
>
> "We are proud of our record. That, we maintain, constitutes real Americanism. Our conduct, our fights, our activities, have been in line with the activities of Washington, Jefferson, Jackson, Lincoln, and Franklin Delano Roosevelt; and we stand on our record."

The turbulent Thirties drew to an end.

PART THREE

21.

War Clouds

Into the Forties

On January 11, 1940, Rep. Vito Marcantonio addressed the House of Representatives to warn against a "serious menace to civil liberties" posed by the FBI's creation a few months earlier of a General Intelligence Division. J. Edgar Hoover, in requesting FBI appropriations, had testified:

> This Division now has compiled extensive indexes of individuals, groups, and organizations engaged in . . . subversive activities, in espionage activities, or in any activities that are possibly detrimental to the internal security of the United States.
>
> "The indexes have been arranged not only alphabetically but also geographically, so that at any time, should we enter into the conflict abroad, we would be able to go into any of these communities and identify individuals or groups who might be a source of grave danger to the security of this country. Their backgrounds and activities are known to the Bureau. These indexes will be extremely important and valuable in grave emergency."

Said Marcantonio: "This language indicates to me the beginning of a disease which will make our democratic body very, very sick . . . if Mr. Hoover has the names of those who are guilty of or suspected of espionage or sabotage, it is Mr. Hoover's duty . . . to immediately apprehend these people . . . If, on the other hand, these people are not . . . then I submit the preparation of these indices is most dangerous to the constitutional rights of the American people."

Elaine and Karl didn't know it yet, but they were among those "indexed" by the FBI.

While increasingly there was talk of impending war, 96 percent of the U.S. people were opposed to U.S. entry into the war in Europe.[1] On April 6, 1940, progressive trade unions and other organizations held peace demonstrations in many cities, several of them embracing the slogan originated by left-wing writer Mike Quin: "The Yanks Are Not Coming!"

The CIO continued to oppose U.S. involvement in "the present horrible war raging in Europe." What the American people needed, it said, were three million more WPA jobs.

ILD Credo

Elaine was still working with the ILD in 1940 and did what she could in the political arena. However, her family demanded much of her time; Tommy was an asthmatic child who required special care and Joyce was in her early teenage years. Karl worked on the waterfront and was still active in the Alaska Cannery Workers Union.

There were "remnants" and "pockets" of court cases in Lodi, Tulare, and in the gold fields, although this legal work had "tempered down," Elaine remembered. Unions had established their own defense funds, but it was still necessary to raise money for political and labor prisoners and their families. Prisoners released on parole needed jobs, and there were mass meetings and benefits to arrange. Elaine spoke when asked, but was unable to do much traveling.

The ILD – 15 years old – continued as a "viable force," she said. Mini Carson, former farm worker organizer, took up the cudgels of leadership in San Francisco, while long-time Los Angeles ILD leader Larue McCormick continued as West Coast ILD representative. In a changing political situation and under Carson's direction, legislative activity to combat repressive and anti-labor legislation increased significantly in Northern California.

"This is a most crucial time in our nation's history," the ILD said, "when the struggle for the defense of our Bill of Rights and the struggle for Peace is decisive for the fate of our country." It continued to urge "every American worker . . . to remember a few practical points about the law and the courts" – what to do if arrested, the right to bail, how to plead, the right to a trial by jury.

Both nationally and in the branches, the ILD issued legislative newsletters regularly. On June 15, the Smith Bill, already passed in the House, won Senate approval. The June 23 ILD Civil Rights Newsletter cited it as a measure that "fires at the Bill of Rights from every direction at the same time."

> It provides for a Federal Criminal Syndicalism Law applicable against "any person who advocates, etc., ANY CHANGE IN ANY GOVERNMENT OF THE UNITED STATES by force and violence . . . PROVIDES FOR THE FINGERPRINTING AND REGISTRATION OF ALL ALIENS WITH DEPORTATION AS THE PENALTY FOR FAILURE TO COMPLY . . .

The ILD credo for the forties was expressed in a "Civil Liberties Assurance Policy" that pledged to:

> Continue to aid labor and political prisoners, and victims of reactionary violence, regardless of race, color, nationality, religious or political convictions, and the defense of democratic and civil rights . . . draw the greatest possible number of people into the fulfillment of these aims . . . aid labor and political prisoners, victims of violence and reaction, families of prisoners, widows and orphans of the victims of labor struggles and the struggles for democratic rights all over the world . . . support the fight against war and fascism . . . organize for the defense of the Negro people and all national minorities against lynching, oppression, discrimination, and for the defense of the foreign born against deportation and for the right of political and religious asylum . . . cooperate with other groups and organizations, for aid to labor prisoners and for the defense of democratic, civil, and individual rights of the people . . .

A Different Drummer

Leaders of the ACLU heard a different drummer. Rep. Martin Dies ceased his red-baiting attacks on the ACLU when it "purged" itself of Elizabeth Gurley Flynn, charter member of both the ACLU and ILD, and first national chairperson of the ILD. Flynn's history in the labor movement and in behalf of civil liberties in the United States was incontrovertible. Even before the first World War, she was an IWW organizer and active in free speech fights, then in the Sacco-Vanzetti and Mooney-Billings cases. She joined the Communist Party in 1937 and was the only Communist on the ACLU board of directors – but one was one too many.

On May 8, 1940, after refusing to resign, Flynn became a victim of liberal anti-Communist hysteria and was expelled from the ACLU. Many ACLU board members, however, protested and ACLU Board Chair Dr. Harry F. Ward resigned. The ILD charged the ACLU with setting "a dangerous example of red-baiting and complete violation of all accepted tenets of fair, democratic processes . . . " Said veteran civil libertarian and ACLU Board Member Corliss Lamont: "The ACLU Resolution of 1940 [under which Flynn was expelled] meant a major setback for civil liberties in America and helped sow the seeds for the U.S. witch hunt that followed World War II . . . culminating in the nation-wide movement known as McCarthyism . . . "[2]

ILWU Women's Auxiliary

During this period, Elaine was becoming more active in the women's auxiliary. The ILWU Auxiliary adopted a uniform and marched in Labor Day parades. Over the years it worked for repeal of the Criminal Syndicalism Act, participated in a Pacific Coast Congress Against War and Fascism, raised funds for the Mooney Defense Committee and collected food for striking gold miners. In 1939 the women circulated a petition to keep America out of war and wrote a Women's Declaration Against War.

In 1940, it protested the Alien Registration Act as well as a "hoodlum" attack on Commonwealth College, a worker's college in Mena, Arkansas. Each year the Auxiliary put flowers on the graves of "Bloody Thursday" victims Howard Sperry and Nick Bordoise. The women raised money for the ILD prisoners fund; they sent a delegate to the American Peace Mobilization in Chicago that year and the next. In October, 1941 they wired President Roosevelt to stop firing WPA workers "on unfounded suspicions . . . and halting of persecutions which weaken the fight against Hitlerism." The auxiliary protested the rising cost of milk and demanded price controls. They supported all workers' strikes. "It is very significant," Dorothy Ray Healey said, that the auxiliaries "were called 'women's' auxiliaries and not 'ladies' auxiliaries because they were never what the word would indicate – an auxiliary to a male-dominated union; they were active participants in every organizing campaign, in all union . . . [affairs] . . . "[3]

J.B. McNamara: 1882–1941

The ILD, especially in San Francisco, worked harder than ever to get Jim McNamara released from prison. He had been behind bars since April 2, 1911, and now he was very ill; there had been too many years of suffering, bad food, and intermittent solitary confinement. A new "Free McNamara Committee" was formed that included Dashiell Hammett, Carey McWilliams, Theodore Dreiser, Lester

Cole, Laura Perelman, Nathaniel West, Eileen McKenny, John Wexley, Robert W. Kenney, Ben Golden, Richard Wright, I.F. Stone, Marie De L. Welch, and Jeanne Reynal.

On visiting the sick McNamara, ILD representatives learned that he was not receiving his mail, nor were his friends receiving letters from him. This was an old prison cruelty – cutting McNamara off from the outside world was the worst punishment the prison could inflict. McNamara's illness became very grave. On February 27, the Women's Auxiliary sent him a telegram, wishing him a speedy recovery from his second operation for abdominal cancer. He died on March 8.

For the last six years of his life, McNamara was a member of the ILD National Committee. To Elaine, he was a very special comrade, a man who "befriended everyone" and with an "acute awareness" of events both in prison and on the outside – both in the U.S. and throughout the world, a man many times "beaten up for standing up for the rights of men in prison." Elaine was to say many times, "I never met a man of his caliber... a warm, kind human being- ... [who] tried to help everyone."

For the first 15 years of his imprisonment, McNamara had been a lonely and forgotten man. It was when the ILD came into existence that "a voice was raised in his behalf."[4]

"Equal Justice" described McNamara:

> ... a shining spirit that 29 years and 11 months of cruel punishment could not break. By killing him in prison, California extracted its last ounce of vengeance and the full measure of the life sentence it had imposed on James B. McNamara ... But they never killed the warmth and radiance of this rare man; his courage, his faith in the people. That never faltered. No steel bars were strong enough to lock away an invincible spirit that roamed the world beside his fellow men.

Tom Mooney said, "Never have I met or heard or read of a man who had such an insatiable hatred of injustice as that which burned in the breast of Jim McNamara ... His heart was in every struggle of the working class ... " And, according to Warren K. Billings, "Prison is no place that leaves sentimental memories. But the privilege of meeting and knowing McNamara was one of the few recompenses for more than 22 years that I spent behind bars."

Mooney and Mini Carson headed up a United Labor Funeral Committee. For two days McNamara's body lay in state at Duggan's

J. B. McNamara's funeral service. A grieving Elaine is at top of stair. 3/15/41

Mortuary with guards of honor standing at attention at his bier. He was buried in Mt. Tamalpais Cemetery in San Rafael, near San Quentin. According to his wishes, his body was laid beside that of Mother Mooney "... whom McNamara loved and revered as his own," the San Francisco *Chronicle* noted in an obituary.

As the funeral cortege left Duggan's and Elaine walked with the honorary pallbearers behind McNamara's casket, tears flowed down her stricken face.

In April, at the Third Biennial National ILD Conference at New York's Hotel Piccadilly, Carson described McNamara's last days. The ILD had won McNamara's transfer from Folsom back to San Quentin, where he lived out the last days of his life. Through the long years, his occasional transfers to Folsom were a punishment for daring to confront prison cruelty and defend his brother prisoners. But San Quentin was his "home" and that was where he wanted to die. The ILD delegates stood in silence to honor their gentle friend and co-worker.

Dies Committee Attacks ILD

Elaine was reelected to the ILD National Committee, and Tom Mooney was among new National Committee members. So were Mini Carson, Paul Robeson, Bella Dodd, Michael Quill, George B. Murphy, and others. Reelected ILD president was Vito Marcantonio and William L. Patterson to the vice-presidency. The brilliant organizer Anna Damon continued as national secretary and Robert Dunn as treasurer.

The conference emphasized legislative work. The ILD *Legislative Letter,* issued weekly when Congress was in session, provided a national centralized source of news and analyses of legislation. While specific measures, like the Anti-Lynch Bill and Anti-Poll Tax Bill – both reintroduced session after session – did not pass Congress at that time, the campaigns around them did educate and mobilize people and lay the basis for future success.

Mini Carson reported on the campaign in Northern California against a state bill requiring "subversive" organizations to register and file for inspection copies of all mail sent through the post office. Legislation that blatantly violated the Bill of Rights was being made law in many states. There was a plethora of bills that legalized wiretapping, established concentration camps, and destroyed labor and election rights. In California the previous year, 19 candidates on the Communist Party ticket had been arrested for distributing campaign literature and making speeches. A policeman told one candidate: "I have orders to keep you people from speaking."

Writer Dashiell Hammett headed up "The National Federation for Constitutional Liberties." To meet the new attacks on election rights, it set up a sub-committee, the "Committee on Free Elections."

In his conference keynote speech, Marcantonio responded to Dies Committee attacks: "Let others play safe. Let others try to be smart... So far as the ILD is concerned, there will be no compromise... Let the attacks come... we are free men and free women in a free nation, and we are going to fight."

Damon, who had been called before the Dies Committee, spoke of the vicious assaults on labor, the Negro people, religious and political minorities and the foreign born. But she told also of defense campaigns that included many victories among several hundred cases handled in Northern California, "the most recent of which was the acquittal of James Montgomery, of Labor's Non-Partisan League, charged under an ancient election law."

Important victories were won, she said, by a combination of "legal skill... supplemented by united mass defense effort." Among these was an attempt in Brooklyn to send a "young Negro boy... on a trumped up charge of rape" to prison; and a case that backfired on the FBI in Detroit, involving the attempt to prosecute 12 citizens for recruiting volunteers for the Loyalist Army in Spain. "So great was the defense protest that the Department of Justice was forced to admit it had no case and to drop all the indictments."

The ILD continued to provide prisoner relief, a function that no other organization even attempted. While 40 ILD-supported prisoners had been released since the ILD conference two years before, the number of long-term prisoners actually increased. The ILD also carried on its support rolls 11 widows and 30 orphans. On November 14, the annual Christmas Drive for prisoner relief was launched. National committee chair Hester Huntington appealed for aid for the "widows whose husbands were murdered in struggles arising out of bettering their living conditions. Eleven of these women have children. Wives of coal miners shut away behind prison bars, wives of sharecroppers locked up on long-term sentences, widows of victims of the Chicago Memorial Day Massacre and many, many others, look to the ILD for support all year round... Now as Christmas approaches, each one of the children will have a toy from us, each person some clothing... none shall be forgotten."

Festus Lewis Coleman

A new prisoner, whose 23-year old wife and two children were added to relief rolls in San Francisco, was Festus Lewis Coleman, arrested in April 1941 for "robbery and rape," tried "before a Negro-baiting judge," and sentenced to 65 years in San Quentin. The only "evidence" against him, the ILD charged, "was presented by the alleged victim and her two escorts, with whom she was spending the evening on a blanket in Golden Gate Park, San Francisco." The ILD entered the case at the appeal stage at the request of the Coleman family and people in the African-American community.[5]

Coleman was a WPA worker. He was arrested after he "stumbled on the trio" in the park and a fight ensued with the white soldiers. Coleman's testimony implicated one of the soldiers in statutory rape, and it was at that point that Coleman found himself charged with rape and robbery. Judge George Steiger offered to drop the rape charge if Coleman would not appeal a robbery conviction. Coleman responded: "I would rather spend ten thousand years in jail than plead guilty to something I didn't do."[6] Actor-singer Clarence Muse became involved; "Again," he said, "the American pastime of railroading Negroes on trumped-up charges of rape is in operation." The popular people's minister, Rev. H.T.S. Johnson, secretary of the Interdenominational Ministerial Alliance in Oakland, became chairman of the Coleman Coordinating Committee. The San Francisco CIO Council endorsed the defense. The case would go on for years.

The Coleman case was only one in the widespread "violent terror against the Negro people" that occurred in the first nine months of 1941. An ILD survey listed "112 examples of unspeakable barbarism . . . based on newspaper reports from a limited number of newspapers," and therefore only a portion of the true number. From July 1 through September 30 – three months – there was a 100 percent increase in incidents of violence against Black people over the first six months of 1941, "involving well over 1,000 men and women of whom at least 700 were Negro soldiers in the uniform of the U.S. Army." These included nine lynch murders, three narrowly averted lynchings and three shootings.

Elaine remembered the "horrendous cases and violations of civil rights of the Negroes . . . a constant battle . . . "

And five of the Scottsboro youths remained in prison.

Elaine, Karl and Tommy visiting Tom Mooney, at San Francisco St. Luke's Hospital, 10/21/41.

22.

A Time of Infamy

Pearl Harbor

Sunday morning, December 7, 1941. As she did the family laundry, Elaine listened to the symphony over the radio. It was a nice day. Karl was polishing their new Studebaker. After the clothes were washed and hung on the line, the family planned to spend the afternoon in Golden Gate Park.

The music was interrupted and "... the news was flashed. I didn't believe it at first and then it was repeated... horrible news was coming over the air."

With Tommy, then almost three, bouncing in and out of the room and 14-year old Joyce doing homework, an alarmed Elaine called to Karl to come quickly. As he cleaned the car, Karl was visiting with Louis Yamamoto,* a young Japanese-American soldier on short-term furlough from a transport ship on its way to the Philippines. Karl and Elaine knew Louie from his days as an agricultural union organizer in the San Joaquin Valley; Elaine had bailed him out of jail. The three listened to the bulletin: "... **This morning at 7:55 Hawaii time Japanese warplanes began attacking Pearl Harbor. Many U.S. warships are damaged with heavy casualties. I will repeat...**"

They looked at each other as Tommy played at their feet. "What is it going to mean for people like us?" Elaine wondered. Karl immediately understood that there could be serious implications for Japanese-Americans. He told Elaine to stay indoors with the children, and the two men left for Japantown to see what was happening. Many news reporters were interviewing people in Japantown. Yamamoto was one of the Nisei GIs who told a newsman that, of course, he would fight against Japan.

That night, Karl prepared a telegram to send to President Roosevelt

*See chapter 7

on behalf of the San Francisco staff and readers of *Doho,* the Japanese-American newspaper on which he worked:

> We pledge full cooperation in all endeavors to secure victory for the democracies. We stand ready to join the ranks of the fighting forces under your command to defeat the vicious military fascists of Japan.

The Japanese-American Citizens League (JACL) and the Oakland Nisei Democratic Club sent similar wires to President Roosevelt. In Los Angeles, in his message of "fullest support," *Doho* editor and publisher Shuji Fujii added: "May I request reiteration of promise of fair and democratic treatment of loyal resident and citizen Japanese?"

The December 7 attack "shocked and enraged the American people, including Japanese Americans," Karl said. "The Communist Party immediately denounced it as the 'culminating outrage of Axis aggression aimed at the domination of the entire world . . . the Communist Party pledges its loyalty, its devoted labor . . . in support of our country in this greatest of all crises . . . ' "

The ILD said: "The defense of democracy and of the Bill of Rights, the defeat of fascism, to which the International Labor Defense is dedicated, demand above all the full defeat of all enemies of the United States and of its people."

A Knock at the Door

Karl had worked on the San Francisco docks since February 1936, the only Japanese-American longshoreman on the mainland of the Pacific Coast. On Monday morning, December 8, he had breakfast and left for work. Shortly after, Elaine answered a knock at the door. The three men standing there identified themselves as FBI agents; they asked for Karl. She told them he was at work.

"I let them in without inquiring whether they had a search warrant – something I would have demanded if Japan's military attack on the United States had not taken place."

"What do you mean, he's at work? He's a Jap, he can't be."

Elaine was indignant. "You must be looking for the wrong person. Karl is anti-fascist. He has been clubbed and jailed for being an anti-fascist . . . " The agents searched the four-room flat.

Elaine had been in the process of preparing Christmas cards. That year their cards were to benefit Chinese War Relief. Enclosed in some was a photo of Tommy with Tom Mooney. Mooney was ill;

the picture had been taken in November in his hospital room. An agent sneered, "Look, Chinese war relief in a Jap house!" Elaine had attempted to cooperate but was "irate at that remark as well as the travesty of their searching for Karl."

"They certainly had a dossier on him," she realized. They knew that "he was anti-fascist, anti-militarist . . . But he also had a record of being a union organizer, being a Communist . . . " Elaine called the union hiring hall to confirm that Karl was working with "Copenhagen" Hansen's gang on Pier 45. The three agents left. Uneasy neighbors told Elaine they saw men on the roof tops of surrounding apartment buildings. The submachine guns they carried were aimed at the Yoneda's front and back doors.

Down on the waterfront, Hansen's work gang had for several days been loading armaments onto a ship scheduled to sail to the Philippines. The workers found nothing irregular about Karl reporting as usual for work and protested when the three FBI agents came onto the job and arrested him. He was taken to the Immigration Detention Center on Silver Avenue, where he found himself among a small group of five anti-fascist Japanese and about 50 "fanatic emperor lovers." Being held in the same cell with them and being threatened was, he told Elaine, the most frightening 72 hours of his life. "Undeniably," according to Carey McWilliams, "there were dangerous individuals among the West Coast Japanese; undeniably there was a strong current of nationalist feeling among certain Issei leaders. But the point is that these elements were well-known to the authorities. They were promptly arrested on December 7 and 8 . . . "[1] Throughout the U.S. and Hawaii 736 Japanese were taken immediately into custody.[2] In subsequent days, however, on the U.S. Pacific Coast the FBI initiated a "ruthless sweep for suspects" and over 5,000 Issei and Nisei were arrested.[3] Most were – like Karl – cleared and released.

"The FBI Had My Husband"

"I was not notified by the FBI that they had my husband," Elaine said. "At noon I learned [it] from a co-worker" of Karl's. She called attorney George Andersen who immediately prepared a writ of habeas corpus for Karl's release.

That day, December 8, the nation's people sat glued to their radios as President Roosevelt made his "Yesterday . . . a date which will live in infamy" speech and Congress declared war against Japan.

This was soon followed by formal declarations of war against Germany and Italy. The Allies – mainly Great Britain, France, the Soviet Union and the United States – made plans for the joint waging of war against the three Axis countries.

Under a banner headline "JAPAN BOMBS U.S.!" the December 8 *People's World* also reported on page one: "Japanese Americans Rally to U.S. Defense." The story quoted Karl speaking for Japanese trade unionists: "We are all for the progressive labor movement, for the defeat of Hitlerism, and now for the defeat of the Japanese military clique." An ominous note was the report that Y. Nishimura, caretaker of a local Japanese cemetery, had been threatened: "You ought to dig a grave."

That same night, with Karl still detained, Japanese members of the Communist Party were hastily called to meet at Elaine and Karl's house. They were informed by the district leadership that all members of Japanese ancestry and their spouses – Japanese and non-Japanese alike – were thereupon summarily suspended from party membership in the interests of "national unity" and "national security." The rationale was that "the best place for any Japanese fifth columnist is in CP ranks . . . "[4] The order was not questioned by the local leadership; there was no time for study or reflection. "There were . . . tears," Elaine said, "and most of us were . . . horrified."

Karl was released from FBI custody the next evening, December 9. Agents told him that he resembled a suspected enemy agent and they had to check him out. This was untrue. In fact, a previously-prepared dossier on Karl had been supplied on December 7 to L.M.C. Smith, Chief of the Special Defense Unit in San Francisco. Some time before, J. Edgar Hoover told the San Francisco office that Elaine would not be investigated "to determine if she has rendered any assistance to any Japanese espionage group" because " . . . there is much evidence available to this Bureau that [Karl] Yoneda is one of those rare individuals who is of Japanese descent, but is open and avowed in his Communist sympathies and anything but in sympathy with the present militaristic regime in Japan. Yoneda is the San Francisco representative of the Japanese language newspaper "Doho", an allegedly Communist inspired publication, the editorial policy of which links Germany, Italy and Japan as the Fascist forces which this country is dedicated to overcome."[5]

E.V. Billaroman, a sympathetic Filipino neighbor, drove Elaine and Andersen to the detention center and they brought Karl home, stopping on the way at Western Union. Karl sent his telegram to President Roosevelt pledging support to the war effort.

Told of the suspension of Communist Party membership, Karl was "just as stunned and speechless as others upon hearing this anti-working class, racist edict. It was so sudden and so unreal that no one uttered a word of protest." A troubled Karl called a meeting of the suspended CP members. "We decided that this was not the time to register a protest against the unwarranted suspension. Our urgent priority was to help carry out the Party campaign: 'Everything for victory over worldwide fascist slavery.' In our case, the task was to help smash Japan's fascist-imperialists . . . We agreed to fulfill our daily activities as Communists in spite of our shock and hurt . . . In retrospect, we made a faulty decision."[6]

The *People's World,* operating under the same edict of suspension, released from her job Nori Ikeda, the only Japanese-American in the employ of the paper. The paper continued to report stories demonstrating the loyalty of Japanese-Americans.

"I Am An American!"

On December 10, Karl attempted to enlist in the Army, believing that his bilingualism would be valuable to the war effort against Japan. He was turned away. The *People's World* reported, "Union man Yoneda freed by FBI, offers to serve U.S."

On that same day, *People's World* columnist Sue Barry wrote:

> There were no children playing on the streets in San Francisco's Japanese community today. Instead there were ominous little groups of overcoated grim-faced G-men, cops strolling in pairs in every block, and here and there a padlock on the door of a bookshop, grocery store or newspaper office.
>
> They are the only outward signs that this is not just another day for the ten thousand Japanese who are jammed into a segregated area in the heart of San Francisco.
>
> . . . In a tiny immaculate drugstore on Post St., pharmacist Maseo Tsujimoto told me: "The only thing we Japanese fear is the possibility of hostility and suspicion on the part of white people who come into the district. On Sunday as soon as the first news of the Japanese attack on Pearl Harbor and Honolulu, thousands of men and women started pouring into the streets around here. They looked at us like we were strange and curious creatures. They did not seem to realize that we were just as shocked and angry . . . as they were . . . " He

> hopes to be called into the Army soon... "Japan is a far-off and strange land to us."
>
> ... Perhaps in a day or so the children can come out of their homes and play in the streets again. And that will be a sign that fears the Japanese-Americans have about suspicion and hostility have been allayed.

On December 11, the *PW* featured on its editorial page the lead article from a special "war edition" of *Doho:* "... this [is a] fight for the freedom of all peoples now oppressed by Japanese and Nazi imperialism, including the peoples of both countries, held in bondage by their war-making overlords... "

The next day, "Jap Hunting License" posters showed up for sale in the community. Karl brought one home. "Some lunatics want to have a lynching party," Elaine said. Karl and *Doho* staff members convinced the printer to stop issuing the posters.

Yellow-colored cards with the inscription "Jap Hunting License ... Open Season Now" also appeared. Japanese-Americans protested to the FBI. The printing was stopped with the arrest of the printers by the FBI – it seems they had also issued counterfeit money orders.[7]

"Remember Pearl Harbor" stickers materialized everywhere, while "I Am An American" buttons appeared on the lapels of Nisei and Issei.*

An atmosphere of racism and "super-patriotism" was beginning to close in on the Japanese community even as young Nisei men joined long lines at Army recruiting stations, only – like Karl – to be turned away. Already in the Army were an estimated 5,000 Nisei GIs who had enlisted or been drafted prior to December 7. Some were summarily discharged. By mid-June, 1942, the War Department had stopped accepting into the armed forces any Japanese, citizen or non-citizen. A few exceptions were made, mostly for linguists in Military Intelligence Service. Not long after, Selective Service banned all Nisei inductions, classifying these as "enemy aliens." German and Italian Americans continued to be drafted through normal Selective Service procedures.

Elaine and Karl were filled with apprehension as rumors of spies and sabotage began to circulate, cultivated and spread by the Hearst and McClatchy newspaper chains. "Yellow peril" journalism was their stock in trade, and they did a good job of it.

---

*U.S.-born of Japanese ancestry

RE: "Alien Enemies"

Under the Alien Enemy Act, originally passed in 1798 as one of several Alien and Sedition Laws, and amended in 1918, when a state of declared war exists between the United States and any foreign nation, "all natives, citizens, denizens, or subjects of the hostile nation can be apprehended, restrained, secured, and removed as alien enemies."[8] To effectuate the Act, President Roosevelt issued Proclamation 2525 immediately after war was declared against the Axis powers, thus authorizing the government to detain enemy aliens. Nationals of Japan, Italy and Germany regarded as dangerous to the nation's security were immediately taken into custody. By January 13, a total of 3,087 were apprehended: 1,287 Germans, 243 Italians and 1,557 Japanese. By February 16, the total was 3,849.[9] An Enemy Alien Hearing Board, the government announced, would determine whether the alien would be "(a) released, (b) paroled under specified conditions or (c) turned over to the Army for continued detention. In all cases the governing policy is to detain enemy aliens only when they are believed dangerous to the peace and safety of the country." Pending that decision, these enemy aliens were to be kept in the custody of the Immigration and Naturalization Service.[10] Careful distinctions, the government said, should be made "between persons who have conducted themselves in a manner detrimental to the United States and those who are loyal aliens."

The ACPFB issued a leaflet reprinting the Dec. 28 statement of Attorney General Francis Biddle: "... it is the stated policy of the Federal Government that there shall be no discrimination in the employment of workers in defense industries because of race, creed, color or national origin... There is no reason in the world why loyal aliens or Americans of foreign birth, should not be employed by American industry; and there is no possible justification for discharging such employees. The Federal Government condemns such discrimination and urges all employers not to adopt such a policy."[11] Biddle added, "I should like to remind such employers that of our total non-citizen population of about 5,000,000, fewer than 3,000 – six out of 10,000 – have been regarded as dangerous to the peace and safety of the United States. These have been taken into custody by the Federal authorities."

The California CIO, too, appealed for fairness, regretting "any hardships which the Nation's crisis must inflict on these aliens of

Axis extraction and their families. Yet... we must support the measures necessary to protect American freedom and what is left of world democracy against the tyrants and butchers of Tokyo, Berlin and Rome... Firmness must be matched with fairness, vigilance and good sense... "

"Help guard at home," said the Department of Justice, "the freedoms our country is now fighting to defend by protecting the civil liberties of our loyal non-citizen population." In the Japanese community, however, people were fired from their jobs, evicted from their homes, and losing their businesses.

Something was going terribly wrong. It was clear that the Japanese were being singled out for special treatment. This was easy to accomplish. The U.S. Japanese population was concentrated on the West Coast; 99.6 percent of the total U.S. Japanese population of 126,947 lived in California, Oregon and Washington – and 93,717 or 73.8 percent of these resided in California.[12] They were an easy identifiable target around which to build racist hysteria, especially when bolstered by the deliberate propagation of wild rumors of fifth column activity – this in spite of the known round-up of suspicious nationals of all three enemy nations.

The 1940 census shows that of a total Japanese population in San Francisco of 5,280, 3,004 were U.S. citizens and 2,276 were born in Japan, while there were 12,000 non-citizen Italians in San Francisco. On the whole West Coast, there were approximately 80,000 alien Italians and Germans. That many older Japanese in the U.S. were non-citizens was largely due to early exclusion laws and "gentlemen's agreements" barring Japanese from citizenship and permanent residency status; the Japanese population, however, was largely young Nisei. Almost two-thirds of the total Japanese population of the U.S. were citizens. What was soon to become apparent was that for all ethnic Japanese, including *citizens,* the 14th Amendment of the Constitution guaranteeing due process and equal protection of the law would – within a short time – be ruthlessly violated.

Mounting Uneasiness

Christmas and the New Year came and went in the Yoneda household, without joy and with mounting uneasiness, not only for themselves but for all Japanese families. Karl and Elaine wondered, too, how would all this affect the waging of a war for democracy against the tyranny and oppression of Nazi Germany, Fascist Italy and Imperialist Japan?

On January 2, President Roosevelt condemned employers' firing of "aliens" as "... stupid as it is unjust ... " He warned the nation, "Remember the Nazi technique: 'Pit race against race, religion against religion, prejudice against prejudice. Divide and conquer.' We must not let that happen here." A few days later, Roosevelt reiterated the government's policy to "encourage full participation in the National Defense program by all citizens, regardless of race, creed, color, or national origin, in the firm belief that the democratic way of life within the nation can be defended successfully only with the help and support of all groups within its borders."

However, it was becoming too little and too late for the Japanese. It was as if the good words were not even meant to apply to them; certainly few were speaking up for the Constitutional and human rights of the Japanese. Throughout the Pacific Coast, anti-Japanese sentiment intensified. It *was* happening even as the anti-fascist forces in the Japanese community continued to declare their loyalty.

The *People's World* continued to reflect a humanitarian approach to the special problems of Japanese-Americans, and a young reader, E.S. Ilyama, wrote a letter to the editor: "Being one who is from a national minority, and an unpopular one at that, I appreciate your understanding of our ... position. I assure you that the vast majority of us are loyal Americans eager to do all we can to defend America, and I would like ... to thank you ... for refusing to reproach us – as so many other newspapers have – for something for which we cannot be held responsible. We have no loyalties other than to this nation."[13]

A January 31 editorial page article reported the "mounting anxiety among Japanese in California [that] was climaxed with a swift series of actions by federal, state and local officials aimed at removal of potential fifth column elements in vital defense areas." That was the January 29 order by U.S. Attorney General Biddle, issued at the request of General John L. DeWitt, Commanding General of the Western Defense Command, that all enemy aliens be removed from certain strategic areas on the coast. The *People's World* concluded that wartime necessity "holds it preferable to inconvenience even one thousand innocent persons than one to remain in a position where he can sabotage the war effort ... " The truth, however, was that there was and had been no sabotage whatsoever, only rumors carefully manufactured and spread. At the same time, the paper warned of the "threat of hysteria, resulting in unbridled punitive acts against enemy aliens or citizens of alien parentage." Also that "some groups saw a chance for personal gain, particularly in rural regions by depriving Japanese farmers of land which they had cultivated and developed."

"Herd 'em up . . . "

The hysteria was unleashed and went wild. "I am for the immediate removal of every Japanese on the West Coast to a point deep in the interior," wrote Hearst columnist Henry McLemore the day the order was issued. "I don't mean a nice part of the interior, either. Herd 'em up, pack 'em off and give them the inside room in the badlands. Let 'em be pinched, hurt, hungry and dead up against it . . . Personally, I hate the Japanese. And that goes for all of them." Nationally prominent columnist Walter Lippmann was among those who advocated setting aside the "constitutional rights" of Japanese citizens and spread the strange reasoning that while "there has been no important sabotage on the West Coast . . . It is a sign that the blow is well-organized and that it is held back until it can be struck with maximum effect . . . The Pacific Coast . . . may at any moment be a battlefield." Labor-hating, racist-baiting Westbrook Pegler said "to hell with habeas corpus . . . "[14]

Worse than all of this, however, were the behind-the-scenes machinations, maneuvering, and retreating by high government officials – from President Roosevelt to Secretary of War Henry L. Stimson and other Administration stalwarts, including the liberal Attorney General Biddle.

> Had the Attorney General vigorously lashed out against the obvious un-Americanism of singling out for especially cruel treatment a colored minority, the President, in turn, might conceivably have had to face up to his nobler libertarian instincts. But Biddle, like the President—while championing the rights of downtrodden minorities abroad—lacked the driving, down-reaching commitment against racism within America's own borders, and the opportunity to assert the very principles for which Americans were then fighting and dying was lost.[15]

Plans were put in place for mass evacuation and internment of the Japanese. Wording for Executive Order 9066, under which this would be accomplished, was even then being prepared by a slick lawyer, Colonel Karl R. Bendetsen, chief aide to General DeWitt. While the order did not contain the word "Japanese" and appeared to apply to all enemy aliens, it was never intended to apply to Italian and German aliens. Bendetsen and DeWitt, his boss, were dyed-in-the-wool racists; DeWitt believed that "the Japanese race is an enemy race" and "a Jap is a Jap."

On February 2, pursuant to Biddle's removal order, the FBI conducted a mass raid on Terminal Island in Los Angeles. Agents, the *People's World* reported, "swooped down . . . arresting over 500 alien Japanese fishermen . . . and interned them . . . the most drastic action against the Japanese population . . . [it] was proposed by the county defense council . . . [and] favored immediate internment of all American born Japanese . . . "

While the order specified aliens of all enemy nationalities, "no mass action was ever taken with regard to Germans and Italians" and they were never the butt of the kind of prejudice and hysteria the Japanese – who had no political voice – were subjected to. Protecting the civil and human rights of the foreign born was a long and legitimate concern of the U.S. Left and progressive movements and undoubtedly helped encourage in the public mind an attitude of fairness toward foreign-born Italians and Germans. What the distinction in treatment shows is the deepseated and historically-rooted racism that made the outrageous actions against the Japanese possible. Rules that previously applied to "enemy aliens" now were "extended to American citizens of Japanese ancestry."[16]

By then, Elaine recalled, "Jobs got scarcer for Karl and in February . . . the Army ordered [that] no one of Japanese ancestry be allowed to work on the waterfront." The February 2 headline of the San Francisco *Chronicle* announced "S.F. May Ask U.S. to Move Japs Inland" while "OUSTER OF ALL JAPS IN CALIFORNIA NEAR!" was the banner headline of Hearst's *Examiner.*

That same day the *People's World* lead editorial said: " . . . of course action must be taken to eliminate danger from actual or potential fifth column elements among Japanese, Italian, and German residents . . . But to fan hysteria . . . will only defeat the legitimate end of strengthening and safe-guarding our defense. Hysteria can only let loose the passions which sow dissension and division among our people . . . " The editorial called for curbing the "politicians and land-grabbers" and said: " . . . only a few of the thousands of Japanese residents in California are fifth columnists. To isolate these few it may be necessary to move many, but it would be wrong to impose economic hardship among these many innocent persons." No source was given for the "fifth column" charge. It just floated in the air.

People's World Foreign Editor John Pittman wrote that the "deep-rooted chauvinism" against "Japanese aliens" was "a byproduct of two centuries of oppression of the Negroes."[17] This connection was made, too, in a racist diatribe against the Japanese by the California Joint Immigration Committee[18] – a report prepared at the request of the Dies Committee: In a long discourse detailing the "determination of Caucasians to keep their country and their blood white . . . a grave mistake," the committee said, "was made when citizenship was granted to all born here . . . Another grave mistake was the granting of citizenship to the Negroes after the Civil War."[19] This report would become part of the Tolan hearings soon to convene.

Contradictions

Articles, columns and editorials reflected the decency and concern of the *People's World* staff, and above all, challenged the racist implications of the mounting anti-Japanese edicts and the hysteria generated. However, the paper did not – due to the policy handed down by the Communist Party – address the tortured reasoning and contradictions of that policy. The policy went unchallenged and, perhaps worst of all, influenced non-Party Leftists and progressives who looked to the Communists for a democratic and reasoned approach to events.

In San Jose, a group called "Knights of Liberty" planned "to drive aliens, particularly Japanese, out of the country."[20] And on Terminal Island, rumors were floated that "all Japanese are to be lined up and machine-gunned and that children are to be separated from their mothers in different internment camps . . . many of the rumors are spread by unscrupulous second hand dealers in their efforts to force the Japanese to sell their possessions for a song."[21]

In a February 20 letter to the *PW,* Karl protested a local radio broadcast of the California Council Table that all "Kibei"* were open to suspicion; " . . . we have remained anti-Japanese-militarist clique and pro-democratic . . . "

---

*Americans of Japanese descent educated in Japan

23.
The Tolan Hearings

Executive Order 9066

On February 19 President Roosevelt signed Executive Order 9066, giving the military the power to exclude from prescribed military areas "any or all persons" and to provide "such transportation, food, shelter, and other accommodations as may be necessary . . . " That night, in Los Angeles, 1,000 people met at the call of the United Citizen Federation, "representing a wide range of Nisei interests . . . Plans were laid to persuade the press, the politicians and the government that their attacks upon the ethnic Japanese were unfounded. It was too late."[1]

Two days later, on February 21 and 23, the Tolan Congressional Committee Hearings on "Problems of Evacuation of Enemy Aliens and Others from Prohibited Military Zones"[2] got underway in San Francisco. Chaired by Congressman John H. Tolan of California, its purpose was to determine the "facts about the war conditions" and make "recommendations that the people of the Pacific Coast want to give . . . concerning the problems associated with evacuations from military areas here, so that we may transmit them to Congress." The decision, however, had already been made. On February 14, "General DeWitt sent a memorandum to the Secretary of War, recommending evacuation of 'Japanese and other subversive persons' from the West Coast."[3] Executive Order 9066, authored by Colonel Bendetsen, was the implementation.

Karl and Elaine did not know yet that Executive Order 9066 would soon translate into something unimaginably terrible: the mass evacuation of more than 110,000 Japanese who would be rounded up, numbered like cattle, and herded into hastily-constructed concentration camps. They would have stolen away from them all of their constitutional rights, their freedom, their land, homes and worldly goods, their pride and dignity.

Elaine believed that each new generation must learn the truth.

And the records of the San Francisco Tolan Committee hearings – the pages permeated and poisoned by anti-Japanese ranting – remain for the generations since World War II as a record of the monstrous racism that with so little protest swept over California and the Pacific Coast. There is page after page of racist diatribe against the Japanese. All this as the nation was feverishly gearing up to fight an all-out war for democracy.

The hearings "served no purpose," Karl wrote in *Ganbatte,* "but to lay down the reactionary political groundwork for the removal of all persons of Japanese ancestry from the Pacific Coast."

San Francisco Mayor Angelo J. Rossi opened by pleading that "evacuation of Axis aliens, other than Japanese, should be avoided unless deemed imperative." Moving Italians and Germans from the city, he said, would cause them "extreme hardship, mental distress and suffering." The Mayor wasn't worried about the suffering of the Japanese. Karl and Elaine sat in the hearing room. They listened to the outrageous hypotheses, the abusive words. Some of it was not surprising; they had years of experience fighting for justice for agricultural workers in the great valleys of California. They had heard it all before. They knew the racism, the exploitation, the avarice and the hatred. They listened, but could do nothing.

The Honorable Attorney General

Those who testified included California Attorney General and star witness Earl Warren,[4] mayors of cities, chiefs of police, Chambers of Commerce officials, ranchers and growers, various state and local governmental officials, and American Legionnaires. Never in Warren's lifetime, including in his later and more liberal days, did he retract his racist testimony. This included an eight-year effort by Edison Uno, well-known Nisei activist, to persuade him to do so.[5] Only in Warren's memoirs, published in 1977, three years after his death, did Warren express regret for "the removal order and my own testimony advocating it . . . "[6] According to Carey McWilliams, Warren was "perhaps the most forceful advocate of mass evacuation."[7] The attorney general told the committee:

> Unfortunately, many of our people and some of our authorities and, I am afraid, many of our people in other parts of the country, are of the

opinion that because we have had no sabotage and no fifth column activities in this State since the beginning of the war, that means that none have been planned for us. But I take the view that that is the most ominous sign in our whole situation.[8] It convinces me perhaps more than any other factor that the sabotage that we are to get, the fifth column activities that we are to get, are timed just like Pearl Harbor was timed . . . I believe that we are just being lulled into a false sense of security and that the only reason we haven't had disaster in California is that it has been timed for a different date and that when that time comes if we don't do something about it it is going to mean disaster both to California and to our Nation. Our day of reckoning is bound to come . . . we are approaching an invisible deadline.

. . . Gentlemen . . . you can't protect against things about which you don't know. We have all been good soldiers out here and we have played the game . . . But when this emergency comes along we are going to have to deal with enemy aliens and those who are acting in concert with them. . . . We have almost 100,000 Japanese in California. The census shows that 33,000 of them are aliens and 66,000 are American-born. But we have no way on earth of knowing who the 33,000 are and who the 66,000 are . . .

So that is one of the things that led us to the conclusion that it was entirely a military problem and entirely a military decision as to what we do with **these aliens. The fact that so many of them are citizens makes the situation far more dangerous.** [Author's emphasis]

I want to say that the concensus of opinion among the law enforcement officers of this State is that there is more potential danger among the group of Japanese who are born in this country than from the Japanese who were born in Japan . . . in the first place there are twice as many of them . . .

Did Warren "have any way of knowing whether any one of this group is loyal to this country or loyal to Japan?" asked Congressman Laurence Arnold.

Congressman, there is no way that we can establish that fact. We believe that when we are dealing with the Caucasian race we have methods that will test the loyalty of them, and we believe that we can, in dealing with the Germans and Italians, arrive at some fairly sound conclusions because of our knowledge of the way they live in the community . . . But when we deal with the Japanese we are in an entirely different field . . . Their method of living, their language, make for this difficulty . . .

Warren was "very happy over the order [Executive Order 9066] of the President yesterday . . . " It was, he said, "most wise and . . . it at least points the way to a real solution of our problem."

Forget the Bill of Rights

The Culver City Chief of Police W.A. McDonald believed that Japanese Americans "should be more than pleased to submit to internment . . . if they should object to such treatment, they could not be looked upon as being true and loyal Americans."

This became a common rationale for the brutal betrayal of civil, legal and Constitutional rights, and the Japanese were expected to acquiesce while the nation was engaged in a just and necessary war. What would be their fate should they *not* behave as true and loyal Americans?

Count such "necessary" evacuation, said one of the country's worst racists, Commission member John Sparkman of Alabama, as "simply . . . a sacrifice necessary in wartime."

Elaine, whose courtroom battles for the Bill of Rights were legend in the Left and trade unions, listened as Madera County District Attorney George Mordecai made it clear that "we must forget such things as the writ of habeas corpus, and the prohibition against unreasonable searches and seizures. The right of self-defense, self-preservation, on behalf of the people, is higher than the bill of rights."

Karl heard the message of the Fresno County Chamber of Commerce: it is the "loyal" Japanese-Americans themselves who should "lead the movement of their countrymen . . . thereby proving conclusively their loyalty as American citizens . . . "

It was of no consequence that there had not been—nor was there to be—a single incident of sabotage by Japanese, every such rumor—and there were plenty as the hysteria grew—having been proven false. [Author's emphasis]

It was a time of lunacy and it was led by Attorney General Warren whose testimony provided a precedent for many others: "Many of our vital facilities," he said, "and most of our highways are just pocketed by Japanese ownership that could be of untold danger to us in time of stress."

It could not be mere coincidence, witnesses averred, that Japanese people, including farmers, lived along roads and highways, rivers, canals, levees and railroads, in West Berkeley and West and South Oakland, near bridges, "overlooking the municipal airport," on bluffs, "farming within a grenade throw of coast defense guns," "surrounding important warehouses," "along Pacific Gas & Electric power line," etc. Oakland attorney Gerald H. Hagar deemed it "quite obvious" that these ownerships and locations "cannot be brushed aside lightly, and it seems quite obvious . . . that it was the result of careful planning."

Semblance of Sanity

Indeed it was only through the testimony of Japanese witnesses that a semblance of sanity was injected into these bizarre claims. Michio Kunitani of Berkeley: "Which came first, the defense areas or the Japanese farms . . . ? I would like to point out that agriculture was the first occupation open to the Japanese people . . . Those fisherman on Terminal Island were there 20 years ago and that military airport that happens to be there was just completed in 1938. I know that for a fact . . . there is no conscious movement of Japanese to these areas. It is just simply a matter of following their occupations – farming."

For the record," said Mike M. Masaoka, national secretary of the Japanese American Citizens League, " . . . many of these places were purchased long before the airports were ever there . . . " Kunitani and Masaoka were two of several Japanese witnesses to appear before the Committee. Masaoka voiced mounting apprehension about evacuation being "aimed primarily against Japanese . . . If, in the judgment of military and Federal authorities, evacuation of Japanese residents from the West coast is a primary step toward assuring the safety of this nation, we will have no hesitation in complying . . . But, if . . . such evacuation is primarily a measure whose surface urgency cloaks the desires of political or other pressure groups who want us to leave merely from motives of self-interest, we feel that we have every right to protest and to demand equitable judgment on our merits as American citizens."

Karl and Elaine – outstanding veterans of the anti-fascist struggle against Japan – sat in silent accord as Kunitani told of the actions of Japanese "against shipments of oil and scrap iron to the Fascist war lords of Japan, and we opposed aggression in Ethiopia." His testimony was echoed by Ernest Iiyama of the Young Democrats and by Karl who submitted a letter to the commission:

> There are many Japanese nationals and Americans of Japanese descent who have openly denounced Japan long before December 7

> and they continue to be antifascist, anti-Axis, and are giving every aid to the United States in order to win the war . . . The Japanese weekly Doho (Brotherhood) published in Los Angeles has carried on anti-Japanese-militarist work . . . the Nisei Young Democratic Club of Oakland, Japanese-American Committee for Democracy in New York and hundreds of Japanese (American and foreign-born) members in the American Federation of Labor and Congress for Industrial Organizations have passed resolutions against Japanese aggression many months before Pearl Harbor.

As Elaine and Karl sat for long sad hours in the hearings, they increasingly developed a sense that plans for evacuation were "an accomplished fact and this was just window dressing." And it was in these terms, Elaine said, that they discussed it between themselves. What they couldn't know was just how quickly it would come and how bad it would be. But there was a great fear spreading among the Japanese.

"Has the Gestapo Come to America?"

Publisher and nurseryman James M. Omura articulated the fears and suspicions of many Japanese Americans in bitter terms:

> Promoters of racialism . . . have enjoyed a virtual field day to date in their vigorous campaign to oust resident Japanese, including bona-fide citizens, from their hard-won economic niche . . . The Nisei Americans . . . are mere stepping stones for political aspirants and self-seekers . . . The future of Nisei Americans is indeed dark. They walk through life in fear, dreading that with each passing moment new restrictions and edicts, disrupting the normal conduct of their daily lives will be adopted. They have watched with saddening brows the pathos and confusion of their alien parents being uprooted forcefully from the homes which took some of the best years of their oppressed lives to build . . . the history of our American Republic will never again stand high in the council chambers of justice and tolerance. Democracy will suffer deeply by it . . .
>
> I should like to ask the committee: Has the Gestapo come to America? Have we not risen in righteous anger at Hitler's mistreatment of the Jews? Then, is it not incongruous that citizen Americans of Japanese descent should be similarly mistreated and persecuted?

Louis Goldblatt

Louis Goldblatt, secretary of the CIO California State Industrial Union Council, is still honored and respected in the Japanese community for representing before the Tolan Committee the "only rational voice," as Elaine expressed it. A few others – mostly religionists and liberal educators – also appealed for fairness and against mass evacuation, urging that evacuation of Japanese be considered on an individual basis, under the same rules that would be applied to Italians and Germans.

But it was Goldblatt who "stood out like a shining beacon in those dark pre-evacuation days," Karl wrote in *Ganbatte.* Goldblatt told the commission:

> The attitude of the CIO on the establishment of restriction governing the movements and work of aliens of enemy nationality stems from the basic policies of the Congress of Industrial Organizations which is committed to the speedy and successful prosecution of the war. The touchstone of this policy is the belief that democracy can wage an all-out war against the Axis Powers, and that the forces generated by a system of free government can and will triumph over fascism.
>
> ... we support the regulation of matters dealing with sabotage and espionage ... Regulation of Axis aliens is regarded in the same light ... Almost immediately following the initial moves against aliens of enemy nationality came a widespread campaign demanding the removal from coastal areas of all Japanese, whether alien or born in this country. The old flames of racial suspicion were fanned to full blaze. Publicity seekers spouted ill-considered and vigilante-inciting epithets against the Japanese born in this country. The Hearst press found new field for its rantings about the 'yellow menace.' Politicians saw a good occasion to garner publicity. Soon the wolf pack was in full cry.
>
> ... Most of our State and local officials, rather than standing as bastions of justice and equal protection under the law, have joined the hue and cry ...

Goldblatt urged the protection of real and personal property and the prevention of land-grabbing. And, he said, there must be "no concentration camps." The CIO, he said, favored "the speedy establishment of governmental machinery to provide for fair hearings and examination to expedite the segregation of anti-Fascists from Fascist elements." He would determine the loyalty of 120,000 Japanese in "exactly the same manner I would proceed to tell who was a loyal or disloyal Italian or German."

Most of all Goldblatt was prophetic: "This entire episode of hysteria and mob chant . . . will form a dark page of American history . . . All of us who failed to speak in time contributed to this victory of the isolationist fifth column in America."

Oakland attorney Clarence E. Rust also saw the future and went on record in utter "opposition to the adoption of a program of hysteria as a national policy." He said, in a statement submitted to the hearing: "At the end of this terrible conflict, some of us are fools enough to hope for a world based on brotherly cooperation. The hate generated now will return to plague us then . . . " The clamor to "drive the so-called alien enemies from California . . . seems to come from chambers of commerce, Associated Farmers, and the newspapers notorious as spokesmen for reactionary interests . . . effort should be made to determine whether there is any connection between the clamor for the dispossession of the Japanese farmers and the desire of these clamoring interests to get possession of the Japanese farms and the elimination of the Japanese competition."

Racism Triumphs

The term "concentration camps" appears at least nine times in the San Francisco Tolan hearing. " . . . Japanese and Japanese-Americans alike should be placed in concentration camps and without a moment's notice," Stuart R. Ward of Menlo Park told the hearing. " . . . all alien Japanese and their descendants [should] be forthwith evacuated to a concentration camp . . . " said a resolution of the County Supervisors Association of California.

After World War II was over, use of the same words – "concentration camp" – on a memorial plaque at the Manzanar camp was resisted by the California Department of Parks and Recreation.

Many Japanese farmers – uncertain and fearful – sold their land and farm equipment for woefully small amounts, while in the cities Japanese families were robbed by greedy buyers who paid a pittance for homes and furniture, precious belongings, automobiles. Elaine often said that the roundup and removal of the Japanese during the second World War was consistent with the U.S. history of exploitation and racism, pointing to the Indian Removal Act of 1830, and the Chinese and Japanese Exclusion Acts of 1882 and 1924. "This was a racial thing. The whole thing was racism . . . You scratched the surface a little bit and you see the hands of

Hearst and all those 'yellow peril' forces... coming out of the woodwork."

She expressed the dilemma facing not only Karl and herself, but all anti-fascist Japanese Americans: "... we did not speak out against the edict [evacuation]; nothing must be done by us to impede the war effort. The immediate task was to defeat the enemy – the fascist Axis... for if they won the war, there would not be a shred of democracy left in this country or anywhere on this earth."

And there was another factor. It also "became apparent that we couldn't possibly fight it... knowing the forces that the United States had at its command, knowing that... [they] would think nothing of dispatching a battalion or two with their guns to evacuate the Japanese should there be resistance... So it was very obvious to us that it could happen, maybe because we... had been involved in all these various struggles of trying to defend the Bill of Rights and knowing how it could be prostituted."

The *People's World* printed Goldblatt's complete statement to the Tolan Committee and editorially condemned the "hysteria... falling in with the race war campaign being incited by Hearst, Martin Dies and others... That's right up Hitler's alley." It quoted a columnist writing in the *Los Angeles Times:* "You can't walk down the street without jumping into Japs. They take the parking space. They get before you in line at the stamp window in the post office. They occupy... space in street cars... This is crazy. We must be done with the alien Jap and everyone with Jap blood in their veins."

This is, said the *PW,* "a wave of filthy race hysteria on which ride the even more dangerous fifth columnists of German and Italian origin... the FBI has nabbed some very dangerous men of recent days, of German origin. Where's the howl... Governor Olson spoke wisely when he said that any regulatory measures against Japanese should be on an individual basis rather than as one racial group?"[9]

Governor Olson, however, soon joined the chorus of local officials clamoring for evacuation. So did liberal Los Angeles Mayor Fletcher Bowran.

With Karl out of a job, things got increasingly difficult. He and Elaine discussed their "future course as a family. With the prospect of no work, car payments on a new Studebaker, plus rent and food," Elaine said, "... where and to whom could we turn to help solve our dilemma?"

Evacuation and incarceration of all Japanese, including citizens, became a constant theme of radio broadcasts and newspaper reports.

In Japantown Karl heard that a camp would be constructed in the California desert and that Maryknoll priests in Los Angeles were coordinating the recruitment of volunteers to build it. He and Elaine decided to move to Los Angeles where she and the children would live with her parents while Karl would volunteer to go into the first camp. This was Manzanar in the Owens Valley, the first of ten such camps to be constructed in seven western states.

Tom Mooney Dies

A few days later, on March 6, as they were arranging for friends to store their possessions, Tom Mooney died in St. Luke's Hospital. He had been seriously ill, and hospitalized, for two of the three brief years since his release from prison. On March 8 Karl and Elaine joined ten thousand people who assembled at Civic Auditorium to celebrate Mooney's life and mourn his death. He was buried beside his mother. "Workers' loving hands carried him there last Sunday," Elizabeth Gurley Flynn wrote. "Flowers covered him. Tears flowed unashamed down the faces of sailors and strong men from shops. They looked long for the last time on the rugged face of Tom Mooney."[10]

Two messages of condolence – among the hundreds – were noteworthy; one was from far-off Moscow, the other from nearby San Mateo. From Moscow, Georgi Dimitrov, hero of the Reichstag fire trial, acclaimed Mooney as "one of the finest sons of the great American people." He said, " . . . Tom Mooney belonged not only to America. His indomitable spirit and courage, his great example of a steadfast fighter, found response in the hearts of all progressive men and women the world over.

"Now, when all freedom-loving peoples, rallied around the mighty coalition of the United States of America, Great Britain and the Union of Socialist Republics are engaged in a life and death struggle against the criminal forces of Hitlerism, the bright memory of Tom Mooney will inspire them to greater and more determined joint efforts to bring about a speedy victory over Hitler's fascist hordes."[11]

Hoko Hideo Ikeda lived in San Mateo, only 20 miles from San Francisco. But he could not attend Mooney's funeral because persons of Japanese descent, citizen or not, were not allowed to travel more than five miles from their homes. Ikeda's telegram noted that "thousands of anti-fascist prisoners were being held in Japan," and pledged that while "we must evacuate . . . wherever we go we will continue to fight against the fascists."[12]

Elaine speaking at Tom Mooney's gravesite on March 8, 1942, Cypress Lawn Memorial Park, Colma, CA.

Elaine spoke at the graveside service and Karl was one of 90 honorary pallbearers. Hundreds of their friends hugged them goodbye, wished them well in their new life, and expressed hope that the war would be won quickly and they would all be together again.

Military Area No. 1

On March 10 the Yoneda family packed themselves and what belongings would fit into the Studebaker and left for Los Angeles. They had, they knew, little time left for voluntary movement. A week earlier, General DeWitt had issued orders designating the entire Pacific Coast and the southern sections of California and Arizona as Military Area No. 1 from which aliens of enemy nationality would be excluded. All Japanese, however, "alien and American-born, are to be the first to be barred, to be followed by the removal of many but not all Germans and Italians." There would be "exemptions for Germans and Italians – no exemptions whatsoever are made for Japanese aliens or for Americans of Japanese lineage. All must go . . . "[13]

In San Francisco, Richard Neustadt, aide to DeWitt, was quoted: "Tell the Japanese not to be worried. Tell them they are not going to be hurt by anybody. Some place is going to be found in the near future where they can go voluntarily and where there will be work for everyone. This will not be a concern . . . there will be regular work for regular money. They can grow crops and sell them." There would be, he said, ten inland "Japanese communities" set up, and " . . . military areas will be created around these places so that there will be no contact with Americans."

"As for the German and Italian aliens," Neustadt said, they can "rest easy and go about their business."[14]

By April 3, farms evacuated by Japanese farmers were getting new tenants. "Farm Security Administration today announced that nearly a third of the rich Japanese and Japanese-American farmlands on the Pacific Coast has been transferred to new operators and that all land will be kept in production for the duration of the war. "Some fear was expressed . . . that the transfer of Japanese-operated lands may bring on a wholesale land grab by the big farm trusts. . . . L.I. Hawes, FSA regional director, said that all agricultural interests in the Pacific area will fully mobilize to meet the emergency and that large canners, packers, processors and land companies had expressed a willingness to work with the U.S. Agricultural Department's war boards in acquiring and operating Japanese farming operations . . . all these groups agreed to give all aid possible, including acquiring and operating, at least temporarily, Japanese land on a large scale."[15] Much of the "Japanese land has fallen into the hands of the Associated Farmers," reported the ACPFB on "Relocation of Enemies of Alien Nationalities."[16]

While the Wartime Civil Control Administration had informed evacuees that they need not dispose of personal property of value at a sacrifice, the Federal Reserve Bank of San Francisco was put in charge of safeguarding the property. The Bank provided no insurance and assumed no liability; rather it "undertook a definite policy of encouraging liquidation and by far the greatest number of evacuees sold their property at distress prices, gave it away, or stored it at their own expense and risk."[17]

Evacuation of Japantown

Mike Quin described the evacuation of San Francisco's Japantown: "American born Japanese children . . . took evacuation in their stride, like some new adventure. . . . [families] had been given six days to finish disposing of their property . . . The old people took it the hardest. For them it was no adventure . . . They stood silent and submissive as if under arrest . . . The tag around the neck was a tough thing for some of the proud young Japanese to take . . . None of them liked it . . . they seemed to understand why it was necessary. That is, except the really old people who were pained and bewildered."[18]

One month later, on May 13, 1942, the Tolan Committee issued its report. "In view of the fact that the final Tolan Committee Report indicates that the evacuation of the Japanese is practically complete," said the IJA in its June bulletin, "we shall give the wisdom of that policy very little consideration. It has become a fact." What must be considered, IJA said, is the "course to be followed in the future." The "objective consideration of the problem," said IJA, "was rendered difficult by the pressure groups . . . [who] became articulate both before and at the Tolan hearings, presented distorted views and took advantage of the predicament in which the Japanese found themselves. Anti-labor groups, such as the Associated Farmers, pleading military necessity, asked not only the evacuation of the Japanese but demanded that these people be placed in concentration camps at forced labor . . . On the other hand, the Congress for Industrial Organizations in California, civil liberty groups, religious leaders, college professors, and liberals came out in support of handling cases on their merits. They asked that 'enemy aliens' be divided into those who were friendly, doubtful, and dangerous. The group of friendly aliens should be undisturbed. Those who were doubtful should be investigated, and those who were dangerous should be interned."

About the problems of Italian and German aliens, IJA said: Without special civilian hearing boards "... some 7,000,000 to 10,000,000 Americans are left terrorized and uncertain because of the 1,000,000 German and Italian aliens in these families who may be immediately evacuated." In the early days of the war, on the West Coast, some Italian and German nationals were unfairly and cruely victimized for a brief period under evacuation and relocation regulations. That it was only for a few months cannot excuse it. However, according to Roger Baldwin, national director of the ACLU, "... perhaps the most striking of ironies was the fact that no evacuation was even suggested for the Germans and Italians, aliens or citizens, on the Atlantic Coast where submarines and defense installations were far more numerous, and the dangers of espionage and sabotage apparently greater. Only racism can explain the discrimination."[19]

There were few who addressed the victimization – the terrorization, fears and uncertainties – of more than 110,000 Americans of Japanese heritage.* It was as if the question did not exist. IJA used a rationale that many progressives followed, and that was in essence to use the patriotism of Japanese-Americans against them: "... whatever measures are necessary for the safety of the country must be approved by all patriotic Americans, just as the Japanese Nisei approved measures even against themselves which were dictated by military necessity, and not by self-interest." That, said IJA, was the "sound point of view." It was also the easy way out.

The U.S. Attorney General freed Italian nationals from enemy alien restrictions in October. Two months later – in December, 1942 – General DeWitt did the same for West Coast German nationals.[20]

The Great Outrage

For the Japanese the great outrage was well underway. But the shame and the tragedy had begun as well for the nation, and

---

*It is generally acknowledged that the accurate number of Japanese interned was 120,000

particularly for its clarion voices of democracy – voices silent in 1942. The great tragedy was not the failure of the victims to speak up, it was the silence – the acquiesence to racism and hysteria – of the anti-fascist, the democratic, the progressive movement – good people all.

It was not until 1959 that the Communist Party acknowledged "serious errors . . . in the failure to oppose the relocation centers . . . " and in 1972 it repudiated the "very grave inroads of racism in our ranks, one of the most serious being our failure to mount a struggle against the racist incarceration in 1942 of more than 110,000 people of Japanese ancestry in concentration camps . . . "[21]

24.

Concentration Camp USA

1st Train to Manzanar

Elaine planned to get a job in war industry while Karl would work at Manzanar and continue his efforts to join the armed forces. They assumed that Elaine and Tommy would live in Los Angeles and have visiting privileges to see Karl at camp. They were confident that sooner or later he would be allowed to enlist.

With 1,000 men and a few women volunteer evacuees, Karl left for Manzanar on March 23. Volunteers were assured that their families would have plenty of time to put their affairs in order and dispose of or store their belongings; the volunteers' families would be the last group evacuated from Military Area No. 1. Karl was with a contingent that traveled to Manzanar by train; another group drove in a long car caravan. Military escorts accompanied both groups. Saying goodbye at the Santa Fe depot was difficult. In addition to families and friends of the evacuees, the area swarmed with news reporters. Elaine later saw a news photo of Karl kissing their son goodbye, and never forgot "the qualms, anguish and uncertainty of that day."

Elaine promised Karl she would not attempt to visit him at Manzanar until he could assess the situation there and feel assured that camp conditions would not aggravate Tommy's asthma. She believed it would be weeks before they would see each other again. In the meantime, she would get a job in war industry; she looked forward to that. She started her job search.

At Manzanar what Karl found were "barracks without window panes, howling dust storms . . . no toilet facilities." To the west was the majestic and forbidding Mt. Williamson and just beyond it – though not visible from the camp – was Mt. Whitney, highest peak in the continental United States; not far to the east, he knew, was Death Valley, lowest point in the Western Hemisphere. Manzanar camp was in between on a bleak and desolate tract of desert.

Those who drove to Manzanar in their own cars were required to leave them outside camp, and they were not allowed to remove their contents – clothes and necessities to make camp life more comfortable. The ability to carry possessions had been the deciding factor in driving their own cars. But by the time they were finally allowed to remove their belongings when the cars were towed away, the contents were dust-laden and the cars' rubber tires had deteriorated in the hot sun.

The promised construction jobs did not materialize. Karl and others decided to clean the camp area and attempt to make it more livable for those to come. It was apparent that they were indeed interned in a concentration camp; the guard towers and barbed wire left no room for doubt.

Elaine Fights to Get In

On the evening of March 23, only six days after Karl left, a sudden radio announcement chilled Elaine.

> "Attention! Attention! All those of Japanese ancestry whose breadwinners are in the Manzanar Reception Center: You are hereby ordered to report to the Civil Control Center at 707 South Spring Street tomorrow from 8 a.m. on for processing to leave for Manzanar by noon, April 2nd, or be in violation of General DeWitt's Civilian Exclusion Order No. 3."

That was only 72 hours. The order didn't apply to Elaine, she realized, but what about Tommy? She was frantic and attempted to call the Army and Maryknoll. She had to have an answer: Did the order apply to a three-year old Eurasian child living with his Caucasian mother?

Finally she got through to a Maryknoll priest. It was, he said, the father's nationality that counted and one-sixteenth or more "Japanese blood" was the criteria. Therefore Tommy, but not Elaine, would be evacuated. There would be a children's village for Tommy. Elaine and her parents agreed that "come hell or high water," she would go where Tommy had to go, and Joyce would remain with her grandparents.

The next morning, Elaine and Tommy joined the long line outside the control station. Suddenly, an Army officer and a priest ran up to Elaine, insisting that she and Tommy leave the line and go with them. She demurred, believing it was her white face that caused this seemingly preferential treatment. They didn't know her – what else could it be? Over her protests, they ushered her inside. Her voice rose as they attempted to appease her – she didn't have to go to camp. They refused to give her two application forms. The "Maryknoll father kept saying: 'We will have a children's village where our well-trained sisters will take care of your son. You needn't, nor will you be allowed to go. It will be too hard for you.' "

But they had a "tiger woman" to contend with. Clutching Tommy and with eyes blazing, she shouted at the Army officer: "As sure as we are standing here, my husband will be in a khaki uniform like yours before the year is out and I'll be there with our son to see him off!"

Nor could the Maryknoll priest placate her. She shouted at him, too: ". . . I'll be with my husband and child . . . " She insisted over and over again: "If he goes, I go!" For Elaine at that moment, that was the one – the only – clear reality. There was no room in her anguished mind to think of alternatives, and no place to turn to for help or advice to seek a possible legal way to keep both Tommy and herself out of Manzanar. The edict of one-sixteenth "Japanese blood" had been established by Colonel Karl Bendetsen, appointed by DeWitt to head up the Wartime Civil Control Administration. Maryknoll Father Hugh Lavery said later that Bendetsen was a "little Hitler" who was "determined that if they have one drop of Japanese blood in them, they must all go to camp."[1]

Later Elaine wondered if she perhaps could have filed an injunction against the Army to stop Tommy's internment. "It was a time of hysteria," she said. "It was a time of not knowing where to turn . . . There was no guidance."[F]

"If he goes, I go!" The authorities' attempt to separate Elaine from her child was sheer madness. Finally, to quiet this perturbed and troublesome woman, they gave in and she signed on for the April 1 train to Manzanar.

Arrival

In the meantime, a letter from Karl told of the terrible conditions. She was not to come for at least a month and then not to bring

[F]Quotations so designated are from an interview conducted on March 3 and 4, 1974, by Arthur A. Hansen for the Japanese-American Project of the California State University at Fullerton.

Tommy. The dust was so bad that, with his asthma and allergies, Karl feared not only for Tommy's health but for his very life. But the order to leave was the harsh reality. On April 1 at 6:45 a.m. Elaine and Tommy reported to the railway station. Amid the bewilderment and confusion, with armed guards posted all around, Tommy was excited and happy at the prospect of seeing his father. Karl did not know they were coming.

Passengers could bring only what they could carry, so with two suitcases and a small bag of toys, Elaine and Tommy arrived at Lone Pine at sunset. With 413 other passengers from Los Angeles, they transferred to buses for the eight mile ride to Manzanar.

At the camp the busses pulled inside the barbed wire fence. Karl was among those who had volunteered to help the arriving internees. About 230 persons had arrived a couple of hours earlier from Bainbridge Island in Washington. Now the volunteers helped unload this new group of internees. Still in the bus, Tommy spotted Karl and yelled happily. Karl "came running . . . ashen-faced," Elaine remembered. "I've never seen him look as ashen, before or since . . . He yelled at me. He used a few waterfront words . . . Are you bringing our son to be killed?"[F]

Elaine handed him a copy of Civilian Exclusion Order No. 3, but, in his own torment, he turned away. Later, after reading DeWitt's order, "Karl's remorse at the way he had greeted me was intense. We had a good, silent cry in each other's arms."

They pleaded for extra army comforters to use as a mattress for the allergic Tommy and filled their own mattress tickings with straw. Apartment 2, in Block 4, Building 2, to which they were assigned was not an apartment at all but a single room to be shared with a 15-year old boy and a blind 75-year old man, the overflow of a large family in another "apartment." Six persons to a room was set as the limit; however, a total of ten persons were crowded into one "apartment," and there were five others that each housed nine persons. There were not even partitions to separate families. The rooms were bare except for army cots and an oil heater.

The wind was relentless. It blew dust through the knotholes and onto every inside surface. Outside there was one cold water faucet at the east end of each barrack and at the west end of the block were six portable toilets. That was all. Elaine "knew it was a prison" the minute she saw the barbed wire and the watchtowers manned by armed guards and with searchlights mounted on the roofs.[F] Elaine and Karl always made a distinction between "American style concentration camps" and the death camps maintained for Jews and political prisoners under the fascist regimes of Germany and Italy. However, Manzanar certainly looked like something out of Nazi Germany.

Dust Storm

The first morning, the camp's faucets were frozen. The internees couldn't wash their hands after using the portable toilets and brushing teeth was out of the question. By mid-afternoon a bad dust storm engulfed the camp. The dust was so thick that "you'd stand in line and not be able to recognize the person in front of you or in back."[F]

Those first days were frightful and the plucky Tommy became ill, his asthma triggered by the dust and close proximity to the straw mattresses, plus his food allergies; he had hives and eczema. He had been allergic to milk from birth and was sensitized to many foods. There were times through the years when it was "quite a horrendous task to keep him alive," and he had been and was yet to be in and out of Stanford Hospital many times.* His Manzanar experience was very difficult; his general health deteriorated and he was in and out of the camp hospital. "You never knew when he might . . . go into a coma . . . suddenly he'd lose consciousness."

The special bread they had shipped daily from a health food store in San Francisco was the main staple in his diet. When the weather got warmer at Manzanar, it arrived moldy. At first they cut the mold off. But as the weeks passed and the temperature climbed, the bread was not edible at all. Fortunately Tommy was not allergic to rice.

He was a valiant little boy, happy to be with both his parents, and accustomed to coping with sickness. They named their quarters "Tommy's Dust-Out-Inn." They were fortunate that Elaine's parents could respond to some of their needs – for example, rope and sheets to make a partition between their cots and those of the other inhabitants of their "apartment." Later on, friends sent a small electric stove on which Elaine prepared supplementary food for Tommy, and little by little they accumulated a few things – pots, "a little worse for wear but usable" – and a pail. Karl, like many internees, scrounged up scrap lumber from which he fashioned a table and

*A few years later, it was discovered that Tommy had internal hives. He would dehydrate and sometimes would have to be rushed to an oxygen tank.

shelves, using empty nail kegs for chairs. At first the barracks had no steps and Elaine didn't know whether to laugh or cry at the spectacle of people attempting to gain entrance to their rooms; they practically had to stand on each other's shoulders.

By early April the latrines were completed: There were separate facilities for men and women but no doors or partitions – just five toilet bowls in a row with another five back to back.

"Because I had been in jails before, in solitary as well as in the main prison tank, I wasn't so appalled by it," said Elaine. But, "I began encountering frustrated, horrified faces, primarily among teen-aged girls, as they came into the latrine, especially if Tommy was with me. Some would run away crying." Perhaps they were menstruating or had the "Manzanar runs," plus a modesty common to young girls.

After a couple of days of this, Elaine talked it over with Karl and then went to see Service Division Director J. M. Kidwell at the Administration Building. She explained the girls' distress; he shrugged his shoulders and said the latrines came up to Army specifications. She pounded on his desk, demanding doors, partitions and shower curtains, and "to hell with specifications. If you don't do something soon, there might be mass hysteria and maybe even some suicides!" It wasn't too long before the doors, partitions and curtains were provided.

Two events marked April 17: the first child born in Manzanar arrived in the midst of a dust storm, and for the first time, there was a flag-raising in the camp. Elaine and Karl had supported this on the basis "that people had to remember that they were part of the United States." The following day they heard rumors that Tokyo had been bombed. "Good news if so," Elaine wrote in her diary. "The harder the better, and where is the second front?" There was a major camp event as well that day: the water system provided hot water to the showers and laundry rooms. Elaine took her first hot shower. "How good it felt."

Until camp elections could be held, Karl was appointed leader of Block 4 – the appointees were sometimes called "Blockheads" by the other internees. They were to set up self-government in Manzanar and handled all manner of grievances and problems. For a 48-hour week, he received wages of $16.00 per month. Elaine went to work, first as assistant librarian, then, in June, producing camouflage nets, a war production project on which only U.S. citizens could work. Five hundred Manzanar internees worked in the net factory.

"I was at that point quite happy, because I was doing something that I felt was going to help beat that damn enemy . . . "[F] Some of the nets were dyed for snow camouflage, some for the desert; working with the dyed strips of burlap hanging from 20-foot ceilings in the huge open sheds was a hot smelly job. Net workers earned $16.00 per month for an 8 hour a day, six-day week. By July they were working in 114 degree weather. They wore face masks to diffuse the fumes and give some protection against the pervasive dust. After a month, Elaine had to take a temporary leave from her job due to a painful rash and swollen arms caused by the dyes; she was hospitalized. Others also had adverse reactions. Net dying was semi-skilled work. The wage scale for unskilled workers was $12.00 per month; doctors, dentists, and other professionals received $19.00 per month.

Elaine, Karl, Tommy at Manzanar, June 1942

Evacuation Challenged

In the meantime, in early June, Gordon Hirabayashi, United States citizen of Japanese descent and a student at the University of Washington, filed a test case through the ACLU challenging the constitutionality of the curfew order against Japanese.[2] Hirabayashi had defied both the curfew and the order to report for evacuation. He was convicted and on June 23, the following year (1943) the U.S. Supreme Court unanimously upheld his conviction. Fred Korematsu and Minoru Yasui were similarly convicted in 1942 in different jurisdictions.

On June 18, 1942, Senate Bill 2293, representing "the first step in the direction of taking away citizenship from those of Japanese ancestry" was unanimously reported favorably by the Senate Committee on Immigration. The Committee "hopes that in some manner the enactment by the Congress of S.2293 may bring about a redetermination of the status of Japanese born in the United States." The bill provided: That during the continuation of the existing war between the United States and Japan, the Secretary of War is authorized to and directed to take into "custody and restrain, to the extent deemed by him to be necessary, any and all Japanese persons residing in or found in the United States, regardless of whether or not said Japanese were born in the United States."

The Secretary of War would be permitted "to release persons so taken into custody if he believes such release will not be inimical to the interests of national defense and to the welfare of the United States, and may require as a condition of such release that persons report personally at such times and places as the Secretary of War shall designate to the military authorities. The Secretary of War was authorized to utilize the services of the armed forces of the United States" to enforce the act.

Because Executive Order 9066 had already been issued and executed, a Department of Justice representative testified that S.2293 was "not only unnecessary but undesirable." Executive Order 9066, he said, "is clear, [and] avoids any question of constitutionality . . . "[3] So it was believed for many years – except, that is, by Hirabayashi, Korematsu and Yasui.

Elaine and Karl wrote to the San Francisco Registrar of Voters for primary election ballots, which they received, filled out and returned for the June 1942 primary. Karl's vote owed no thanks, however, to the Native Sons of the Golden West, who sued the San Francisco Registrar of Voters in an attempt to prohibit from voting "2600 Japanese of the full blood born in the United States and the State of California, of alien parents born in the empire of Japan." The registrar, however, asked for dismissal of the petition on the basis "that Japanese born here are citizens of the United States and as such are entitled to be registered as voters." The dismissal was granted on the basis of three previous cases which had also unsuccessfully attempted to deprive U.S. born Japanese persons of their right to vote.[4]

Manzanar Black Dragons

A July 4, Independence Day picnic had been planned but was cancelled because of a severe dust storm.

Karl and Elaine did not have a radio, but they did subscribe to San Francisco newspapers. They also carried on extensive correspondence with friends outside who clipped and sent news articles. They read a lot and Elaine did some typing for the *Manzanar Free Press,* the camp newspaper. Karl wrote a letter to the camp administration, requesting consideration for himself and others of like mind to join the armed forces.

It was when the camouflage net program started that leaflets signed by "Patriotic Suicide Corps" and the "Manzanar Black Dragons" began to appear. The Dragons were mostly Japanese-born Kibei; they were loyal to the Emperor and used as a symbol a black pirate flag with a white painted skull and crossbones. There were never many of them and these "pro-Japan-fascist-hoodlums never reflected the majority of Manzanar concentration camp 'residents,'" Karl said. But they were vicious.

They beat up James Oda, trade unionist and anti-fascist from Los Angeles, and attempted to ram a truck into Karl and Tokie Slocum, an older man who had served in World War 1 as a regimental sergeant major with the famed Sergeant Alvin C. York. Karl and Slocum were able to jump aside just in time but the steps they had been sitting on were demolished. A report circulated that the Black Dragons had a "death list." They threatened camouflage net workers and incited teen-aged boys to throw stones at them. Elaine came home with bruised legs and a cut on her forehead. However, "we found more workers signing up for camouflage work despite the warnings . . . "

The attacks were reported to the camp Administration who chose to ignore them, the rationale being, as Assistant Manager Ted Campbell told Karl, "You are all Japanese and will have to live together."

Had early action been taken, the terror that was later to engulf the camp could have been avoided. With urgent requests to remove the Black Dragon group from Manzanar ignored, Karl and Elaine wrote to the FBI asking them to "clean out the handful of fanatics who were making life more miserable than it already was and hindering the U.S. war effort as well."

Manzanar Citizens Federation

To counteract the Black Dragons, Karl was one of a group of 15 who formed the Manzanar Citizens Federation. It held its first public meeting on July 28 and 500 attended. In spite of the cutting of the building's electric wires and heckling, they held their meeting and discussed how to improve camp conditions, help the war effort, initiate leadership education, and prepare for life after the war.

Attacks on the Manzanar Citizens Federation continued. By this time, Manzanar's population was 10,000 people who lived in rows of identical barracks cheaply constructed of green lumber. The unseasoned lumber was the reason for the profuse amount of knotholes and the big cracks that appeared in walls as the lumber dried.

Sixty-five percent of the population were U.S. citizens, 2,300 were under 16 years of age, 4,100 between 16 and 65. Of those born in Japan, there were 2,100 men and 1,300 women, mostly elderly. Racist U.S. laws had long barred these "aliens" from becoming citizens.

Karl celebrated his birthday by writing a letter to his union asking about enlistment in the "Dock Battalion" he read about in the union paper. The following week, he and Koji Ariyoshi, also an ILWU member, drew up a petition, and Elaine typed it onto a stencil and ran it off in the *Manzanar Free Press* office. It was addressed to President Roosevelt:

> We, the undersigned Americans of Japanese ancestry, relocated at Manzanar, California, herewith add our voices to the millions of other peoples in the United Nations and the conquered countries to OPEN THE SECOND FRONT NOW for a decisive Victory over the Tokio-Berlin-Rome Axis.
>
> We also urgently and respectfully request that the citizen manpower, now residing in evacuation camps, be utilized to the fullest extent in contributing to the national war effort by accepting us as draftees and enlistees for frontline duty in the U.S. Armed Forces.

A cover letter, accompanying the 24 petitions signed by 218 men and women citizen internees – most of whom were eligible to enter the armed forces – told Roosevelt "that we are willing and ready to service our Country and the United Nations, to our utmost, in preserving our democracy and extending the 'Four Freedoms' to the four corners of the earth."

The petition was still being circulated in camp on July 31, the day Manzanar Director Roy Nash went to San Francisco to speak before the Commonwealth Club of California. At the end of a long speech, in which he assured his audience that "Manzanar is not a concentration of idlers and boondogglers," Nash told of the petition.: "It was the deliberate act of mature men, American men, born in California, who know no other country than these United States, and who are willing to lay down their lives for their country's cause. There are many men in Manzanar whose loyalty is no more to be questioned than that of any of us here."[5]

While there was no response from Roosevelt, the internees' action inspired favorable editorials and stories in many newspapers. The petition and cover letter are now in the Franklin Delano Roosevelt Hyde Park Memorial Library.

Children Suffer

The Black Dragons continued to threaten Karl and other antifascists. On August 23, fourteen invaded Karl and Elaine's room, arguing with Karl in Japanese – which Elaine did not understand – and "making threatening gestures."

"Tommy sat cowering on his cot as I tried to calm him." Worried about Tommy's fears and the danger of bodily harm to Karl, Elaine got more bad news. A troubled Joyce had run away from her grandparents' home. Elaine was filled with apprehension; her daughter could be in danger.

"She had asked to go to camp with us and I had told her I didn't think it was the place for her and that she had better stay with Grandma and Grandpa. The school was close by. I didn't know what conditions were going to be like at Manzanar, I would probably have my hands full taking care of Tommy . . . That was, perhaps, an error. I don't know."[F]

Elaine immediately applied for a leave and received permission to join her mother to search for Joyce. She took the train to San Francisco and spent the following three weeks tracing her daughter's movements. When Joyce was found, a relieved but still troubled

Elaine had several visits with her. Then, before returning to Manzanar, E.V. Billaroman, her former San Francisco neighbor, drove her to the Tanforan evacuation assembly center where she visited Japanese friends who had not yet been assigned to permanent camps. Tanforan was a former racetrack. Elaine's visit was on September 6; by then the Tanforan evacuees had been living in horse stables for a long time.

Back at Manzanar, she found that Tommy was having more frequent attacks of asthma. While Elaine was gone, he had to be hospitalized twice and had cried for his mother constantly. Elaine returned to her job at the net factory, trying as best she could to protect her arms from the caustic effects of the burlap dyes. "It was hard to see and hard to work because of another [dust] storm that was raging . . . "

She was relieved to receive a letter from her mother saying that she and Joyce had returned to Los Angeles. Elaine hoped things would be stable for awhile.

Friendships

Elaine was well-accepted by the young adults in camp, especially the women. Some became close personal friends. There was a constant stream of people in and out of the Yoneda apartment, and there were many whom Elaine felt free to visit or call on for help with Tommy at any hour. She and Karl were in a group who saved their hard-boiled breakfast eggs for a Sunday deviled egg party.

Laundry day would see Elaine and Karl doing their laundry together. "Not only would he carry Tommy on his shoulders, but he would help me carry the laundry." This was a reversal of the traditional male-female roles in Japanese families where "most of the scenes . . . were of the wife carrying the child, the wife carrying the soap, the wife carrying the laundry . . . " Karl sometimes got Elaine "uptight, too," by laundering her underthings, making "the point that . . . it doesn't make less of a man out of you if you help equally."[F]

While Elaine was, in her words, a "seasoned" person, able to take "more blows" than some, she also sometimes felt a tension around her and tried to be sensitive to the other women and their family situations. As time went on, there were women who maintained their traditional roles but told Elaine, "I wish I could speak like you." "Try," Elaine would respond. "I bet you could, even better."[F]

The whole camp knew about – and appreciated – the fuss she created with the administration for privacy in the toilets. However, there were times when she walked a line between her propensity for lusty struggle and her awareness of the subdued role of women in many Japanese families.

She attended meetings and affairs when Tommy was able to go and one thing she was not reluctant to speak up about was the need to defeat fascism and win the war. Elaine felt that the ability of the Black Dragons to cause as much damage as they did was due to a laxness by the camp administration in establishing better living conditions. She had little rapport with the administration and had as little to do with them as possible.

Betty DeLaSada in later years listened in fascination to Elaine tell stories about camp life:

> What courage and initiative she demonstrated! . . . Elaine exhibited here, as she did throughout so much of her life, a total commitment: as a political actress, as a woman, as wife and mother. She never seemed to have any ambivalence about her identity—she was a total woman . . . she committed herself wholly to everything she did, and she did, simultaneously, a great many things.
>
> Elaine was such a warm person as well; I get a kick out of thinking about her funny, Jewish sense of humor. She would tell anecdotes about episodes in camp that would make my hair frizzle, but she could recount these stories with humor.

Saving the Sugar Beet Crop

By late August, farm workers were in short supply in various parts of the nation. In Idaho the sugar beet crop was in peril for lack of adequate "stoop labor." A committee of the Manzanar Citizens Federation, including Karl, wrote another letter and petition to President Roosevelt, urging that internees be permitted to do farm work. This time 793 internees signed. Again, there was no reply from the President; however, it wasn't long before the War Relocation Authority was allowing farm work furloughs.

Temporary leave was granted to several hundred internees to work in the sugar beet crop in Idaho and Montana; in early October, Karl signed up to do sugar beet topping on a ranch near Idaho Falls. Prevailing farm labor wages were paid and while these were low, Karl sent war bonds, toys and candy to Elaine and Tommy plus a crate of apples to share with Manzanar neighbors. For a month's work, Karl and each of his crew members made $222.17. "It was the hardest work I had ever done," Karl said.[6] Still in Idaho for the November general election, Karl cast his absentee ballot from there. When internees wondered why Karl and Elaine exercised their vote in view of the loss of their freedom, Elaine responded that "we have to take our side, yes, we have to line up either pro-fascist or anti-fascist. We can't be sitting in the middle . . . It may be very hard at times, especially here in this environment . . . "

Elaine and Karl were fortunate in having moral and financial support from her parents and relatives as well as scores of friends whose letters and gifts helped ease the burdens of Manzanar. They sent magazines, books, clothing and toys, often filling orders for needed items for other internees as well. Friends in San Francisco sent a portable record-player and records, including "Ballad for Americans" sung by Paul Robeson. "It was a joy for us to be able to hear that powerful voice again and have it right there with us," Elaine said. The Yonedas received and sent enough mail to keep the post office busy all by themselves.

There were occasional weddings and sometimes they helped to organize picnics when they were allowed to go outside the barbed wire fence and "climb toward the majestic mountains to a creek where trout were caught and roasted, along with hot dogs we brought up with us." They were careful to be back in camp before curfew – back behind the barbed wire and under the constant gaze of the armed guards in the watchtowers.

25.

Keep the Home Fires Burning

Karl Joins the Army

Karl was still in Idaho working in the "Food for Victory" program when Elaine heard that a recruiting team from the Military Intelligence Service Language School had scheduled a trip to Manzanar. She wired Karl to return to camp immediately; he arrived on November 18.

In the meantime, she had her hair done at a new beauty parlor on Block 15. The weather got very cold. There was ice on the water barrel and snow in the hills. Sometimes during raging dust storms, the electricity would go out.

About 50 men applied for enlistment in the Army even as Black Dragons cruised through the camp, urging internees not to cooperate. To qualify for military intelligence training, applicants had to be proficient in both English and Japanese, and pass a physical and oral examination. Karl was one of only fourteen to pass the bilingual requirement. He was very happy. He and the others were immediately inducted into the U.S. Army. Those who didn't make it were urged to study hard and perhaps they would be able to pass the next time.

Although she could have done so, Elaine decided not to follow Karl to Minnesota where he would train at the Camp Savage Military Intelligence Language School. She applied for a travel permit for Tommy and herself to return to Military Area No. 1 in Los Angeles and planned to stay there or return to San Francisco. In either case she would get a job in war industry. She told Manzanar administrators who seemed to be pushing her to go with Karl: "I want to do war work! I want out! I want a place where . . . my son can have adequate housing and care . . . "[F]

Elaine faced the uncertainty of not knowing what the situation was outside or what work might be open to her. She had been out of the job market for a long time. Workers had flocked into California from all over the country. Perhaps there were no openings for office workers in war plants and she had no experience in factory production work. But she would find something and was encouraged to know that child care centers had been set up for children of war workers; there would be good care for Tommy.

A few days before Pvt. Karl Yoneda left for Camp Savage, they were notified that before Tommy could be issued travel documents by General DeWitt he would have to be photographed; "he was still a potentially dangerous enemy." Elaine said derisively. It would take about 30 days to process the required papers.

Elaine wrote in her diary that on November 30, "about ten to twelve guys are skulking around our barrack. They followed us a couple of hours. Karl notified [camp Police Chief] Gilkey. From then on we had to have people posted around our barrack" for protection from the Black Dragons.

Leavetaking

Karl and the other recruits left for Minnesota on December 2. Not a single camp administrator joined well-wishers to see them off. Military Police were posted along the camp exit to keep the recruits' families and friends inside the barbed wire. "Tommy cried miserably. The parents, wives and sweethearts of the men who were leaving were not allowed to go with them to the bus, which was parked right outside the barbed wire gate. We had to stay on the other side of the barbed wire, so our last farewell to each other was through the barbed wire."[F]

That night Tommy became very ill. "He was very distraught about his daddy leaving him behind. He wanted to go . . . his last words were screamed through that barbed wire fence." Awesome and terrible for such a little boy and indicative of emotional strain, hurt and fear, Tommy screamed, "I want to go with you and help you kill the fascists!" As it pulled away, Elaine heard suppressed sobs from inside the bus. Everyone was weeping.

"So much," Elaine said, "was working on Tommy . . . " There was the hurried preparation for Karl's departure, the arrangements for Tommy's and Elaine's departure for Los Angeles, the photography session, the threatening presence of shadowy figures outside their barrack, being guarded by friends armed with baseball bats, the awareness that strange and fearful things were going on. Elaine tried to avoid any confrontation because of how he was feeling. The strain Tommy was under manifested itself in diarrhea and a high fever and he was hospitalized that night and for three days more. He wasn't quite four years old.

Terror

Elaine learned that Fred Tayama had been viciously beaten when he returned to Manzanar from a meeting of the Japanese American Citizens League in Salt Lake City; the JACL had urged the military drafting of Nisei. Tayama was former president of the Los Angeles JACL and, with Karl and a few others, a founder of the Manzanar Citizens Federation. He was hospitalized with head injuries.

On December 5, Tommy was released from the hospital. Tension was building in the camp. The Black Dragons spread rumors that Karl had joined the Army in order to leave Elaine, that Elaine was trying to get "Reds" assigned to Block 4, that Karl was afraid of the Black Dragons. It was well known that the Yonedas were on the Black Dragons' "death list."

A telegram from Karl on December 6 said he had arrived in Minnesota; the temperature was below zero and it was snowing. In the early afternoon, at Manzanar, Elaine and Tommy headed for the administration building to check the status of Tommy's travel permit. A crowd of about 1,000 persons was gathered in front of the building, listening to the exhortations of Joe Kurihara, a Black Dragon leader. Elaine heard him say the name "Yoneda." A friend translated: "If Karl Yoneda was here we would kill him!" The crowd was growing larger.

An administration staff member hurried over. "Elaine, they are in an ugly mood and Joe is saying that Yoneda ran away from them to hide in the Army but Yoneda's son is still here so we can still 'get him.' " Elaine stood there unbelieving and stunned. Satoru Kamikawa, a *Manzanar Free Press* reporter, also hurried to her side, confirming what she had just been told. He urged, "Go back to your apartment, lock yourself in, and don't even go out for meals." Elaine ran to the Camp Police Station, requesting protection "but none was offered. We proceeded at a run to 4-2-2 [their apartment], barricading the door with the inside bolt and the table."

Toward dusk, Yo Ukita, a good friend, came to say she would bring some food and spend the night with Elaine and Tommy. She returned later with food, but her father had forbidden her to stay due to threats against his entire family. At nine o'clock that night,

Elaine became aware of movements outside, then loud banging on kitchen utensils came from Mess Hall No. 4. After midnight, she heard anguished screams from the direction of the Ito apartment in Barrack 1. "Not able to contain myself, I warned Tommy not to make any noise nor put on a light. I moved the table and ran across to the Itos . . . I heard the horrifying news that their youngest son, James, a signer of the petition to President Roosevelt, was shot and killed by an MP as he headed to his Administration building night job." James was killed in the confusion of events as Black Dragons "commandeered a truck and started to run down the MPs who were guarding the police station. That's when the firing started."

The Ito family and Elaine embraced, weeping. They told her to hurry back to Tommy and to "watch out." Elaine ran back to her apartment, aware of shadowy figures prowling around. Tommy was sobbing. At about 4:30 a.m. on the morning of December 7, the first anniversary of Pearl Harbor, Elaine knew she couldn't stay in the apartment. She tied a scarf on Tommy's head and put on his coat with the shiny lining outside "to give him a little girl's appearance." And, "with nothing but my son and purse in hand, I began running in the darkness toward the Administration Building."

Elaine couldn't know, but "MANZANAR RIOT" was the December 7 headline of the newspaper Karl saw on his second day in Minnesota. Thoroughly alarmed, he wired immediately to Manzanar Director Ralph Merritt demanding protection for his family, whom he knew would be targeted for terrorism. It was, Karl said, an "inevitable riot."

Halt! Who Goes There?

Martial law had been declared in Manzanar, but Elaine didn't know it as she ran with Tommy. "Near the west end of Block 4, Barrack 1, a voice called out: 'Halt, who goes there?' A soldier appeared with a drawn, bayonet-equipped rifle, flashing a light in my face."

Elaine explained that she and Tommy needed protection at once. Tommy was shrieking, "My daddy's a soldier! My daddy's a soldier!" The MP took them to the next guard down the line and she and Tommy were passed from one guard to another until they reached the Administration Building. "It was surrounded by troops clustered around machine guns." Escorted into the building, "Campbell came over to me and said, 'Oh, I forgot to send you protection.' "[F]

Desks had been pushed back to make room for about 60 cots and people were trying to sleep. These were all internees and their families who had been threatened, old and young, even babies. Fred Tayama was there with a big bandage on his head. At daybreak, they were all transported by Army trucks to the small dispensary building, fed, and told to rest. At night they were returned to the Administration Building to sleep. They thought of themselves as a "clan," Elaine said, and worried together about their friends. More people were brought in for a total of about 67.

The "dust was raging, and it was cold. It got very, very cold!" On December 8, "It was reported that no one was working – only the kitchen and hospital crews." Additional troops arrived from Reno. After three days, Elaine was driven under armed guard to her apartment to get clean clothes for herself and Tommy. As she hurriedly packed some belongings and a bag of toys for Tommy, a crowd gathered outside; her military escort urged her to be quick. That was to be the last Elaine was to see of their apartment.

Escape

On December 10, under heavy guard, they were evacuated to an abandoned Civilian Conservation Corps (CCC) camp in Death Valley. The buildings were in bad disrepair and Elaine and others stuffed broken window panes with newspapers and blankets. They all rolled up their sleeves and cleaned and patched as best they could.

"Life at the CCC camp was one of waiting and more waiting for my son's pass and Karl's letters while I worked as one of the kitchen crew." Death Valley Park Rangers led short, guided tours of the area, which broke the tension. However, "Tommy landed in the makeshift hospital with a high fever . . . crying for his daddy."

On December 16, Campbell and E.R. Fryer, regional director of the War Relocation Authority office in San Francisco, traveled from Manzanar to the CCC camp to notify Elaine to be ready to depart for Los Angeles the following morning. Tommy's travel permit had finally arrived! With it was a letter of instructions: "I must complete an affidavit each month . . . attesting to the fact that Tommy had or had not been in any fight because of his ancestry [and] had done nothing to endanger national security. I was to report all address changes. He was to always be in a Caucasian's custody, namely his mother." Elaine protested the last restriction. "If Tommy was to spend weekends . . . with any of our Chinese, Filipino or Negro friends, would he be in violation of his right to be in Military Area No. 1?"

Campbell: "You always raise unnecessary questions."

Elaine: "Not unnecessary; I'm just trying to avoid any misunderstandings that might lead to his return to a concentration camp." Fryer tore up the instruction sheet, telling Elaine just to be sure to get the affidavits in and to keep General DeWitt's headquarters informed of any change of address. Elaine bade a tearful farewell to her friends at the CCC camp. She and Tommy were in Los Angeles for Christmas.

A news clipping from a Minneapolis newspaper, dated December 25, gave her – and the nation – its first news of the secret mission of the Military Intelligence School: "Sgt. Fred Nishiuji, the first graduate of the Military Intelligence School was dispatched to the U.S. Army in Australia in May, 1942. In September he was sent to Buna, New Guinea as a frontline interpreter. In order to safeguard Sgt. Nishiuji, his commanding officer assigned a Caucasian, First Class Albert Johnson, for 24 hour duty."

Where would Karl be assigned after he graduated? Elaine wondered.

As for Tommy, the notarized reports on his status and movements continued until October 1944, even as Karl was serving with the China-Burma-India Office of War Information Psychological Warfare Team.

When Karl left for Minnesota on December 2, Elaine was a brunette. The next time he saw her, her hair was completely white. Poet Janice Mirikitani wrote:

A sky opening,
sunlight strikes a stretched white wing
of swan's sudden flight.
One moment becomes presence.
Elaine's hair, breathing with light.

26.

Meanwhile—Other Battles

Grim Facts

Meanwhile, there were other battles. The nation mobilized its armed forces to fight the enemy overseas, and industry and labor combined efforts to win the battle for production at home: to build ships, planes and tanks to smash the Axis.

Trade unions, with some exceptions, voluntarily gave up the strike weapon and wages largely remained static. While corporate profits skyrocketed, employers attempted to outlaw the 40-hour week and eliminate time-and-a-half for overtime. Patriotic sacrifices were all by working people. Talk of "big wages" was more talk than substance, but workers who had been jobless and had lived through the hard Depression years now got jobs and regular paychecks and could even – especially with overtime pay and with more than one wage earner in the family – bank some money or buy a house. National War Labor Board figures showed that 21 percent of U.S. workers got less than 50 cents an hour and 54.3 percent received less than 80 cents an hour. "Big wages" was essentially an employers' fable and got off the ground only because war jobs replaced no jobs. Living costs soared.

The population shifted as hundreds of thousands of Black and white workers migrated – mainly from the South – to northern centers of industry like Detroit where tanks instead of automobiles rolled off the assembly lines; to port cities like Oakland and Richmond, California, where the great cargo ships were built and launched; to Seattle and Los Angeles where the fighter planes were fabricated and assembled.

In 1940 when the government first established defense-related job training programs, only 4,600 of the 175,000 trainee workers were Black. A 1941 threat of a March on Washington by Black workers spurred President Roosevelt to issue an executive order barring discrimination in defense work. A. Philip Randolph, head of the Brotherhood of Sleeping Car Porters and chief organizer of the march, called it off on June 28 when he announced:

> The march of 100,000 Negroes on Washington for jobs in national defense which was scheduled for July 1 is off. The march is unnecessary at this time . . .
>
> The reason for this decision is the issuance of an executive order by President Roosevelt banning discrimination in defense industries on account of race, creed, color or national origin, the attainment of which was the main and vital aim of the march-on-Washington movement. This is the first executive order which has been issued by a President of the United States in behalf of Negroes since the immortal Abraham Lincoln issued the Emancipation Proclamation in 1863.

After Pearl Harbor, whatever impeded the war effort had to be addressed. Eleanor Roosevelt knew that when she spoke – though mildly – at a Salute to the Negro Troops in New York City in January, 1942, one month after Pearl Harbor. "Today we are facing a great challenge," she said. "We know that although we have made great strides, we still have much to do before we can say that for all of the people this country is a true democracy."

The ILD put the stark facts on the record and forced the issue: "Major attacks on Negro troops occurred at Fort Bragg, N.C., Gurdon, Ark., Alexandria, La. Six Negro soldiers have been killed – in North Carolina, 2, Louisiana, 2, Kentucky, 1, and New Jersey, 1. At least four have been shot or stabbed in Louisiana. Scores were severely beaten in North Carolina, Arkansas, Florida, New York, South Carolina and Texas. Hundreds arrested in the same states." One victim was Pvt. Felix Hall, who disappeared on February 14, 1941, from Fort Benning, Georgia. On March 28, his decomposed body – in Army uniform – was found near the camp hanging from a tree.[1]

Saboteurs of Democracy

Violence against Afro-Americans – civilians and military personnel – continued unabated, and in the spring of 1942, ILD President Rep. Vito Marcantonio addressed a petition to President Roosevelt asking that "the strong voice of the Commander-in-Chief of our nation at war be heard in sharp, unmistakable terms against the activities of that small handful of saboteurs of our democracy who are responsible for wave upon wave of terrorism against the Negro people."[2]

Attorney General Francis Biddle also received a letter. In addition to the ILD National board, it was signed by 600 individuals and 42 organizations and applauded "the recent energetic action of the Department of Justice in apprehending the eight Nazi spies landed here by submarine, their direct accomplices, and numerous members of the Nazi Bund, also agents of our country's Axis enemies." However, it decried "the singular lack of energy shown by the Department of Justice" against internal hate-mongers like the Ku Klux Klan, Charles Coughlin, the Christian Front, Gerald L.K. Smith and others who "promote disunity, breed internal hatreds . . . "[3]

In summer 1942, the ILD published more "grim facts" proving beyond all doubt that terrorism and violence against Black Americans was at a stage that "cannot be tolerated any longer by a country at war for its survival . . . "[4] It recounted incident after incident in all parts of the country of killings and woundings, beatings, and mob violence against military personnel, workers in war industry, sharecroppers in the South.

A "Japanese Problem"

And in California, there was a "Japanese problem." Led by the same groups that fomented hysteria against Japanese Americans prior to and during the evacuation process,* an organized campaign was initiated in January 1943, to prevent the return of the Japanese to California after the war. "We should strike now," said C.L. Preisker, chair of the Santa Barbara County Board of Supervisors, "while the sentiment over the country is right . . . if we begin now to try to shut out the Japanese after the war, we have a chance of accomplishing something . . . I think the state legislature should memorialize Congress for action. We don't want to see the time return when we have to compete with the Japanese again in this valley."[5]

Hearst's San Francisco *Examiner* eagerly took up the cause, editorializing on January 25:

> Bad as the situation is in Europe, the war there is between European Occidental nations, between white races. Antagonisms, hatreds and jealousies, no matter how violent, cannot obscure the fact that the

---

*Mainly, these were the American Legion, Native Sons of the Golden West, California Joint Immigration Committee, Associated Farmers, State Grange, and the Hearst and McClatchy press.

> warring nations of Europe stem from common racial, cultural, linguistic and social roots. It is a family affair . . .

And, said Los Angeles *Examiner* on March 23: "The war in the Pacific is the World War, the War of Oriental Races against Occidental Races for the Domination of the world."

So it went. The same rabid forces that campaigned – with little opposition – to drive the Japanese out of West Coast areas at the beginning of the war were at it again. However, by December of 1942, the Los Angeles *Examiner* was bemoaning the "amazing lack of public interest" in the subject. According to Carey McWilliams, the "anti-Japanese forces really do not represent the people of the West Coast, not even in the state of California."[6] All the same, when the evacuees did return there would be violent, even murderous, attacks against them.

27.

Return to San Francisco

"Your Wiffle—Elaine"

Elaine and Tommy returned to San Francisco and a severe housing shortage. She rented a room with kitchen privileges from a longshoreman friend and she and Tommy settled in, being just two of several tenants who shared an old Victorian mansion.

Elaine wrote to Karl almost every day. She signed her letters: "Your wiffle – Elaine," and sometimes included a red lipstick kiss.

"January 30, 1943

"Jobs are more plentiful in S.F., especially in warehouse and office – either place I could work because of Tommy; could go to work in shipyards which would be direct war work but having the sole care of Tommy . . . shipyard work and hours, while more money, would, I think, be too hard.

" . . . Yes, we are proud of our fighters against the fascist Axis, let's hope with increased activities in the European theater of war, Africa and the Pacific, the United Nations will soon crush the fascist monster and its satellites and all of us will be able to take up our normal lives again as free people all over the world – free from want and fear and free for the pursuit of happiness as sane men and women, building a better future and no fear of having to destroy or be destroyed.

And dear, I know that is your main aim in life to preserve a happy future for our son and all other children . . . "

ON FEBRUARY 2, THE GERMAN SIXTH ARMY SURRENDERED TO THE RUSSIANS AT STALINGRAD, AND THE RUSSIAN OFFENSIVE THAT FOLLOWED PUSHED THE GERMANS WEST AND SEALED THE FATE OF FASCIST GERMANY.

"Feb. 3

"Dad's business in January alone was $800 less than last January, and every day it gets less and less, because he cannot get any merchandise such as candy bars, cigars or gum, so he's almost just a cigarette man and that's the least profit ... You can spend about two hours waiting in a butcher shop and then no meat ... and bacon – what does it look like? Glad your food is improving, that's how it should be – our soldiers need and deserve the best."

"Feb. 13

"Yes, Tommy is getting bigger – he no longer cries or gets scared when Manzanar is mentioned as he did ... he used to tell me not to talk, and that he did not like Manzanar because there were Nazis there ... "

"Feb. 18

" ... it's terrible in Manzanar ... kids who want to enlist in U.S. Army are still scared. When is the WRA and FBI really going to weed out those pro-Axis b______s?

International Women's Day

International Women's Day on March 8 was commemorated in wartime 1943 by progressives calling for rationing of commodities and establishment of strict price controls; more nurseries and child care centers; ending discrimination against Negroes in the Army and in war industry; and opening a Second Front.

> We greet our sisters who are fighting all over the world. Our admiration is boundless for the courageous women of China who work and sacrifice so much to beat back the Japanese bandits. We greet our sisters united against fascism in Central and South America ... We pay tribute to the young Russian women—Pavlichenko and the sainted Tanya who was caught and hung by the Nazis—and thousands more who battle Hitler's fiendish hordes ...
>
> We women of the United Nations can build a chain around the world that will bind us together in victory and in the peace to come.[1]

On March 16, Elaine wrote Karl that her mother, Mollie, had gone to work in the needle trades industry. Also, "she was called in last week to immigration officials and asked whether or not I was a citizen ... she writes me not to be scared if I'm called in ... I wonder what's up?"

On the Belt Line

Through the ILWU Local 6 hiring hall, Elaine got a job at the Hills Brothers coffee plant. It was a novel experience for her. "I never worked on a belt line before . . . they were jarring coffee. There was one hour that you did a certain job, and then you went on to another because, otherwise, it would be like Charlie Chaplin in *Modern Times* . . . So, we had one hour spent taking jars out of the case and flipping them on to the belt line. Well, I was taking one jar, or two jars, at a time, and I saw other women and men, flipping six at a time; I couldn't imagine how they could do it . . . but finally managed . . . Then we went to where we saw the coffee going into the jar, to make sure it went to a certain level. If it wasn't . . . we had to pull that jar off before it went to the next stage. Then [we had] a coffee break . . . Next we got these little mallets, and . . . [hit] the top of the jar, to hear whether or not the vacuum was sealing. If it didn't sound right, we had to make sure that jar didn't get beyond that position on the belt line. So there were these three different motions all day long."[F]

For working eight hours, Elaine received $5.60 – less than $35 for a six-day week. She promised Karl that she would "try and save every penny possible [although] prices are impossible." She worked three months for Hills Brothers.

Reunion with Karl

On April 11, after getting military permission to take her small son out of state, Elaine and Tommy boarded the Challenger for the three-day train trip to Minnesota where Karl had a four-day furlough. She was still sending monthly reports to General DeWitt swearing that Tommy had not been in any fights, had not committed any acts of sabotage and was behaving himself. The reunion with Karl was joyful; it was difficult to part.

"May 5

"Tommy and I arrived safely [home] last night . . . don't worry about me – I shall cherish our furlough, it was memorable for me also and your closeness warmed me and will keep me warm until we can be together again and raise our darling son together in a democratic world . . . I'll go to work as quickly as possible and save for our future together."

The Yonedas, Ft. Snelling, Minn. 4/15/43

"May 6
". . . saw a Denver *Post*. . . it had almost one-half front page, one-half of page 3 and one-half the letter page, all viciously anti-Japanese-Americans . . . "

Through friends, Elaine heard that the CIO United Electrical, Radio and Machine Workers of America (UE) needed an office manager. The office was across the bay in Oakland. Under wartime regulations she was "frozen" to the Hills Brothers job but obtained a release; the union job, too, was essential to the war effort. She enrolled Tommy in a nearby child care center for working mothers and went to work for Sandra Martin, UE business agent.

"May 31

"My day starts at 6:30 when the alarm rings – sometimes I dress first . . . then breakfast for Tommy and getting Tommy to school not later than 7:50 so I can make the 8:29 bus which gets me to work at 8:50 and, of course, I work until 4:50 and catch 5:09 bus to S.F. and pick up Tommy at 6 or 6:05 p.m. and get dinner for Tommy first . . . we eat about 7:30 or 8. When I get through eating, I put Tommy to bed and then read, listen to radio and write letters. Last week two nights, I had some overtime work I did at home – in fact 7 hours of it . . . How are you, dear – did you get paid – hope you're not broke again like last month; please let me know because there is no need for it, dear . . . "

The following month, Elaine received good news from Karl. After six months of intensive study at the Military Intelligence School, he and 435 other students graduated on June 18, 1943, and were promoted to T/5 – Technical Sergeant. Some were sent immediately overseas but most went first to Camp Shelby, Mississippi, for two months of basic army training. Colonel Kai L. Rasmussen, school commandant, called Karl to his office. The few Communists among the students were all capable and he would like to keep them as instructors. Karl told the colonel that he preferred an overseas assignment, and so was sent to Camp Shelby.

Elaine's letters to Karl related all the minute details of everyday life: whom she saw, where she went, Tommy's health status, what they ate, what she bought, the movies she and Tommy saw, Tommy's response to them, and numerous drawings and "letters" to Karl from Tommy. What she kept from Karl was the extent of Tommy's trauma after his frightening experience at Manzanar.

"July 22

"Dear, I personally disagree with WRA choice of Tule Lake for segregation camp; it will keep the damn reactionaries in the backward counties around Tule and other places worked up about the "Jap" menace."

"July 29

"Dear, I know I should write more often but gosh I just don't seem to have the time or the pep . . . but dear, I love you . . . "

In early August, Elaine was a delegate from UE to a Conference on Minorities called by the CIO. Paul Robeson was the keynote speaker. "His every word," Elaine said, "was a nail in the coffin of the Axis . . . "

ILD Writes the President

In the summer of 1943, the ILD circulated an "Open Letter to President Roosevelt from 800 United States Civic and Labor Leaders."

> We call your attention to a series of outbreaks of violence against Negro people and other minority groups in the country which have developed in various sections of the United States. The mass murders and anti-Negro rioting in Detroit, the lynching of Cellos Harrison in Marianna, Florida, and the riot of ten thousand whites against the Negro population of Beaumont, Texas, are but the latest in a mounting series of grave incidents of similar nature, which includes the so-called "Zoot Suit—Sailor War" in Los Angeles, the strikes against upgrading Negro war production workers in Detroit, Michigan and Mobile, Alabama, the pitched battles between Negro troops and white military police at Camp Wheeler, Georgia, the slaying of three Negro soldiers at Camp Van Dorn, Mississippi, the clash of Negro soldiers and civilian police at Collins, Mississippi, the shooting of four Negro soldiers at Riverside, California and numerous other instances of riots, lynch mobs, police terrorism and incitement to anti-Negro strikes, all occurring within the short span of the last few months.

It urged President Roosevelt's personal intervention to "thwart the designs of enemy agencies to create racial strife . . . "

While the letter commended Roosevelt's reaffirmation in Executive Order 9346 of the federal principle of no discrimination in employment in war industry and his recognition of the heroism of Negro troops, it urged him to make "an historic fireside chat" on these issues in order that:

> Negro people and other minority groups will be freed from every hindrance which prevents their full participation in our war effort; that every member of our armed forces will be given full and adequate protection by the federal government wherever he may be. And we urge you to effectuate these vitally necessary declarations with proper directives to the various agencies of government under your direction.

> Such action will sustain the morale of thirteen million Negro people and millions of other minority groups whose labor and devotion are essential to victory . . . [2]

The Detroit strike referred to in the open letter took place at the Packard Plant in July 1943, when 25,000 workers left their jobs – manufacturing engines for bomber planes and marine engines for PT boats – in protest against the upgrading of three Black workers. The racist sentiment was whipped up by KKK members among the mostly white Southern workers at the plant although: "Subsequent investigation indicated that only a relatively small percentage of the Packard workers actually wanted to go on strike," wrote Walter White, executive director of the National Association for the Advancement of Colored People. The CIO United Auto Workers Union quelled the short-lived strike, and the Black workers were not demoted.

"The racial hatred created, released, and crystallized by the Packard strike played a considerable role in the race riot which was soon to follow. It was the culmination of a long and bitter fight to prevent the employment of Negroes in wartime industry," said White.[3]

On July 6, from his hospital bed at Camp Crowder, Missouri, Corporal James E. Ferriero wrote a letter to the *Detroit Times.* "Why are these race riots going on there in Detroit and in other cities in this land – supposedly the land of freedom, equality and brotherhood?

"We who are doing the fighting . . . shed the same blood – one kind of blood – red . . . In this hospital ward, we eat, laugh, and sleep uncomplainingly together: Jim Stanley, Negro; Joe Wakamatau, Japanese; Eng Yu, Chinese; John Brennan, Irish, Paul Colosi, Italian; Don Holzheimer, German; Joe Wojiechowski, Polish; and Mike Cohen, Jewish."[4]

Life Goes On

"Aug. 18
" . . . spent all afternoon shopping, bought a black dressy dress (and spent more for it than I have for one dress in over 15 years – $23) and it isn't much to look at but clothes are getting harder to get and the prices outrageous . . . "

"Aug. 22
"Glad to hear that you are going back to the U.S.A. and leaving the Confederacy of the South... Got your nite club letter – who did you go nite-clubbing with?"

"Aug. 25
Just got through listening to the rebroadcast of the President's speech – to me it seems he took a slap at the Hearsts and Dies without mentioning names..."

ON SEPTEMBER 3, AN ARMISTICE WAS SIGNED BETWEEN ITALY AND THE ALLIED POWERS, BUT GERMAN TROOPS STILL OCCUPIED TWO-THIRDS OF ITALY, INCLUDING ROME AND NAPLES.

"Sept. 6
"It was delightful to us to hear your beloved voice over the phone... the [Russian War Relief] meeting at the Civic Auditorium was thrilling... over $15,000 was collected for the Leningrad Military Hospital... Tommy fell asleep but before that when the meeting opened, a color guard of U.S. soldiers and Coast Guards marched in carrying the Stars and Stripes and some Russian Red Navy sailors marched in with the Hammer and Sickle and the audience stood up – Tommy jumped on a railing and stood at attention..."

"Sept. 16
I certainly will be glad to see you again even for one day, I'll settle even for one hour just to be with and near you again..."

"Oct. 3
Yes, Tommy and I eat out a great deal, not so much because of the time I would have to spend in the kitchen but under the present arrangements (no frigidaire) it is hard to shop... I am sure when I get another place to live it will be better."

"Oct. 6
"The war news still is very encouraging on all fronts – sure hope there'll be Victory by '44 or soon thereafter."

"Oct. 13
"... got your letter – it sure was a love letter... anytime you return we'll be waiting for you, have no fear..."

"Oct. 27
"We sure had a terrific earthquake here . . . I was just through washing my hair when the lights began swaying and the ironing board jumping around . . . Tommy didn't wake up . . . it shook again, his bed moved back and forth and hit the door . . . lots of broken glass windows and dishes . . . yes, Tommy knows as I do that you are coming back to us and we will again be a happy family . . . "

"Nov. 11
"Yes, dear, something must be done to combat anti-Semitism . . . that's why I was so happy when the President took such a firm stand that his Fair Employment Practice Proclamation was mandatory and not just a directive . . . it was one of the President's strongest stands on internal policy yet."

"Nov. 15
"Am definitely asking the executive board for a raise to 85 cents an hour, 40 hour week, or $40 for a 45 hour week . . . "

"Nov. 25
"The war news is again very encouraging, especially the continuous bombing of Berlin . . . "

"Dec. 6
"Dear, I'm very happy at your delight in your assignment and promotion – congratulations."

"Dec. 12
"I was thrilled to hear your beloved voice this morning . . . I will always love you and await your return . . . "

On Dec. 15 Karl and his teammates were sent to Camp Anza near Los Angeles; they expected to be shipped out soon. He got a two-day pass and Elaine and Tommy met him in Los Angeles. The team sailed for India in January 1944, arrived in March and were flown to New Delhi where they were attached to the China-Burma-India Office of War Information Psychological Warfare Team. They were first based in Ledo, India. Karl's main assignment in Ledo was the writing of propaganda leaflets and radio broadcasts; he also interrogated Japanese prisoners of war. Over the following two years, he conducted broadcasts to enemy lines in Myitkyina, Burma and was stationed as well in Kunming, China where he wrote propaganda leaflets for air-drops to enemy troops.

Tommy's Trauma

Many of the drawings Tommy did for Karl represented themes of death and destruction. They showed bombs raining down on Tokyo and the Japanese flag going up in flames. He wanted to fight the Nazis, liked knives and wore officers' bars on his little boy's Army uniform. And he got sick. He had nightmares, would wake up crying, terribly afraid for his daddy. He distinguished between fighting Hitler and the Japanese who were, in his mind, the "mean ones like those who came to our room in camp." He wanted Karl to fight Hitler; he would be safer.

After he overheard a conversation with friends about Karl's determination to serve in the Pacific, the nightmares increased in intensity. A friend wrote to Karl on June 11, 1944:

> . . . I found an American shell case . . . for him to play his favorite game of war with. A truck went by near work and some of these cases fell off and I picked it up after another truck ran over it. He will like it that way as it looks as though it had been used . . . I feel very flattered as he drew me a picture of an airplane shooting another one down. I asked him why he did not send it to you but he said you didn't want war pictures and he was drawing you something else . . .

From Elaine to Karl – "June 22:
"He gets spells where he keeps on drawing endlessly, and almost always the same theme – a Japanese plane or a Nazi plane on fire – a tank, etc. I have written you about this . . . "

"July 6
"When Tommy saw pictures of two GIs carrying the little Japanese kids, he said, "See American soldiers aren't Nazis – they don't hurt little Japanese kids – or their mothers."

"July 21
" . . . got a telegram from Sarah . . . she was worried about Tommy and me because of explosion at Pt. Chicago . . . a terrible thing . . .

thought it was an earthquake . . . looked out the window and could still see the glare in the sky . . . "[5]

" . . . Tom, I believe, would like to have a Japanese helmet, sword or gun . . . says other kids have gotten "helmets" from daddy and brothers in service!!

Tommy's physical health deteriorated and after being held under observation at the San Francisco French Hospital, he was admitted in October to the Stanford Convalescent Children's Hospital in Palo Alto for asthma, allergies and suspected rheumatic fever. He had his sixth birthday in the hospital. He remained there for eight months, until mid-June 1945. Doctors discovered that he had internal hives; his diet was stringently restricted and three times a week he received allergy shots.

Initially, he was too ill to draw or write. Karl knew something was wrong when Tommy's letters and pictures stopped coming. Elaine had tried to protect Karl but finally had to tell him of the seriousness of Tommy's illness. Finally, over the long months, he began to improve and the letters and pictures to Karl poured out like a torrent. His drawings became more detailed and sophisticated; war was still the main theme. In his young adulthood, Tommy would become a pacifist.

Death of Anna Damon

Anna Damon, national secretary of the ILD, died on May 18, 1944, after a long illness. It was an irreparable loss. Tributes poured in from trade unions, labor prisoners, the NAACP and National Negro Congress, civil rights organizations, attorneys, elected officials, artists and writers.

"Anna Damon will live in the hearts of workingmen and women . . . " said Harry Bridges.

"I feel heartbroken and my grief is too great to express," said Scottsboro defendant Haywood Patterson from Kilby Prison in Montgomery, Alabama. "She drew upon her love of people and hate of oppression . . . " said Ina Wood, Oklahoma criminal syndicalism defendant. The ILD was, said ILD Secretary Louis Colman, Damon's "living monument."

She was, said the ILD National Board, "a peerless leader and organizer . . . Anna Damon always took a personal interest in the campaigns to bring aid and cheer to those who were imprisoned for campaigns to bring aid and cheer to those who were imprisoned for their part in the struggle for freedom... We would stress also her valiant efforts on behalf of the Negro people beginning with the Scottsboro and Herndon cases and continued through the fights against discriminatory legislation, lynchings... struggle to abolish the poll tax... Our loss and our country's loss... is truly great." "Anna Damon is mourned by thousands who have only heard of her," said Mini Carson.

Damon had come to the ILD from the trade union movement, having been business agent for the Hat, Cap, and Millinery Workers Union in Chicago. She was a member of the Communist Party for the last 25 years of her life.

The ILD established an Anna Damon Fund and in Decem ber, 1944, posted a $500 reward for "information leading to the arrest and conviction of members of the mob who lynched James T. Scales, 17 year old of Pikeville, Tennessee, on Thanksgiving Day."

Congressman Vito Marcantonio continued to fight in the Congress for the ILD legislative program. A main campaign was the establishment of a permanent Fair Employment Practices Committee (FEPC) with powers of enforcement; the ILD was the first organization to project this goal.[6] Other objectives were:

- Abolish the poll tax
- Outlaw segregation in travel
- A GI Bill of Rights
- Abolish segregation in the armed forces
- Investigate Jim Crow baseball
- A Full Employment bill
- A minimum wage bill
- Improve unemployment benefits
- Equal pay for equal work
- A Seamen's Bill of Rights
- Federal aid to education
- Maternal and child welfare programs
- Independence for Puerto Rico
- Naturalization rights for Filipinos

Second Front

ON JUNE 6, 1944 THE ALLIES OPENED A SECOND FRONT ON THE BEACHHEAD OF NORMANDY. GERMANY WAS FORCED TO FIGHT NOW ON TWO FRONTS. A LARGE SEGMENT OF THE U.S. PUBLIC HAD LONG CAMPAIGNED FOR A SECOND FRONT.

Marcantonio observed the historic day by urging President Roosevelt to set up mechanisms to rescue Jews who survived the death camps:

> In this hour of the liberation of the Continent of Europe from the ravaging hand of Hitler and Hitlerism, I join with all Americans in the expression of the deepest appreciation for your leadership in this most critical period in the history of our Nation.
>
> It seems fitting to me that on this significant day (D-Day) I should address you about the problem of the Jewish people now prisoners in Hitler Europe. For on this day the signal for the struggle for their liberation was given. Now at last it is possible for America to offer the long-oppressed Jewish people the aid and succor we have long been prevented from giving them because of the conquest of Europe by Hitler . . . there will be tens of thousands of Jewish war refugees from every section of Europe . . . They were the first to feel the heel of Hitler tyranny and should be the first to be freed from Nazi oppression.

Marcantonio urged the establishment in the United States of a "refugee rescue camp or 'free port' where these refugees may find sanctuary from the horrors of war . . . "

"Army Scottsboro Case"

On June 10, a few days after D-Day, Rep. Marcantonio, as president of the ILD, and William H. Hastie, chairman of the NAACP's National Legal Committee, jointly filed a petition with President Roosevelt. It urged clemency for Black Army Privates Frank Fisher, Jr. and Edward R. Loury, convicted of "rape" in an Army court-martial at Noumea, New Caledonia in the South Pacific. Sentenced to life imprisonment at McNeil Island Federal Penitentiary in Washington, the two men appealed to the ILD for help. Marcantonio and Hastie argued before the War Department, causing "a furious struggle inside the department between the forces of unity and decency and those who stood for white supremacy . . . "

A compromise decision reduced the sentences to eight years for Fisher and ten for Loury, and reflected a recognition of "the important effect of whatever action was taken on the morale of the Negro troops who constitute one-tenth of the armed forces, and on the morale of Negro people on the home front." Marcantonio and Hastie continued to press for complete freedom and exoneration for the two men, the ILD obtaining more than 1,100 signatures of leading individuals and organizations to an appeal to President Roosevelt.

Roosevelt's "efforts for unity," the ILD said, had been "given a most recent expression in the War Department's order forbidding segregation of Negro and white in post exchanges, movies, and transportation."[7]

ON JULY 23, KARL AND KENNY YASUI WERE IN MYITKYINA ON THE IRRAWADDY RIVER IN NORTHERN BURMA BROADCASTING TO JAPANESE TROOPS: "... THOUSANDS OF YOUR COMRADES HAVE DIED LIKE INSECTS ... THEY HAVE BEEN ANNIHILATED ON ATTU ISLAND AND THE MARSHALL ISLANDS AND HERE IN NORTHERN BURMA SEVENTY-FIVE HUNDRED OF YOUR COMRADES HAVE ALREADY BEEN KILLED ... COME OVER TO OUR SIDE WITH A SURRENDER LEAFLET ..."[8]

ACCORDING TO GENERAL CHARLES WILLOUGHBY, GENERAL DOUGLAS MACARTHUR'S INTELLIGENCE CHIEF OF STAFF, THE INTELLIGENCE WORK DONE BY JAPANESE-AMERICANS IN THE PACIFIC THEATER OF WAR SHORTENED THE WAR IN THAT SECTOR BY TWO YEARS.[9]

AND IN ITALY, THE HEROIC "GO FOR BROKE" 100TH INFANTRY BATTALION AND THE 442ND REGIMENTAL COMBAT TEAM, BOTH COMPOSED OF JAPANESE-AMERICANS, WERE LIBERATING ITALIAN TOWNS FROM GERMAN TROOPS. ON OCTOBER 27 THEY RESCUED 300 INFANTRYMEN OF THE TEXAS 36TH DIVISION, SUFFERING 60 PERCENT CASUALTIES. THE 442ND WAS THE MOST DECORATED UNIT OF THE WAR.[10]

"Defend Every Step Forward"

No organization in the nation more consistently fought against racist practices in the armed services than the ILD. It commended the War Department for issuing a general order forbidding some Jim Crow practices in Army base transportation facilities, theaters and post exchanges. It was "a step required by the principles of progress, decency and human dignity." But the ILD also noted the "hue and cry" and calls for suspension of the order by intransigent white supremacists.

Meanwhile, the *People's World* editorialized that President Roosevelt was being subjected to tremendous pressure to "go backward instead of forward to eliminating racism – foundation stone of fascism – from our armed forces." And the ILD called for the defense of "every step forward."[11]

Help the Boys Overseas

On September 19, 1944, Elaine wrote to "The Friends of the American Way:

> . . . thank you for your continued correspondence with Karl . . . letters such as yours help the boys overseas, particularly of Japanese ancestry, keep up their spirits and reaffirms belief that their sacrifices will not have been in vain.
>
> The work of your committee . . . deserves support, therefore will you kindly forward the enclosed $5 to them . . . Karl was in Burma from sometime in July til August 6. Photos he sent home indicate that he lost considerable weight during those trying days in Burma. He wrote about the "true soldiers" on the Burma front—little Burmese children who crossed the paddy fields under cross-fire of Japanese and American machine guns . . . These little children reminded him of our son Tommy who will be six in January and made him take heart, for his son is safe in America which, with all its faults (evacuation, lynching in the South, discrimination . . .) is still a wonderful country with great possibilities for all.
>
> I do not know what Karl will write . . . about your suggestion that perhaps a contribution . . . to the ACLU would be a good gesture at this time. but may I say for myself that for many years Karl and I were active in defense of labor's rights and this work very often brought us into close contact with the ACLU . . . many campaigns were jointly conducted; however, I strongly believed then and I do more so now, that the ACLU negates its good, by in the same breath, linking the rights of persons of Japanese ancestry . . . to the rights of a Gerald L.K. Smith . . . leading fascists of these days and their counterparts in past years—the campaigns of obstructionists to the war effort . . . does not help the cause of re-establishing the rights of Americans with Japanese faces to return to their homes on the West Coast . . .

On September 25, Elaine wrote to Karl from the CIO Servicemen's Canteen (at 150 Golden Gate Avenue) where she was a hostess. The center attracted trade unionists serving in the armed forces from all over the country. It was immensely popular. All servicemen were welcome, including merchant seamen whom the CIO always considered part of the armed forces.

"October 19
"Am sitting here listening to the thrilling news about the invasion of the Philippines – this time by an Army of Liberation! Do you remember how we sat huddled over the news of Pearl Harbor . . . Democracy is on the march . . . we'll be together sooner than we dared hope . . . "

"Nov. 27
" . . . stopped to have a cup of coffee and right there beside me was a Hawaiian Nisei with all sorts of medals and a Purple Heart; he lost his right leg in Italy . . . he is the first returned Nisei that I've seen . . . Tommy was proud as a peacock that you liked his drawing . . . I told him to draw a streetcar next time."

"Nov. 30
"Tommy drew your streetcar . . . "

"Dec. 7
"Dearest, do you remember three years ago about this very same hour? You and Lou talking . . . Tommy running around and I washing clothes – how stunned . . . the radio reports . . . now you are in India or perhaps Burma again doing your great share to help smash the Axis monster. And two years ago, Tommy and I were huddled at the MP barracks, wondering what was going to happen next . . . "

1945: War and Peace

ON JANUARY 27, 1945 RUSSIAN TROOPS CROSSED THE ODER RIVER IN EASTERN GERMANY, ONLY 100 MILES FROM BERLIN, AND BY FEBRUARY 8 THE ARMIES OF GENERAL DWIGHT EISENHOWER WERE APPROACHING THE RHINE RIVER IN WESTERN GERMANY.

"Feb. 26
" . . . UE [Local] 1412 passed a resolution of welcome to the returning Nisei . . . "

"March 8
"Cathy and I just came home from seeing ... "Othello" with Paul Robeson ... went backstage and spoke to Paul for a few minutes – he sends his best wishes to you."

"March 11
"This is one of the busiest nights at the Canteen. Paul Robeson just sang and spoke here – he is wonderful!"

Elaine was asked to take over the Festus Coleman Defense Committee as executive secretary. On March 16 she wrote Karl:

> I consented on condition that the committee assign at least one other person for technical help since I do not have more than about three evenings and Saturday afternoons to give to the committee. Coleman has gotten a rotten break right from the start and now to add insult to injury the Adult Authority has set his term at 25 years with good time, if granted—it means 15 years and three months—so we are to appeal, etc. the Adult Authority to rehear his parole plea and grant immediate parole ... I visited Coleman at San Quentin ... he has been terribly depressed, but since people such as Rockwell Kent, Henrietta Buckmaster, Rev. Richardson, Paul Robeson and other outstanding men and women have taken a renewed interest ... he has picked up in spirits ... [in] May he is supposed to appear before the "Authority" ...

Coleman was a young San Francisco Afro-American railroaded to San Quentin in 1941 on "rape and robbery" charges after a fight with two white soldiers in Golden Gate Park. In a 2-1 decision, the District Court of Appeals refused a new trial, Judge Ray Peters dissenting because "... the trial shows evidence of prejudicial error." By 1945, Coleman had been behind bars for almost four years.

From the March 23 *CIO Labor Herald:* "Best seller along the Ledo Road is ILWU Longshoremen 10's monthly servicemen's newsletter, and ex-longshoremen, a shipowner's son and former San Francisco newspapermen read it for news of home. That's the report of S/Sgt. Karl Yoneda, Japanese American longshoreman now with the Army Psychological Warfare Team in Burma. The shipowner's son in question is the son of Almon Roth, Waterfront Employers' kingpin."

On April 12, President Roosevelt died suddenly of a cerebral hemorrhage. That night Elaine wrote to Karl: "Words fail me in expressing the deep personal loss I feel at the death of our President FDR. He has left a heritage that we must all endeavor to live up to... We must mobilize our full strength and back Truman in his pledge to carry out the tasks before us as Roosevelt wanted them... we must crush the Axis so that it will never raise its ugly head again. We must make the United Nations conference work. I know you are doing your share and I shall try to do more. We have lost a friend."

"April 15
"... a pall has hung over the nation... the radio has been playing nothing but hymns and solemn music... went to the city Hall SF memorial service for FDR..."

U.S. TROOPS REACHED NUREMBERG ON APRIL 16 AND ON APRIL 21, RUSSIAN TROOPS WERE ON THE OUTSKIRTS OF BERLIN. ON APRIL 25, RUSSIAN AND U.S. INFANTRYMEN MET AT TORGAU ON THE ELBE RIVER.

On April 25 the United Nations Conference on International Organization opened in San Francisco to draft the Charter of the United Nations. It would establish a security council of five permanent member nations – China, France, Great Britain, the Soviet Union and the United States – and six elected non-permanent member nations. Fifty-one countries participated in the San Francisco conference. Main objective was to maintain international peace and security and to achieve "cooperation in solving international problems of an economic, social, cultural, or humanitarian character, and in promoting and encouraging respect for human rights and for fundamental freedoms for all without distinction as to race, sex, language, or religion."

Concurrent with the UN meeting, across the San Francisco Bay in Oakland, trade unionists from many Allied nations met to lay the basis for establishing a World Federation of Trade Unions (WFTU). Its purpose was to preserve international working-class unity "to build a lasting peace, root out Fascism and establish new relations among the nations..."

"After all the sacrifices readily accepted during wartime, it was essential to obtain for the workers a radical improvement in their living conditions, draw up a programme of economic reconversion and reconstruction and achieve the economic and social needs of and reconstruction and achieve the economic and social needs of the working class," according to WFTU President Louis Saillant. Saillant, a French Socialist, credited the Red International of Labour Unions (known in the United States as "International Red Aid"), in its brief 14 years of existence, with establishing "a clear, still applicable approach – that of the class principles which underlie any policy of unity among trade unions, nationally or inter-

Elaine's Busy Schedule

By April 30, Elaine was busy packing to move, keeping up with U.N. developments, and helping with a union reception for WFTU delegates. She also attended a mass meeting at the Civic Auditorium where actor Orson Welles, screenwriter John Howard Lawson, CIO President Philip Murray and "heartbeat Charles Boyer" paid tribute to the lofty aims of the new U.N.

Tommy was still at Stanford Hospital and Elaine visited him regularly.

ON MAY 7, GERMANY SURRENDERED UNCONDITIONALLY.

"May 8
"Today the fight is half over. Let us hope that V-J Day isn't too far off."

"May 16
"Just got through stamping, stuffing and sealing 764 Coleman Defense letters – so part of those old campaign days are back!"

"June 10
"Yesterday went to San Quentin and visited Festus Coleman, his little four and three-quarter year old son and his sister were along. Ronald, the son, is sure cute and clever. Festus hasn't come up before the parole board yet – they are only in the middle of their April calendar now and he is No. 77 on the May docket. He sends his best wishes to you."

"June 19
" . . . went to several stores looking for stockings . . . at Lerners there

was a line at the stocking counter . . . two pair each we got and who cares . . . sheer or heavy . . . stockings they are . . . !"

"July 14
"Last night I attended, partially . . . the southern half of the state [Communist Party] convention . . . Mother is a delegate . . . saw many old timers . . . "

"July 21
" . . . Dr. Wolf thought it might be a good idea for me to get Tommy in [summer camp] . . . but when I told them that the child was Eurasian with his daddy in the U.S. Army somewhere in China, the woman said she would have to take that up with the head of the camp . . . ' [got] a nice note, 'we will be happy to have your little son at camp . . . ' don't let the bedbugs get you down . . . keep as well as possible under the conditions you have to live."

Hiroshima—Nagasaki

ON AUGUST 6, AN ATOM BOMB WAS DROPPED ON HIROSHIMA, FOLLOWED BY THE ATOM-BOMBING OF NAGASAKI ON AUGUST 8.

"Aug. 8
"Awaiting your reactions to the atomic bombs and Russia's entry into the war [against Japan]! Much speculation going on now how long it will be before you and others can come home!!"

"Aug. 11
"Momentarily we are expecting the news that the fighting is over . . . when we can again be a happy family . . . "

Karl, stationed in Kunming, China when the atom bomb was dropped didn't know what an atom bomb was any more than anyone else. "Along with the rest of the world, little did we realize the horrendous deadly force that had been unleashed upon humanity."[13] But his mother lived in Hiroshima and he was terribly worried. It was not until two months later that he found out that she been at work several miles away and was not injured. Where her home had been she found "just flat, bare land."

She described what she saw: " . . . a dark cloud covered the sky and black rain started to fall. Hundreds of half-naked people, some with horrible burns on their bodies, walked... like a parade of ghosts, all pleading for water. It was hell created on earth."

JAPAN SURRENDERED ON AUGUST 14.

PART FOUR

28.

The War is Over!

Wanting to Cry

"Aug. 16
"My reaction to the news on Tuesday was one of pent up emotion, I wanted to cry but the tears wouldn't come but I still have the feeling of wanting to cry. I think I would feel better if the tears would come . . . it took two hours to get home . . . we walked through Chinatown – it was bedlam . . . "

The atom bombing "was not necessary," Karl said. "We at the OWI office knew as did other U.S. high ranking officials that Japan was defeated militarily by the end of July 1945 and that its ambassador to Moscow . . . was asking the Soviet Union to act as a go-between to the U.S. in order to negotiate 'face-saving' surrender terms . . . However, Truman wanted to test the bomb's destructive power and chose to use it on populated Japan areas, rather than some barren islands. He had a two-fold purpose – kill off as many Japanese as possible and to stop any Soviet move into Asia."*

Elaine to Karl on Aug. 24
"I have high hopes we may spend Xmas together!"

"Aug. 27
" . . . your happiness . . . was equal to mine, but dear, you expressed it so much more beautifully . . . [each] "passing minute is a diamond to me because every move of the clock's hand brings me closer to you."

"Sept. 3
" . . . Labor Day parade – Tommy rode in a car in the UE contingent

*Interview with Karl Yoneda by Yvonne Yoneda, April 22, 1982

and I walked with the UE... saw Harry B. [Bridges] who says hello, Lou Goldblatt, Paul and Ruby Heide and many other people we know... there were about 50,000 in this first Labor Day parade since Pearl Harbor."

"Sept. 7
"... dear, my postwar plans include a place to live... and a car, but we'll discuss that together in each other's arms... "

"Sept. 10
"... I, as alternate, attended County [Communist Party] Convention; you... got nominated for County Committee... I declined for you... Enclosed is excerpt of Oleta's speech dealing with Nisei – that is the first official statement from any source, national, state or county – also the [racial] minorities report had strong section on this question – will get excerpts later. Voting was by secret ballot!!!"

Oleta O'Connor Yates was chair of the Communist Party of San Francisco County. Her report included the following section:

> ... Side by side with activities on the Negro question, we must take up the fight against anti-Semitism, and revise our work among the Chinese, Mexican and Filipino groups. In connection with the American Japanese, who are returning to San Francisco, the Board has a particular point to make.
>
> We believe that it was a mistake to have dropped all Nisei from the Party immediately after Pearl Harbor and that the reasons given were not sufficient to justify the fact. We believe that the Party failed to carry out in practice a program around the problems within the Relocation Centers following the evacuation, and continued its mistakes in not becoming a leading force in fighting for jobs, housing and security for the Nisei who began to return many months ago. A sharp turn in this approach and outlook is now necessary... [1]

"Sept. 13
"Yes, dear, I'll be glad when I'll not have to write you letters but just tell you what's on my mind and together we can be with our son. My daughter dropped into the office yesterday – she looks real good... "

GI Rights—and Wrongs

With the war over, veterans' rights became an immediate issue. Wartime pledges that veterans' jobs would be waiting for them were often violated. The ILD national office established a GI Rights Bureau and appointed Milton Becker as director.

Elaine wrote to Karl: "If you want to go back to the waterfront, I'm sure there'll be no problem there and no discrimination either, except from... ignorant people who may be members or are probationary members... don't worry they'll be straightened out immediately."

In the union's Stockton division, when several members refused to work with a returned Nisei warehouseman, the ILWU international officers, headed by President Harry Bridges, took quick action. Lou Goldblatt was sent to straighten things out. Goldblatt, who had deplored wartime hysteria against U.S. Japanese more than three years before in his Tolan Committee testimony, now told the Stockton members: "Race discrimination knows no end. It starts off with the Japanese, then the Filipinos, Catholics, Protestants and pretty soon it will wreck your union."[2]

The local union set up a rank and file trial committee; the accused were ultimately found guilty of violating the union constitution and expelled. The principle of "An Injury to One Is An Injury to All" remained inviolate.

Most returning Nisei, however, did not have a union like the ILWU to protect them. As they left the camps and attempted to return home and restore their lives, there was vandalism, shooting, arson, dynamiting, desecration of Japanese graves, and intimidation and threats. In California, the groundwork for a campaign to keep the Japanese from returning had been prepared during the war. New organizations were founded: The California Citizens Association of Santa Barbara, Pacific Coast Japanese Problem League, No Japs, Incorporated, Home Front Commandos and Americanism Educational League. There were also established hate groups like the Native Sons of the Golden West, Associated Farmers, California State Grange, and the American Legion. Slogans were: "No Jap is Fit to Associate with Human Beings" and "Slap the Jap Rat." The Home Front Commandos issued a flier: "... Lend your help to Deport the Japs – if you can't trust a Jap, you won't want him as a neighbor... a Jap is and always will be a Stabber-in-the-Back gangster..."[3]

In Hood River, Oregon, the American Legion removed from the

town's Honor Roll the names of 17 Nisei soldiers who gave their lives in the war against fascism;[4] Secretary of War Henry L. Stimson condemned the attack on Nisei veterans' homes in Madera, California; and two Nisei soldiers appealed to Secretary of the Interior Harold Ickes for protection for their parents from terrorist shootings in the small farming town of Livingston, California.[5]

"Cry Out, America!"

During the same time in 1945, returning Afro-American veterans were being killed in the South. According to an ILD representative, "In the Georgia county where I went, it is openly admitted that the landlords have set a policy of killing the first Negro veteran who returns to any community, as a warning to all other Negro veterans. This is generally understood down there to be a Southwide pattern, at least in rural communities."[6]

The ILD charged that the Department of Justice stood by while Black men were "wantonly murdered." Among them were:

- Veteran Moses Greene murdered by two deputy sheriffs on his farm near Ellenton, South Carolina on September 9.
- Jesse James Payne, taken from jail and lynched in Madison, Florida, on October 11.
- Veteran Sam McFadden lynched in Suwanee County, Florida, on October 21.
- Veteran St. Claire Pressley, shot dead by a police officer in Johnsonville, Carolina, on November 17.
- Edgar Thomas, Black merchant, shot dead by two police officers in his own store in Union Springs, Alabama, on October 7.
- Veteran Ed Day Gary's eye shot out by a police officer in Union Springs, Alabama, by one of the same police officers who killed Thomas.

This "homicidal strain of the 'white supremacy' virus has spread to Los Angeles, Portland, Seattle, New York and other places," the ILD charged. "IT IS TIME FOR THE PEOPLE OF AMERICA TO FORCE THE DEPARTMENT OF JUSTICE TO ACT. THE DEPARTMENT HAS THE POWER TO ACT IN THESE CASES. THE POWER OF THE PEOPLE CAN MAKE IT GO TO WORK."[7]

Urged the ILD: "CRY OUT, AMERICA!"

29.

Adventures in Chicken Farming

Karl's Return

Karl returned home to Elaine and Tommy. They were a family again! He enjoyed renewing old friendships and being brought up to date on events and politics. The Communist Party of San Francisco gave a big party for its returned veterans. Karl was received warmly back into the party, some members apologizing for the wartime suspension of Japanese-Americans. Friends were fascinated when they learned of his wartime assignment with Military Intelligence, and saw his large collection of propaganda documents and materials.

Karl's military service didn't help, however, in obtaining housing. He was shocked and angry at the racism he encountered while trying to find a decent place for his family to live.

Nor did the Waterfront Employers Association welcome Karl, turning down his application for registered longshoreman status, as it had turned him down in 1936 when he had had to use a work permit to get waterfront jobs. It didn't matter that he had six years of longshore experience or that he was a war veteran. The union, however, challenged the rejection and his case went to arbitration in early February of 1946. Two weeks later the ruling came down: he was entitled to full longshoreman status.

Karl worked for a brief period, then collapsed with what doctors diagnosed as a kidney problem. Longshore work was impossible. He and Elaine had an immediate problem of how to earn a living. And they had not yet found a place to live.

Therefore, when Elaine's parents recommended that they take up chicken farming in Sonoma County, it seemed to make sense. Some of their friends were making a nice living. And, they said, it wasn't hard work, "... surely Karl, who had been a longshoreman, who had fought in the jungles... would be able to endure chicken work. Little did we know what we were getting into." Elaine laughed about it later with some chagrin. "... I couldn't see myself in the country...

Country Girl

I'd never been a country girl... had always lived in a city..." But Elaine became convinced it was the thing to do, for Tommy as well as Karl. With the help of a GI loan and Nathan and Mollie, they bought a ranch and in April moved to the country. Since Karl and Elaine "knew from nothing" about chickens, her parents moved in with them.

That's how they became chicken ranchers, a time Elaine would describe later as one of the most difficult and unsatisfying periods of her life. Elaine, however, didn't allow herself to indulge in regret or self-pity.

She and Karl settled down on their six-acre chicken ranch on Petaluma Hill Road, Penngrove, and learned together – the hard way – about chicken farming. Karl threw himself into it, even becoming a member of the Board of Directors of the Petaluma Cooperative Hatchery.

For their first chicken "raise," they ordered 6,000 birds. Until 1949, when they also raised laying hens, these were solely meat birds. The price of chicken feed almost doubled when wartime price controls were lifted and the work was harder than they had imagined. Essentially it was a 24-hour a day, 7-day a week job. They couldn't afford to hire outside help so had to "feed the bins and change the water and vaccinate... whether you knew how to do it or not." Nor did they know that "... you're supposed to give them corn... so we didn't... [and] our 'raise' wasn't so hot as far as weight" was concerned.

They made a modest living, however, later raising 30,000 meat birds a year and collecting eggs from 1,000 layers. Petaluma was still the "egg basket of the world." All this changed later as mechanized ranching by big feed companies took over and the main raising of meat chickens moved out of state.

It was hard work, "harder than longshoring," Elaine said. They lifted 100-pound sacks of feed to fill the hoppers in the chicken houses, and the never-ending cleaning and vaccinating made for a constant dirge of toil. The family worked together, Tommy growing well and working diligently. In addition to helping with the chickens, he joined the 4H and raised pigs. He was a brilliant student and later excelled in sports, particularly basketball.

Tommy Deals with Racism

The Yonedas became part of Sonoma County's political Left; they knew most of the progressive Jewish chicken ranchers – some were old family friends – and Elaine also had ties in that area from her days in the ILD, including the "tar and feather" period. In the '30s during the apple workers strike, strike sympathizers were seized, beaten and tarred and feathered.

"So we didn't feel isolated," Elaine said, in spite of the intolerance and racism of a section of Penngrove's population. During the period of evacuation of Japanese-Americans, the Japanese Buddhist Church had been burned down, and there were other acts of vandalism. There was still much hatred against Japanese and Tommy had to deal with that at school as early as the second grade. He had fights when schoolmates made racist remarks about Black people and one day he came home and told Elaine that a German family around the corner had a swastika over their fireplace.

Seven-year-old Tommy knew what it was. "He had drawn many swastika pictures with the boat sinking to send his father while he was overseas. And Nazi airplanes being shot down." Before the war, the German-American Bund had been active in Penngrove, even maintaining a big swastika embossed on a mountain in the area, and "they used to have their meetings with swastikas flying . . . "the sentiment was there . . . hidden, but it was there."

Political Life

While chicken ranching was a difficult and dreary way to make a living, their political life was full and the movements and campaigns waged in San Francisco had their counterparts in Sonoma County. Neither Elaine or Karl were constituted to be politically lethargic. They helped to organize a branch of the California Labor School and raised money for the *People's World,* putting on big cookouts – with barbecued chicken, naturally.

Friends visited constantly; Bill Reich remembered "how Elaine would always welcome me . . . after a hard and frustrating day trying to educate and organize poultrymen and other farmers in Sonoma county. She was the perfect hostess and activist, always engaged in one campaign or another, yet never neglecting her home and family."

Bernard Martini lived across the highway; he had known Elaine during the ILD days and remembered that "she was active all the time." During San Francisco waterfront strikes of 1946 and 1948, Elaine and Karl went together from ranch to ranch, collecting truckloads of fruits, eggs and chickens for strike relief. Their rancher friends had a good understanding of unionism. They were old time radicals and remembered the days "when they had been cloakmakers or shoemakers or butchers..." They remembered even though they had become "land owners" with their five- or six-acre chicken farms, Elaine chuckled. They also remembered the Scottsboro case and the campaign to free Tom Mooney. "So there was that heritage there and that understanding..."

Elaine and Karl were involved in organizing a big Santa Rosa rally for the 1948 Progressive Party campaign. Paul Robeson was the main speaker and filled the junior college auditorium. They also had meetings for Communist Party candidates. They attended meetings of the Jewish Cultural Club, and participated in PTA affairs. Elaine organized a Sonoma County Kaiser prepaid medical group among the poultry farmers, recruiting nearly 100 members.

ILD to Civil Rights Congress

When a chapter of the Civil Rights Congress (CRC) was organized in Sonoma County, Elaine became chairperson. The CRC came out of the 1946 merger of the ILD and the Federation for Constitutional Liberties. The Civil Rights Congress "was dedicated to the victims of racist persecution and of those who were hounded for advocating peaceful co-existence," according to William L. Patterson. Patterson, previously national secretary of the ILD, became CRC national executive secretary in 1949.[1]

The transition from ILD to CRC almost immediately after the war was necessitated by the organized and growing racist terrorism in the nation. It was exacerbated by a drive to wipe out the modest economic and social gains that Black people won during the war. The racists were active in every section of society, every institution, every city and small town. And not only in the deep South; "southern justice" had traveled North. "Jim Crow and Discrimination is a national policy of government enforced by terror at federal, state and local levels," Patterson said.[2]

The CRC – like the ILD before it – was a national organization with chapters in many states and most large cities. Paul Robeson was on its national board; so was author Dashiell Hammett; so were trade unionists and civil libertarians. It had a three-fold program:

> Defense of the rights of labor; of Negro, Mexican and other national groups, and the rights of political minorities.

This meant fighting for national and local Fair Employment Practices Committees. In the San Francisco Bay Area, it became common to see picketlines demanding equal hiring in food chains, banks and transportation systems; these were Black community efforts supported by CRC and the whole spectrum of the Left and they were ultimately successful. So were the struggles of Black workers to eradicate Jim Crow locals in the Boilermakers Union.

The CRC fought for repeal of anti-labor measures, against Jim Crow and anti-Semitism, against police brutality, for the rights of the foreign-born, for repeal of the Smith Act and McCarran Law. In most areas the CRC maintained a lawyers' panel and a bail fund.

Cases of several victims of racist oppression defended by the CRC became, like the Scottsboro case before them, national and international in scope. These included the Trenton Six, and the Willie McGee and Martinsville Seven cases. In Northern California, there was the Wesley Robert Wells case. The CRC supported the Hollywood Ten, campaigned against loyalty tests in the universities, against deportations of the foreign born and the continuing persecution of Harry Bridges, and for the right of free speech and thought for 12 national leaders of the Communist Party indicted under the Smith Act.

Free At Last

The case that perhaps most of all – through all the years – stained the fabric of American life was that of the Scottsboro Nine. It was a direct link between the great civil rights battles waged by the ILD and the campaigns developed by the CRC. The CRC would bring the Scottsboro case to conclusion. Charges against four of the Scottsboro youths had been dropped in the late 1930s, and in the mid-'40s, four of the five still in prison had been paroled. Only Haywood Patterson, serving a 75-year sentence, remained in jail, and he escaped in July 1948.

Two years later the FBI captured him in Detroit and attempted to extradite him to Alabama. The CRC said it must not happen. The pressure on Michigan Governor Mennen Williams to deny extradition was so great that he did refuse, and finally all of the Scottsboro youths were free. The CRC's William L. Patterson assessed the case:

> It took seventeen years! It took all kinds of court maneuvers, all kinds of struggle outside the courts; it took tremendous sacrifices of time and energy by thousands of good people around the world—many of them Communists, many of them not Communists—to win that great battle. But at the end, not one boy was lynched. All were freed. And the South has not been quite the same ever since.[3]

30.

The Cold War Years

Tradition of Radicalism

During the Cold War years of the late 1940s and the 1950s, the Yonedas continued their political activities, remaining staunch members of the Communist Party. They circulated the Stockholm World Peace Appeal in 1950, opposed the Korean war, anguished over the executions of Julius and Ethel Rosenberg in 1953, and heard their son, at age eleven, worry about "going to another concentration camp because my grandparents came from Russia."

Nori and Travis Lafferty, Oakland friends, recalled Elaine's "kindness when our sons were born and how she and Karl 'harbored' us in Penngrove when we were victims of the California Un-American Committee." Elaine "cared for her many friends."

In 1952 Alexander Saxton* visited Elaine and Karl in Penngrove, planning to write a novel on California labor in the 1930s. Elaine's experiences in the ILD would be invaluable. Saxton and his wife Trudi last saw Elaine at a Manzanar Pilgrimage. "Her face was as lively as ever. Failing health and physical pain had not dimmed her marvelous enthusiasm ... When we are depressed, we like to think of Elaine because she was so vital and happy. Karl was lucky to find her but then we think she was lucky to find Karl, too ... We are all lucky to have known such people ... we grieve ... [but] can rejoice that she lived her whole life as she lived it. She contributed her piece to the great tradition of American radicalism."

During the McCarthy era two men, claiming to be from Army Intelligence, visited Karl at the ranch. He was vaccinating chickens. The men said that Karl's name had been given as a reference by someone reenlisting in the military. Karl knew this was a lie and sure enough, they attempted to question him about Harry Bridges. Elaine quoted Karl: "Now if you want to know why I'm sticking this

*Alexander Saxton is a novelist and UCLA history professor.

chicken in the ass I'll tell you. Otherwise I'll meet you in my attorney's office." The men left and didn't return.

Marcantonio Mourned

Like people from all corners of the country, all walks of life and many political viewpoints, Elaine sorrowed when Vito Marcantonio died suddenly of a heart attack on August 9, 1954. He was 51 years old. His death left a deep void in the political fiber of the nation. "Marc" had decided to run again for Congress after being defeated in 1950 when the American Labor Party suffered a split, the result being that three political parties joined forces for the express purpose of getting rid of him. Prior to that, he had served seven terms. The people who mourned him most were his constituents in East Harlem: Afro-Americans, Italians, Jews, Poles, Hungarians, Puerto Ricans, Irish, West Indians, Latinos. He fought for them, he loved them, they were his people.

In his last term in Congress, he provided his own epitaph:

"...I have stood by the fundamental principles which I have always advocated. I have not trimmed. I have not retreated. I do not apologize, and I am not compromising..."[1]

Chicken Ranch for Sale

Tommy graduated from Petaluma High School in 1957, a straight "A" student, three letter man in basketball, football and track, and student body president. He won the Petaluma B'nai B'rith Frankel-Rosenbaum Award for outstanding scholarship, leadership and athletic skills and the Private Ben Frank Masaoka Memorial Scholarship Award from the National Japanese American Citizens League (JACL). He also received an academic scholarship to Stanford University.

With Tommy through high school, the distaste for chicken farming and the lure of the city got stronger for Elaine and Karl. They gave up raising chickens and commuted to jobs in San Francisco – Karl on the waterfront and Elaine doing office work. In 1960 they sold the chicken ranch. Elaine gave hardly a backward glance to Penngrove as they moved back to San Francisco and became city folks again. Hallelujah!

"Life of the Party"

Elaine and Karl always assumed that the FBI kept them under surveillance. What they didn't know was the extent of it or the number of agencies that kept track of their activities. The FBI supplied information on Elaine to six agencies: Department of the Air Force, Passport Office, Department of State, Immigration and Naturalization Service, Department of Justice, United States Army, and Central Intelligence Agency.* She was on the FBI's list for "custodial detention in the event of a national emergency" under the Internal Security Act and considered to be a "possible candidate for prosecution." The FBI bureaucracy kept busy over the years updating Elaine's file, reinvestigating her activities, duplicating previously gathered data, and keeping informers occupied in spinning out all kinds of tales from the imaginative to the ludicrous to the obvious:

> . . . one of the Communist Party women who will start the 'whispering campaign' sponsored by the Communist Party against the FBI.
>
> . . . Stated to be a professional prostitute . . .
>
> . . . when there is a demonstration of Communist agitators, she will usually be one of the most active.
>
> . . . is one of the most ardent and militant of Communist agitators on the Coast of either sex and has a long police record of arrests for disturbing the peace, vagrancy, failing to move on, seditious utterances, inciting to riot, unlawful assemblage, resisting an officer, etc. as well as an unenviable record as an organizer and a disturber.
>
> active member of . . . flying squad of agitators.
>
> In her brushes with the police, by demanding police trials, arranging postponements, writs of habeas corpus, taking appeals and militantly 'insisting upon her rights,' she has generally succeeded in 'beating the rap' but has been convicted by juries on several occasions.
>
> . . . she must know the provisions [of McCarran Act] because she usually does more talking than anyone else.
>
> . . . the life of the Party.

"DETCOM"

In 1955, when Elaine was president of the Civil Rights Congress in Sonoma County, the FBI determined that the ". . . scope of her

*FBI files obtained under the Freedom of Information Act

activities falls within the criteria governing the retention of subjects on the SI [Security Index]." Her file was tabbed "DETCOM" which meant "DETAIN COMMUNIST."

Through the years, she alternately would be added to and removed from the "DETCOM" status as the FBI figured the designation was or was not "warranted" by her activities at a specific time. In addition to the "Security Index criteria," there was also a "Key Figure" list to which she was added in 1957 when she became financial secretary of the Sonoma County Communist Party; for that reason, too, it was recommended she be again considered for the "DETCOM" program. But when she had "not attended the three most recent meetings of her [CP] club," she was removed – temporarily – from the "key figure" list. One update concluded: "It has been established that any contact with Yoneda would be reported to CP officials and it is certain that she would be hostile in any contact by FBI agents." And another: " . . . still no indication of any disaffection toward the CP."

When, years later, Elaine got her FBI files, she took its 600 pages in stride; approximately half of the pages were blanked out for "security reasons" and to protect informers' identities. One thing she never forgave the FBI for was its description of her as "chunky." Now *that* was an insult! But then it also gave her credit for five feet five inches of height, six inches more than she possessed. The report that her hair was black was also untrue; since her concentration camp experiences, her hair had prematurely turned snow white and, realizing how striking it was, she never tinted it.

31.

Marching in Sisterhood

The Women's Auxiliary

"Auxiliary members must help every member of a trade unionist's family realize that the benefits of strong and effective unions flow directly into our homes and communities," Elaine once said.[1] A woman's auxiliary is as relevant, as pertinent, as militant as its membership. The ILWU Federated Auxiliaries came into existence wherever the ILWU had locals, up and down the Pacific Coast. The first originated in San Francisco when "a small group of strikers' wives helped obtain food and donations for the strike kitchen and needy families during the famous 1934 strike." They formed an organization in early 1935.[2]

The auxiliaries were composed of wives, mothers, sisters and daughters of longshoremen and warehousemen. These were women intimately involved in the life and death struggles of their men for militant trade unionism, and against gangsterism on the docks, including the dreaded shape-up, the play-off of union against union and worker against worker. These women were all colors and nationalities, active in church and community affairs, in education and legislative matters. They came from all parts of the country; their personal politics varied.

In the beginning, they had one thing in common: they were the women of good trade union men and they valued their men's union because it brought their families a good life and security. If the men had security on the job it meant a decent education for their children, a health plan for the whole family and safeness in old age. The women took their place alongside their men; they marched with them, but they marched together as women, too. And as they developed programs in the auxiliaries made up out of their own militancy and concern for the world, they marched in sisterhood.

Tom, Karl, Elaine with Karl's mother, Kazu, Hiroshima, August 1963

Karl and Elaine at Gensuikyo—Conference against A and H Bombs, Tokyo 1960

Life Never Dull

Life for Elaine was never dull. Back in San Francisco, she became active again in ILWU Federated Auxiliary No. 16, and was at different times its secretary, publicity chair, legislative chair, and president. In 1960 she was the auxiliary's delegate to the Sixth World Conference Against A and H Bombs (Gensuikyo) in Japan; Karl represented ILWU Local 10. On this trip Elaine and Tommy first met Kazu Yoneda, Karl's mother, in Hiroshima, and other relatives – all of whom warmly welcomed their American family.

In 1963 Elaine was one of 19 auxiliary members to receive an honor pin for 25 years of continuous service to the auxiliary. Twelve years later, only two members of Auxiliary 16 were left who went back to the beginning – Elaine and Asta Harman. The Eleventh Biennial Convention of the Federated Auxiliaries in 1963 supported repeal of anti-labor legislation such as Taft-Hartley, and urged the establishment of friendly relations with the Republic of Cuba.

Auxiliary No. 16 collected signatures that year to the "Ban the Bomb" petition, supported a scholarship fund for the children of slain civil rights leader Medgar Evers, participated in a conference on "Disarmament and the Abundant Life," and opposed capital punishment.

On February 14, 1965, Elaine, auxiliary president, spoke at a Negro History Week meeting at the Mt. Zion Baptist Church:

> "I do want to take this opportunity to say a few words in tribute to some of the outstanding Negro women who have long fought and been in the front ranks of every struggle to gain human dignity for all mankind.
>
> "Many thousands of the Negro wage-earners in the mid-1800s were women and they belonged to the trade unions of that day . . . 300,000 of the million-strong Colored Farmers Alliance were women. The National Association of Colored Women was organized in the late 1890s, some 10 years before the NAACP.
>
> "The names of Harriet Tubman, Sojourner Truth, Mary Ellen Pleasant, Charlotta Bass, first Negro woman to run for vice-president of these United States, are well-known . . . but I wish to dwell on the great loss the Negro community as well as the whole world suffered this past month when the life of one of America's brightest young writers was snuffed out [by cancer] at the age of 34. Lorraine Hansberry—author, playwright, humanist—was an outstanding fighter . . . an eager participant in all that was good . . .

"Elaine quoted actress Shelley Winters who had eulogized Hansberry: 'Nobody can make me understand why we spend millions of dollars for instruments of war and we don't find out how to cure disease and hate and selfishness. I'm unreconciled to her death.' "

In 1965 the auxiliary got involved in the anti-[Vietnam] war movement. A letter signed by Elaine as auxiliary president reminded President Lynden B. Johnson of his election promise to "... make any plan, go any place, play any part that offers realistic prospects of peace. We want no wider war."

Tocsin

Tocsin, an anti-Communist hate sheet which specialized in naming names, was published across the Bay in Berkeley, and made note of Elaine's peace activity:

> Identified Communist Elaine Black Yoneda is serving as spokesman for Auxiliary 16 of the International Longshoremen's and Warehousemen's Union in a protest to President Johnson about Viet Nam ... sent a resolution ... this month assailing American anti-Communist efforts in the war-racked country ...
>
> Identified as a Communist at 1953 hearings of the House Committee on Un-American Activities, Mrs. Yoneda has been active in party activities for her adult lifetime. She was a militant leader of the old International Labor Defense.
>
> ... Mrs. Yoneda was among persons listed as supporters of an Easter "peace" demonstration in San Francisco in 1963.

In turn the FBI made note, in Elaine's file, of *Tocsin*'s concern; Elaine was up to her old activist tricks. Over the years, as protests against the Vietnam war mounted, there wasn't a peace rally or parade that she and Karl didn't attend. There wasn't a petition demanding that the U.S. get out of Vietnam that she didn't circulate. And as duly recorded in her FBI file, she regularly attended her Communist Party club meetings, including one in 1966 at which a peace conference was discussed, "the aim of which was to stop the war in Vietnam as an unjust imperialistic war."

She was an accredited representative of her auxiliary to the planning sessions of the 1967 Spring Mobilization against the Vietnam war, and a member of Women for Peace and the Women's International League for Peace and Freedom.

San Francisco anti-Vietam War march, 4/15/67. Elaine is in 2nd row, 3rd from left, holding placard with 3 children

Elaine's Human Touch

Wenonah Drasnin, of Oakland Auxiliary 17, illustrated Elaine's concern for the "human touch":

> During the 1967 Federated Auxiliaries Convention in San Francisco we left the convention at the noon hour to join a Local 6 picket line. We picked up our placards, joined the line and began our walk. Elaine "tapped-tapped" along on her high-heel pumps. She spotted a woman striker seated on the steps of a building and sped to her side. She began an animated conversation, touched on the reasons we joined the line and then inquired how things were going for this woman. The public statement of support had been made by the picket line—Elaine saw the need for the human touch. With a warm embrace she left the woman and returned to the convention.
>
> Elaine is not a memory to me but one whose vibrant personality influenced the communities of neighborhoods and unions, auxiliaries and individuals. That influence stemmed from the heart and to me that heart still lives. To Elaine "issues" were not just intellectual statements—"issues" were people—their problems, the personal way in which poverty and injustice beset them. "Issues" were also their hopes and aspirations. Elaine had an appealing directness of approach and speech, whether to groups or individuals. Always the core of her concern was untimately the person.
>
> The list of causes and issues she supported is endless. The picket lines, demonstrations, marches, community appeals for relief for the impoverished in which she appeared and gave of herself was awesome. This tiny little body ignored fatigue and illness to give heart to another's cause.
>
> On a family level she spoke to me with loving pride of Karl, his lectures, his books. Like other mothers she worried about the health of her daughter Joyce and together we rejoiced at her recovery. Her son Tom and his daughters were a source of joy and anecdote and as grandmothers we shared stories.
>
> In all things, Elaine was HEART. And she never gave up.

A Force to be Reckoned With

The April 1967 Report of the ILWU Officers to the 17th Biennial Convention said of the Auxiliaries:

> . . . it is well recognized that the ladies, who are always so quick to make themselves available for "coffee and" at caucuses and other

> functions, and are pledged to back up their men if and when there is a strike, are also the most outspoken in speaking for peace on earth and decent conditions at home. Peace and civil rights are a high priority for the ILWU auxiliaries who have been working to end the war in Vietnam, prevent nuclear war and prohibit nuclear weapons.
>
> They have protested police brutality against Negroes and other minority groups, have vigorously supported every movement that will win equality in the job market, and strengthen the health and education of the children of the country, in particular the disadvantaged children of minority groups.
>
> . . . whenever there has been a cry for help they have spoken up and acted . . . it is these women who very often carry into the communities the social and humane program that best reflects the meaning of ILWU.

The effort never ebbed. The Auxiliary urged its members' participation in events opposing the military draft, including "Stop the Draft Week" and draft card turn-ins, and encouraged the understanding that ending the war in Vietnam and the struggle to end poverty in the United States were inextricably linked.

Its April-May 1968 "Newsletter" contained a resolution to ". . . support to the fullest all efforts of organized labor to improve living standards and bring peace to the world . . . be a full time citizen, and be active in the affairs of my community, my country and the world . . . "

Elaine addressed the June 22, 1968 auxiliary meeting decrying the assassinations of Rev. Dr. Martin Luther King, Jr. (who was an honorary member of ILWU Local 10) and of Robert F. Kennedy. "Unless we and others work to turn the tide," she said, "democracy will vanish . . . and we will become a nation at war with itself." It was a time of turbulence with marches and rallies, student strikes, "Black power," "flower power," peace vigils, sit-ins, Welfare Rights organizing, Black community demands for an end to police brutality and for the right of self-defense. The people had taken to the streets and the police reacted with more force.

The auxiliary didn't believe in mincing words. It didn't like the actions of the police "TAC" squad, so its letter to the San Francisco Police Commission said the city should get rid of it: "Students, Black people in the ghettos, peace workers and draft resisters are the special targets of the Tactical Squad now. In time of strike it may be our husbands and sons in the ILWU and our own members who will have their heads beaten . . . We call for the abolition of the Tactical Squad . . . "

Mervyn Dymally, former Lt. Governor of California, once remarked about the auxiliary, "They aren't a bunch of dumb broads, but a force to be reckoned with."[3]

Elaine Loved her Auxiliary

In 1968 Clydenia Austin, vice-president of the Northern California District, ILWU Auxiliaries, first joined Auxiliary 16 and met Elaine, then auxiliary president.

> I worked under her leadership with joy . . . She has always had a way with people—getting them to work for the cause and to work together for unity . . . she believed in giving all she could to help one grow . . . You couldn't slow her down. She knew time was precious and she tried to make every moment count in an unselfish way . . .
>
> She loved her Auxiliary and all its members . . . We were a part of her life. I know that because she loved me and my family as her own.
>
> When I first joined the Auxiliary, she put her arms around me and welcomed me with a beautiful smile. That smile will live on with me forever . . .
>
> She never gave up—she always had hope. She gave hope to others for tomorrow . . . Like God never stops loving his children, Elaine never stopped loving people. She had love to give when everything else ran out . . .

Austin remembered the good times she and Elaine had together. "She taught me along the way and she loved to put young people to work. We traveled together. She was always my roommate and we were a special team. Even when I didn't want to go, she would encourage me to go and help fight for peace and justice. Just as Martin Luther King had a dream 25 years ago, Elaine also had a dream. I am sure that she knew within her heart that one day her dream would come true . . . She is at rest now . . . Thanks for letting her be a part of our lives. We promise to carry on the great works that she had started with the Auxiliary . . . "

Raising Bail Again

"From protest to resistance" was now the battle cry of the militant youth movement. More and more protesters – on college campuses and in working-class communities – were arrested. In response, in September 1968, the Bay Area Committee to Defend Political Freedom was established with a component Bay Area Movement Bail Fund. Elaine was a bail fund trustee. Under special attack were the Black Panther Party and participants in the draft resistance movement, with "The Oakland Seven" especially targeted. The seven young men were indicted for "conspiracy" during the huge October 1967 Stop the Draft Week demonstrations at the Army Induction Center in Oakland.

"The true history of the United States is replete with long and courageous struggles in which black and white working people, students, and the families of the victims, have contributed defense funds to save the leaders of progressive movements," said a Bail Fund appeal. "... Whether it is outright political prosecution, frame-ups, harassment on technical violations, or whatever, legal repression drains seriously the movement's finances, picks off its leaders, and diverts it from its main task." Elaine worked with the bail fund for the four years of its existence, raising and posting bail for civil rights activists, Black Panther Party members, student strikers and draft resisters.

Unfair is Unfair

Elaine was a member of AFL-CIO Office and Professional Employes Union Local 29. In early 1968 the union was shocked when the ILWU fired five women members of Local 29 for attending a stop work meeting in support of a fired shop steward. Elaine joined her union sisters in a 50-woman picketline in front of the ILWU.

She was one of the determined pickets who demanded that the ILWU reinstate the women and settle the grievance. Unfair is unfair even when the boss is a trade union. After three days of picketing and leafletting, the ILWU met the women's demands and the strike was settled. Helpful, too, were concerned longshoremen and warehousemen who stopped by the picketline to express support, and ILWU Business Agent Bob Hipps who helped lead the strike.[4]

Edith Withington, former Local 29 president, remembered walking that picket line with Elaine "making her presence felt" and, "at union meetings, always speaking for the rank and file... Elaine alerted the membership of Local 29 on the Japanese-American internment during WWII, and presented up-to-date resolutions on every phase of the struggle for reparations. When her health started to deteriorate, she had Karl drive her to union meetings, and her

Elaine, member of OPEIU Local 29, picketing ILWU Local 10 in 1968 over labor dispute between Local 29 and ILWU

dynamic espousal of issues she so fervently believed in drew rounds of applause from the membership.

"Those of us who knew Elaine personally know how passionately she believed in the progressive union principles to which she devoted her life. She communicated these beliefs to the membership. People who did not know her personally knew the 'dynamic little white-haired lady who sure knew what she was talking about.' "

"Women Seize Podium"

A favorite story of Joyce Maupin, Local 29 member and long-time trade union activist, was of Elaine's involvement in hearings to defend California's protective labor legislation before the Industrial Welfare Commission in April 1974. Union WAGE (Women's Alliance to Gain Equality) was one of 29 organizations that petitioned the IWC "to rehear proposals that would permit a 10-hour day without overtime pay, eliminate rest periods, allow employees to work through their lunch breaks and require them to pay for uniforms."

WAGE organized a picketline; Elaine "never missed a demonstration," Maupin said. "Picket signs had been prohibited as dangerous on grounds they could be used as weapons . . . We wore sheets and painted slogans on them. 'Shroud for the 10-hour day,' 'Shroud for rest periods' . . . frustration grew as the Commissioners denied one appeal after another. Noisy shouts of protest arose. As usual, when the meetings became 'unruly,' the Commissioners called a recess. Elaine and I looked at the empty chairs on the podium. We signalled two other women and the four of us went through the crowd, seating ourselves in place of the absent Commissioners and declared, 'The meeting is now open for discussion.' " "WOMEN SEIZE PODIUM," said a newspaper headline the next day. The Commission denied all 29 petitions, but at the last minute a lawsuit prevented their implementation. "The case dragged on in the courts for years, but in the end we won."

Once, Maupin related, she and Elaine were walking to the Labor Temple in Oakland to attend a Local 29 meeting when Elaine "let out a shout that could be heard for blocks. The startled purse-snatcher fled and Elaine smiled . . . she had a remarkable voice!"

"When the mike went dead in the 1934 longshore strike," Elaine said, "they put me on the platform." Elaine, with Maupin and Jean Maddox, was among the "caucus of militant unionists [who] challenged the conservative, male-dominated leadership, introducing new ideas." Maupin continues:

> This was when Jean Maddox first became president and sought help from the women's movement in the strike against Lucky Stores in 1970. The issue was equal pay for women and, with the Teamsters supporting our all-night picket lines (we locked ourselves in cars and stuck the picket signs out of the window), we won. We raised demands like maternity leave (we had not yet thought of paternity leave), child care on the job and at union meetings and putting women organizers in the field to lead new, aggressive office worker organizing drives.
>
> One tactic of the opposition was to prolong union meetings so that members would leave, one by one, until we no longer had a

> quorum. To be in Local 29, one needed a strong backside and the ability to stay awake until one or two in the morning. I remember Elaine coming to the "ladies" [room] where I had fallen asleep on a couch, "Wake up! We're going to vote!"

Young women had a special regard for Elaine. As they "learned about her turbulent life, her lifelong struggle for justice, freedom and peace, she became a role model for many of them," Maupin concluded.

Labor for Peace

In 1970, April 15 was set by national and local peace organizations for mass demonstrations in many cities to demand an end to the war in Vietnam. By then, there was a "Labor Assembly for Peace" working with the New Mobilization Committee to End the War in Vietnam, a coalition composed of women's peace organizations, pacifist and religious groups, welfare rights and community organizations. Elaine, as auxiliary president, was involved from the beginning in the building of unity between labor and community organizations.

"Stop Work – Stop War" was the slogan of the April 15 San Francisco rallies. One of several actions was a Ferry Building rally sponsored by the Labor Assembly for Peace. Labor was getting more involved in the peace movement; 123 leaders from 22 unions demanded in a full page Washington *Post* ad the "immediate withdrawal" of all U.S. troops from Vietnam. "A rich man's war and a poor man's fight. Hawk or dove, we are all clay pigeons," they said. "We are active trade unionists who are convinced that every dollar spent in Vietnam inflicts a scar on our nation and our economy. We share a common determination that the war in Vietnam must end now."[5] ILWU Auxiliary No. 16 urged participation in the day's activities:

> Don't you agree that IT'S TIME TO STOP THE BLOODY COSTLY WAR AND SEE THAT THE 80 BILLION A YEAR IT DRAINS FROM THIS COUNTRY'S ECONOMY IS PUT TO WORK ON PROJECTS TO END POVERTY, IMPROVE HOUSING, EDUCATION, MEDICAL AND HEALTH COVERAGE, TO SEE THAT CITY AND GOVERNMENT EMPLOYEES ARE NOT GIVEN PAY CUTS TO "help stem inflation" WHILE THE ORDINARY WORKER PAYS MORE AN MORE IN TAXES!!??[6]

The women's auxiliary was known as the "conscience of the ILWU" and all the strong women over the years made it so.

32.

Redress and Reparations

Emergency Detention Repealed

In September 1971, the Japanese American Citizens League won a four-year campaign to repeal Title 2 of the Internal Security Act (McCarran Act) passed in 1950. The repeal bill had been introduced in the Senate on April 18, 1969 by Senator Daniel K. Inouye of Hawaii. Other organizations were also involved, notably the Citizens Committee for Constitutional Liberties, organized in 1961 to work primarily for the repeal of the entire McCarran Act, which it termed "the extension and legal arm of McCarthyism." The CCCL commissioned Charles R. Allen, Jr. to write *Concentration Camps – USA,* exposing in detail the FBI's plan to subvert the Constitution through its detention program.

Title 2 provided for:

> EMERGENCY DETENTION: In the event of . . . Insurrection . . . the President is authorized to make public proclamation . . . of an "Internal Security Emergency" . . . and . . . "acting through the Attorney General, is . . . authorized to apprehend and . . . detain . . . each person as to whom there is reasonable ground to believe . . . PROBABLY WILL . . . CONSPIRE with others to engage in acts . . . of sabotage . . . Persons apprehended . . . shall be confined in . . . places of detention . . . prescribed by the Attorney General.

Under Title 2 the FBI had for many years maintained Elaine on its list for "custodial detention in the event of a national emergency . . . " This information was exposed only when Elaine got her FBI files under the Freedom of Information Act. At the actual time of listing, it was a secret closely guarded by the FBI. It was, however, deduced that thousands of people were on the list, Hoover having told Congress in 1950 that "there is a potential fifth column of 550,000 people..." of which, he said, 55,000 were Communists, and of these, of which 12,000 were "hard core."[1]

The JACL's role in repeal of Title 2 was primary. Long before there was a McCarran Act, more than 110,000 U.S. Japanese were arrested and forced into concentration camps. That meant it could happen again.

ILWU members Karl Yoneda and Taro Tsukahara and Elaine played important roles in bringing trade union support to the repeal campaign. A resolution passed by the ILWU and all of its affiliated locals and councils reaffirmed the union's consistent opposition to the McCarran Act, specifying the experience of citizens and non-citizens of Japanese ancestry incarcerated "without hearing or due process of law because of racism and war hysteria." The union helped put the issue before the whole labor movement, representing more than 1,700,000 unionists in California, while the Federated Auxiliaries reached many women's organizations.

Pilgrimage to Manzanar

The first organized pilgrimage to Manzanar was in December of 1969. Elaine and Karl, like other former internees, had visited the site before that and many times more in subsequent years. Sue Kunitomi Embrey[2] recalled that first time:

> "It was a bitterly cold morning, two days after Christmas, when over 200 people gathered on the desert floor of Owens Valley, in the shadow of Mount Whitney. Many of them were strangers to each other. Most were not prepared for the biting, penetrating wind that blew off the Sierras. The day would get darker and colder. All of us would remember it as the most significant event to occur in the recent history of Japanese America. It was the first Pilgrimage to Manzanar.
>
> "On that eventful morning, I met Elaine Yoneda. I had argued with my then husband that the man at the wheel of the Volkswagen Squareback was a famous Asian actor. For wasn't he handsome with his sharp and alert facial features... For the moment, the woman with her white, wispy hair, the sparkling eyes and the wonderful, unforgetable smile went unnoticed.
>
> "But later, as the crowd milled around at the cemetery area, we began to talk... I was bundled up in a scarf, overcoat, long under-

wear beneath my pants. Elaine had a knitted cap on her head. We both wore mittens, which many of the young organizers did not. Yet we were numbed by the cold.

"Warren Furutani . . . was busy gathering people to clear out the sagebrush and the manzanita branches. The group wanted to plant a tree there. The television crews from the major networks were in the way. Warren shouted at me to take care of them. Elaine and I did. We reminisced about the cracks in the walls and knotholes in the floors of the barracks. We spoke of the piercing wind, the mess hall lines, the unappetizing food. And so it was Elaine and I who showed up on the 6:00 o'clock evening news . . .

"For the next 19 years, Elaine was more than a friend and staunch member of the Manzanar Committee. She was a role model of a liberated woman, an optimistic, encouraging individual who smiled, charmed, suggested and prodded us to greater things. She organized people to write letters to declare Manzanar a State historic landmark. She gave us suggestions for pilgrimage themes. And most importantly, she and Karl were there at Manzanar supporting the volunteers on the Committee. She was consistent in her goal—to educate the American public about the World War II internment, to spread the word about redress legislation. How sad that Elaine did not live to see the Civil Rights Act of 1988 signed by a President she opposed.

"More than any other quality, Elaine possessed a warm and caring attitude which extended out to those who didn't know her . . . Elaine Yoneda was a gallant lady who was my friend and a friend of all who seek justice around the world."

Duet for Elaine

In a "Duet for Elaine," poet Janice Mirikitani and Cecil Williams* wrote:

> *Because you dared to go beyond limits*
> *set like walls by society,*
>
> > *you never kept your silence*
> > *locked in by safety or expediency.*
> > *Like thunder, uncontrolled,*
> > *you spoke terrible truths.*

---

*Rev. Cecil Williams is pastor of Glide Memorial Church in San Francisco

Elaine, you broke through the status quo
of what was "acceptable" of your day,
made things happen. Beyond your time,
with boundless energy and commitment, you fought to
bring justice to all communities.

Workers, students, veterans, teachers,
seniors, hotel maids, the poor, poets,
peace activists, warriors for liberation
and self-determination here and abroad—
White, black, yellow, red, brown . . . your
compassionate voice, healing spirit provided
a home for our struggle against injustice.

Elaine, your presence was penetrating.
You touched us all.

You touch me, your beautiful fury,
your irrepressible fire, your capacity
for love embraced us all . . .

You made us more humane, more perceptive,
and we are rewarded by your unrelenting spirit.

We love you.
Raise our individual voices
to become a chorus
for passion, for peace, for justice . . .

A Talkative, Vivacious Lady

San Francisco attorney Dale Minami met Elaine and Karl in 1972 at a meeting of the Bay Area Chapter of the JACL:

"Our chapter was considered a "renegade" group since we raised and supported issues far outside the JACL mainstream, including the farmworkers' struggle, the Black Power movement, ethnic studies, and redress for Japanese Americans which was, at that time, a radical idea. We attended meetings, rallies, demonstrations, together. We fought against racism, the Vietnam war, the conservatism of JACL and social inequality . . .

"My first impression of Elaine was . . . a friendly, talkative, vivacious lady supportive of our progressive ideas. But the impression did not begin to convey Elaine's depth and breadth of experience and character. Only after working with her did I begin to see her strength, political acuity and total commitment to justice for the poor. I remember several meetings where Elaine would voice her position with a clarity and resolve which was totally persuasive. Several years passed before I learned that the strength of her ideas and commitment came from a lifetime of struggle and dedicated work.

"I heard a saying . . . about elder statesmen who pass away in rural villages. Villagers say that their death is like a library burning down. I feel that way about Elaine because of all the knowledge and experience lost with Elaine but I also feel Elaine has left us with much more than a library—a legacy of caring, sharing and hope for a better future."

Lynne Horiuchi remembered "her critical sharpness and her intelligence in sorting out important issues, viewpoints and feelings. She is a historic figure in the Japanese American community."

The Manzanar Plaque

With other Manzanar Committee members and the JACL, Elaine and Karl worked on the wording of the plaque that the State Department of Parks and Recreation placed at the Manzanar camp site in 1973:

> In the early part of World War II, 110,000 persons of Japanese ancestry were interned in relocation centers by Executive Order No. 9066, issued on February 19, 1942.
>
> Manzanar, the first of ten such concentration camps, was bounded by barbed wire and guard towers, confining 10,000 persons, the majority being American citizens.
>
> May the injustices and humiliation suffered here as a result of hysteria, racism and economic exploitation never emerge again.

It was by then acknowledged – except by diehard racists – that the camps were in fact "concentration camps." It took a long time for the Department of Parks and Recreation to agree to the words that meant official acknowledgement of the fact. The Manzanar Committee refused to allow the state to duck the issue. The bronze plaque can be seen at the old stone guardhouse at the camp entrance, one of the few remaining vestiges of the huge campsite.

There are left only traces of guard towers, barbed wire fences and a cemetery. The dust blows relentlessly over the lonely desert.[3]

Internees still remember when the mother of a Nisei soldier, killed while fighting the war for democracy, was transported to Washington D.C. to receive her son's medal for high valor and bravery – and then transported back to the concentration camp.

Never Again

Elaine's last major work before her death was participation in the campaign for Redress-Reparations for incarcerated Japanese Americans. The JACL led the campaign, and a National Coalition for Redress and Reparations was formed to bring about a unified effort and conduct an educational campaign, both in and outside the Japanese community. The campaign was carried to the halls of Congress, to the courts, to the media, and to the streets.

JACL National Director Karl Nobuyuki wrote in *Pacific Citizen,* JACL newspaper, that redress was "one of the greatest tests of the American political system in modern times," the "painful fact" being that the action could recur due to the precedent set in World War II when "the ability of the Constitution to protect its own citizens in this bleak hour was tested – and failed."

The Congressional Black Caucus supported redress-reparations, as did numerous national and community organizations and progressives generally. Like the Title 2 repeal campaign, Elaine and Karl's special contribution was in getting trade union support.

The 23rd Biennial Convention of the ILWU in 1979 supported the JACL's nationwide campaign for redress-reparations of $25,000 "to each person unjustly incarcerated" and reaffirmed its stand "against any form of racism, [and] concentration camp incarcerations." Its 24th Biennial Convention in 1981 cited not only the injustice of the incarceration of persons of Japanese ancestry into American-style concentration camps, but the $400 million in property losses suffered as well as the "destruction of personal human dignity, the loss of income and disruption of careers and the psychological trauma of having been innocent victims imprisoned up to three and a half years."

Between the two conventions (on July 13, 1980) President Jimmy Carter established a Commission on Wartime Relocation and Internment of Civilians to conduct an inquiry of events leading to Executive Order 9066 and make recommendations to remedy the injustice.

The San Francisco hearing was held on August 19, 1981. Elaine and Karl were among the 100 persons to give testimony. Elaine described the hardships of camp life, and told of Tommy's nightmares. But the main question, she said, was that "... we must see that it is made impossible for such racist, repressive edicts to be issued and used ever again against any group of people in these United States."

The redress campaign took 12 years of persistent hard work. There were three stages to the victory: In 1983, in a preliminary finding, the commission admitted that the removal of Japanese Americans was not a military necessity but "a result of racial prejudice, war hysteria and a failure of political leadership"; in August 1988, Congress passed the Civil Liberties Act of 1988 which mandated monetary compensation and an official apology for the injustice of internment; on November 21, 1989, President George Bush signed into law the entitlement bill providing payment of $20,000 each to the 60,000 surviving internees.

Elaine testifying at Industrial Welfare Commission hearing as member of Union WAGE, 9/13/73

33.

ELAINE BLACK YONEDA
Sept. 4, 1906—May 26, 1988

"Many Tomorrows"

All the rest of her life, Elaine lived the lessons she learned in her work with the ILD in the 1930s. Sometimes, she said, there is a tendency to think "that the revolution should have happened yesterday. There may be many tomorrows. You have to work with the people . . . their needs . . . and see . . . that things do not happen overnight . . . If it's the right objective, eventually you'll get it."

Elaine was well aware, as she got older, that she and Karl had lived a good life working for a better society. Staying in there "pitching and fighting" uplifted them. She acknowledged working within the structure of the system. "I would like to see a complete change but it not going to come tomorrow" and whether it is called "reformism, revisionism, or whatever . . . while we are struggling for our ultimate goal we also have to try to make things more bearable."

Elaine had no illusions about the system and fought tooth and nail against those things that helped capitalists make more profits off the backs of workers. Racism, "still so prevalent in this country . . . brings about conditions that the employers use [to] divide and rule . . . we must fight racism, fight all those things that make more profits for the employers . . . "

"Bloody Thursday" Observance

Elaine's participation in annual "Bloody Thursday" observances was tribute to the unique and leading role she played in the 1934 general strike. She was a regular speaker at the yearly July 5 rituals – these were emotional occasions for her. Yet, besides remembering Howard Sperry and Nick Bordoise, the labor martyrs gunned down by police, she used the platform to address current issues of concern to labor and to reiterate that women's supportive role was crucial to the strike.

On July 5, 1980, a "Bloody Thursday Memorial Plaque" was unveiled at the intersection of Steuart and Mission streets where the two men were killed. Elaine participated along with union officials, waterfront pensioners, auxiliary members and city officials.

The plaque reads:

> In memory of Howard Sperry and Nick Bordoise, who gave their lives on Bloody Thursday, July 5, 1934, so that all working people might enjoy a greater measure of dignity and security.
>
> Sperry and Bordoise were fatally shot by San Francisco police at the intersection of Mission and Steuart Streets when longshoremen and seamen attempted to stop maritime employers from breaking their joint strike. Community outrage at these killings sparked a general strike by all San Francisco unions.
>
> The maritime strike continued through the middle of the summer, concluding with a union victory which brought decent conditions to the shipping industry and set the stage for the rebirth of a strong and democratic labor movement on the West Coast.
>
> An injury to one is an injury to all.

Each July 5 the site is covered with flowers.

At the 1989 observance, Karl took the platform in Elaine's stead, relating the events 55 years earlier when his gallant wife defended the strikers, represented them in court, raised and posted bail, and was often jailed. "No wonder the Hearst press labeled her as 'Tiger Woman' and the *Western Worker* called her 'Red Angel,' " he said.

"Elaine was a truly unique individual," said ILWU International President Jim Herman. "She had an amazing record of service and commitment to the ILWU and to the cause of social justice and peace. With all that, she was a warm, humorous and caring person. She is irreplaceable."[1]

" . . . a born fighter for peace and civil rights," the San Francisco ILWU Pensioners Bulletin described her.

"It is rare," said Gene Vrana of the ILWU Library, "to be able to die as we have lived, but Elaine was always special."

"When we remember Elaine, we remember Joe Hill," San Francisco Labor Council Secretary Walter Johnson said at her memorial.

Harry and Nikki Bridges, Elaine, 7/5/80

"Bloody Thursday" Memorial Service, 7/5/80.

"You can bet," wrote Dawn Rutter from Australia, "Elaine is unionizing Heaven . . . "

The San Francisco Board of Supervisors adjourned its meeting of July 28, 1988, "conscious of the many fine qualities of heart and mind which distinguished and brought justifiable appreciation to Mrs. Yoneda in the community."

"Kept Feminist Standard Flying"

Elaine fought all of her life for equal pay for equal work, for child care, for women's equality in all spheres of life; yet she did not consider herself a feminist. "Some of it I can agree with and some of it I just look the other way," she said.

She was class conscious rather than gender conscious. Men were never the enemy and she had little patience with "the thing of saying it's the female that's going to bring . . . [progress] about. It's not going to be just the female that's going to bring anything about. It's going to be the joint action of male and female . . . a joint endeavor." Yet, as women in more recent years have taken up the old and constant fight for equality, feminism has in life assumed a broader characterization.

Susan Musicant wrote:

> That Elaine is a feminist, I have no doubt, but I know that feminism was never a central issue in her struggles. She viewed sexism, like racism, as a tool of capitalism to degrade and dehumanize people for its own purposes. Her vision is of people starting to believe in themselves and fighting for their rights, then standing together and fighting off our common oppressor . . . it won't be an easy fight, just ask Elaine.[2]

And according to R. Holliday Cullimore:

> Even though these women [Communists active in the ILD] did not take up the banner of feminism, their actions show that they kept the feminist standard flying by providing continuity, and laying the groundwork for the revival of feminism thirty years later.
>
> Communist Party Popular Front activism . . . was central to the radicalism of the thirties, and provided the stage on which many women activists performed . . . This form of political activism provided women with an arena in which to put forth demands for social, material and political justice in the face of the depravity presented by the depression.

> . . . the experiences of women leaders, and their rank and file sisters in the popular front organizations such as the ILD, reveal that women attained feelings of self-mastery and personal fulfillment in their radical political activities, thereby opening up the political arena to allow greater participation by women. Additionally, it must be recognized that despite the sexism in the CP, women enjoyed a higher degree of egalitarianism in the party and the popular front organizations than they did in mainstream American society.[3]

Elaine believed that working class women played an effective role in the class struggle even when, as she said, that role was "staying home, sticking by the men, sticking by the union." This was especially clear at times when strike strategy would necessitate that women walk the picket line, "the women and children being about the only resource" striking men sometimes had. Too, women and children have been attacked and killed right alongside men in strike struggles. Certainly the employers made little distinction.

According to Cullimore:

> Feminist separatism had no purposeful meaning . . . because the goals . . . worked toward to achieve socialism, were to better the lives of all working people. So distinctions were not made between whose liberation should come first: men's or women's. It was widely held, that when the working class rose to power, so too would women be ensured equality in the society.[4]

Elaine always credited Karl with making it possible for her to carry on her own political work, never attempting to hold her back, always putting their interests and work on an equal par. "I certainly couldn't have done the things I did if I didn't have an understanding person like Karl. He was very active in his own field . . . Our activities weren't often the same although the end results, we hoped, would be the same."

Communist Commitment

Said Kendra Alexander, Northern California Communist Party chair:

> Elaine Black Yoneda will be remembered as all of us, especially politically active women, would like to be remembered after our life struggle ends. Elaine will be remembered as a trail blazer in the fight

for women's equality. She was the only woman on the leadership committee of the 1934 general strike. Elaine will be remembered as an uncompromising enemy of racial and political repression. From the battle to save the Scottsboro Nine to the struggle to free Angela Davis and the San Quentin Six.

Elaine will be remembered as a wife and mother whose love knew no limits. She insisted on being interned . . . But she went fighting mad and determined to one day see justice done for the shameful racist internment of thousands upon thousands of Japanese Americans.

Elaine will be remembered as one of the most effective fund raising speakers for the *People's World* newspaper . . . Elaine will be remembered for her unshakeable commitment to the Communist Party, USA. She was a proud active leader of the Communist Party for 57 years.

Elaine Black Yoneda will be remembered as the "Tiger Woman" and the "Red Angel." She will be remembered for her love, commitment, courage, politics, and her fighting spirit. Elaine Black Yoneda will be remembered always. But perhaps the greatest tribute to Elaine's memory will be the many women who will stand in her place and continue to fight like hell to make this world a better place.

On the Lecture Circuit

In later years, Karl often lectured on Asian History and U.S. Japanese Labor History, appearing on college campuses throughout California. Elaine accompanied him on the lecture circuit and curious students often wanted to know about Karl's and her relationship. She was nothing if not candid: "Because of the California anti-miscegenation law we shacked up, but after a couple of years we made it legal in Seattle."

While many of their activities were in different fields in the earlier years, taking them to different places, Elaine and Karl were inseparable as they got older. They attended international peace congresses and ILWU conventions, carried on their Communist Party activities, participated in civil rights campaigns and activities in the Japanese American and Asian communities, and were active together in the Bay Area Community Chapter and later, in the Golden Gate Chapter of the JACL. Elaine didn't drive so Karl was resident chauffeur and Elaine was back-seat driver. It was no problem; "she's just a bit nervous," Karl would explain.

They cared for each other, each worrying about the other's health. Elaine suffered her first heart attack in 1977 and was thereafter fragile, but remaining active was the only way she knew to handle life. In 1980, during a Local 2 Hotel Workers strike, Elaine and Karl, together with Jean Worthimer and Jack Olsen – all residents of the St. Francis Square Co-op Apartments – formed a Residents' Hotel Strikers Support Committee which supplied coffee three times a day to strikers at the Miyako Hotel and Kyoto Inn, located in their community. At the strike's successful conclusion, Elaine wrote to the Co-op Board of Directors: "This support made possible having a pot of coffee going in our Social Hall and some of us carrying a 30-cup pot of coffee and thermos of tea to the multiethnic women and men on the around-the-clock picket line, every night of the strike at about 8 and midnight on those cold, foggy nights during their strike and lockout. Altogether 52 trips were made to the lines – the Yonedas twice every night assisted by 10 others . . . at various times . . . The report of our support efforts met with much cheering and applause."

Supervisors' Salute

On May 26, 1983, 600 people converged on the Longshoremen's hall to celebrate the Yoneda's 50th wedding anniversary. Their lives "almost synonymous with labor organizing, civil and racial rights causes and an unceasing commitment to involvement," San Francisco *Examiner* staff writer Dexter Waugh wrote of the gathering.

A certificate from the San Francisco Board of Supervisors saluted "their effort, both together and individually over the past 50 years for Labor, Civil Rights, Peace and Against Racism. They have dedicated their life together to fighting for the betterment of other people's lives. Their example has been an inspiration to many of us."

Shirley Nakamura helped organize the celebration. "I know a lot of Asians who are active and have done a lot of things, it's just that I haven't met one couple who – Karl being Asian and Elaine being Jewish – are so involved," she said. "Even at their age they are just going stronger and faster than me, and I'm only 38. They are just totally involved and very, very committed."

By that time, both had "suffered debilitating illnesses – Elaine Yoneda, a triple heart bypass operation a few years ago, her husband, malaria in the Pacific theater in World War II and other illnesses right after the war. They've always bounced back."[5]

Elaine and Karl receive a Certificate of Honor from S.F. Board Supervisor Nancy Walker. May 22, 1983

"I Cry in my Heart"

Sataye Shinoda, instructor at the Tokyo Kasei University, met Elaine and Karl for the first time in the summer of 1981; Shinoda was researching Japanese American history and was familiar with Karl's work and anxious to meet the author. "I knew a lot about Elaine and Karl through some books and articles written in the *Akahata,* Communist paper in Japan. I also knew someone called Elaine a Red Angel and someone, a Tiger Woman. I wondered which she was. When I saw her, my worry melted away, She was a beautiful lady worthy of the name, Red Angel! From that time we became good friends."

Keiko Fukuda traveled from Japan to San Francisco to be at Elaine's memorial. A writer, Fukuda was a small child in Japan during World War II when Karl gathered intelligence materials from the bodies of Japanese soldiers after the Battle of Myitkyina, Burma. One of the dead soldiers was Fukuda's father; among the materials Karl found was a packet of postcards sent to him by little Keiko. Karl had a five-year old, too, and sensed it would be helpful to the child to have the cards returned. So he kept them and when he and Elaine went to Japan in 1960, he found Fukuda who gratefully received the cards and kept in touch thereafter.

She told the memorial meeting, through an interpreter: "I wanted to meet Elaine and Karl again and give them my first published documentary book, *Flowers of Burma,* personally. I cry in my heart for sadness... Elaine was my American mother and Karl is my adopted American father... Now even though I've lost my American mother, Elaine and Karl had planted a seed among us in Japan... The tree from the seed is growing well because many people throughout Japan are nurturing the tree by giving it water, loving fertilizer and understanding and love. The tree has many buds, which we call 'peace' and it will bloom beautifully very soon."

Sharing Life

Karl wrote:

> *"Oh, my beloved comrade . . .*
> *We cried, laughed, argued, and criticized each other,*
> *and then made up with kisses . . . "*[5]

Historian-writer Anne Loftis, who "found it difficult to write about Elaine apart from Karl who shared her life and work for over fifty years," first met Elaine in 1974. She interviewed both Yonedas in connection with a book on farm labor organizing. Loftis was struck by the "sheer drama" of their stories. "It is a chronicle of risk and daring, of ingenuity and courage."

> I have been thinking about the significance of this history. Through their organizing, legal defense work and Communist affiliation, the Yonedas formed connections with workers from a number of racial and ethnic backgrounds. This experience in conjunction with his own bilingual heritage led Karl to write about labor organizing

among immigrant workers in California. As he has lived long enough to see colleges take an interest in ethnic and labor studies, he and Elaine have witnessed an evolutionary process at work in the political sphere: the process, which was particularly evident under the New Deal, by which social and economic problems first articulated by the Far Left have been taken up and addressed by elected officials of the government.

Dorothy Ray Healey, too, considered it "impossible to think of Elaine without Karl . . . my first impressions of their companionship was that this was one collective that was truly comradely." So it remained for all of their 55 years together. They never lost that comradeship, nor did they lose the romance and passion of their great love for each other.

Elaine's young friend, Wendy Yoshimura, found it "so reassuring to see such great love as the one Karl and you have. If I didn't know any better, watching Karl and you, I would have thought you've just met!" she said in a letter to Elaine. "It's so wonderful to see two people loving and caring for each other . . . not only you, as a woman, a person, is inspirational to me, but also the marriage, the relationship, the love Karl and you have . . . "

Al Buckman, Elaine's brother, said: "Their marriage brought two kindred spirits together in a most happy, enduring and loving relationship that was the envy of all who knew them."

Poems for Elaine

Her family grieved and wrote poems for her.

> **Remembrance . . .** by Tamara Yoneda:
> *Elaine was wise before I was born.*
> *She ran through life with anticipation.*
> *She'd greet me with wet kisses and soon would be*
> *Questioning me about my private secrets with a gleeful curiousity . . .*
> *I gained personal confidence in her love affair with Grandpa Karl,*
> *And love between them wasn't always pretty.*
> *When I was little, Elaine's anxious personality would sometimes*
> *Anger and scare me. I remember going to Karl to ask*

why she was "that way."
He looked at me matter of factly and said, "That is her nature."
When I got older she became entertaining to me;
I began to appreciate . . .
Her split-timing reactions and beauteous pride . . .
She suffered through many operations;
I held her in my arms when she had blacked out . . .
. . . her body was often weak.
Elaine loved to gamble.
She enjoyed a good party.
She looked forward to saying "I told you so!"
(I heard her say it often.)
Her temper could burn like fire,
And she always came from the heart.
I honestly grew close to her,
Attracted by her wild vitality and deep intelligence.

Quiet Memories . . . by Yvonne Yoneda:
The quick clack of her shoes
Echoes in my mind
The memory of her soft snooze snore
Tickles my inner ear . . .
She was a lover of the world
A lover of clothes
A lover of Karl
A lover of life
Contagious loves, all . . .
She hated to miss a thing
And rarely she did
Now we miss her
Inquisitive looks
And ringing laughter . . .

Tommy wrote A Eulogy: "Grandmother, Mother has Joined You."

Grandmother Kazu, I always thought it a miracle that you survived
The atomic bombing of Hiroshima. And Grandmother, forever I will remember that while the other children cheered that bombing, I sadly wondered if you were alive.

Then, Grandmother . . . years later when we met in Hiroshima, it seemed I had known you all my life . . . Grandmother, we managed to communicate what needed to be said . . .

And now, Grandmother, Mother Elaine has joined you, her portion of work having been completed as yours was some twelve years ago.

Grandmother, I will remember Mother for being my first teacher and showing me her own particular love.
How hard it must have been, Grandmother, for Mother to leave sister Joyce with Grandmother Mollie and Grandfather Nathan when we were forced to go to Manzanar . . .

And Grandmother, never could Mother forget sister, and she always reminded me to call her . . .

Grandmother, Mother loved people, especially little children, and she loved flowers and plants and rocks. She wanted to see everybody happy, but she would amaze me most with her love of nature . . . she would hurry off in her high heels right into a wavering field of green grass . . .

And Grandmother, Mother enjoyed to cook borscht and to create with her hands, crocheting with nimble fingers . . .

Grandmother . . . I was able to see you together, both so slight of stature, unable to say much to one another but joined through your own particular expression of inner calmness and love for son and husband . . .

How blessed I am, Grandmother . . .

Last Days with Karl

On Wednesday, May 25, Elaine and Karl attended a Jesse Jackson for President Rally at the ILWU parking lot on San Francisco's waterfront. Karl told of that day:

> Elaine was getting weak and not able to walk even a block, however her mental attitudes were clear and alert . . . In the morning I told her I would shop around for a wheelchair and take her any place she wished to go—to a movie, to an opera, to a demonstration, out

shopping and even to a heaven if there was one . . . She laughed . . .

It was beautiful May weather except for a windy side. I told Elaine to dress warmly . . . I covered her legs with a blanket . . .

Suddenly Jesse and his entourage showed up, Elaine's face lit up with excitement. We watched a good hour . . . I lifted Elaine and walked over to Jesse for handshaking. She was very tired but expressed great satisfaction that her mission for the day was accomplished.

That night we went to bed early because we had to get up early to make a trip to Lake Tahoe to celebrate our 55th wedding anniversary. In my heart I knew she would never make the five hour long trip . . . I had told our son Tom many days ago to not be surprised if something happened to Elaine this year.

I knew death was closing in each day, yet we never talked about our eventual passing. One time we had jokingly talked about dying together, holding each other's hands tightly.

Death Came So Quietly

"She was up at 6 a.m. . . . I went to her and said: "Happy Anniversary. Thank you for these 55 years you stood by me . . . Are you sure you feel like going this morning? "Yes, I am going." With that she laid out an evening dress, jewelry, purse, and shoes to match. She always dressed nicely . . .

"As she began to dress she complained that her chest was in pain. She collapsed in my arms and said faintly: 'I love you' and kissed me. I didn't know death comes so quietly, as if someone had stolen the life from her . . . I still had hope of reviving her and called 911. They came worked on her for half an hour with no results. She was gone forever and I felt I had lost both my arms . . . I couldn't cry any more from exhaustion. . . .

"That night I couldn't sleep because she wasn't there in the bed. I cried for love."

Karl wrote many poems for Elaine during their years together. In the last one, he said:

Birds are singing
and hummingbirds are flying
in our backyard.
They are looking for your smiling face
and wanting to talk to you.

WE HEAR ELAINE'S HEELS

By Janice Mirikitani*

March 2, 1991

There are those
who do not accept tides of history
to carry us, passive as bundles.
    Elaine,
your voice like a sword
or an oar,
        cuts through
the overgrowth, hypocrisy's maze
of rules;
        slices the waves
that beat us, as we swim,
upstream, against convention.
        You did not have to go.
You fought to go.
Your eyes widen and you grasp your son's
arms, all that you could carry
and went to Manzanar Concentration Camp.
        To separate you from your child
        and your beloved Karl would be to separate
        the root from the tree,
        the lioness from the lair.
You did not have to go,
        packed your knitting,
        a vase to hold fresh flowers,
        your heavy sweater and small high-heeled
        shoes in which you marched.

---

*Janice Mirikitani is author of "Shedding Silence," Celestial Arts Publishing, Berkeley, CA, 1987; and "Awake in the River," Isthmus Press, 1978.

(She marched for miles, Elaine did.
In rain and whipping wind, in those
clicking high heels, demonstrating
against unjust incarcerations:
the Scottsboro Nine, Tom Mooney, Harry Bridges.
Leading labor revolts,
protesting imperialism.)
But you fought
to go to Manzanar.
We learn a lot about a strong back from you.
Work to be done,
barracks to be washed,
bedding to be aired,
children to be taught,
meetings to be organized,
gardens to be planted, and a husband to stand beside,
while causes were proclaimed and accomplished.
There in camp, freedom shouted from your block.
Elaine,
We learn a lot about a strong voice from you.
I could wear your words
in my hair like hibiscus over my ear.
You grew protest and passion like blooming trees
in the orchards.
They do not die with your physical departure.
(In Baghdad, women
keen for their dead children.
In Soweto
they weep no less loudly
for bread and freedom.
In Hiroshima
the salt of her tears
mingles with hers in San Salvador
and hers in the hospitals
of Harlem, Oakland, Newark,
Jackson, and too many other cities
where more infants die than in any
other industrialized nation.)
Your words
become seeds.
In the turning seasons, pear trees blossom,

bear fruit.
You grow from the edges of sidewalks where we march.
We hear your heels clicking.
Peace. Justice. Non-intervention. Self-determination.
Socialism.
Elaine, we learn much about the strength of a woman from you.
You will not be passive, lifted by the harsh winds
of executive orders,
wafted like a feather subjected to brute force.
You won't stand for the bombings, the napalm,
gang rape, or police squads clubbing workers and women.
We hear your heels
clicking, clicking
as we continue to demonstrate
against military budgets and massacres in oil fields,
apartheid, racism and nuclear proliferation.

Elaine, we learn much from your courage.
I remember your beautiful smile
and know you would do it all again.
You didn't have to go to Manzanar.
You did.
And from the verdant fields of farmworker labor,
from purple deserts with barbed wire rusting,
from mountains with wild flowers, from shipyards
and cement streets of our inner cities,
the insistent need for freedom,
essential as water,
and justice as urgent as breath
call us.
Dignity, a woman with white hair
marching in small high heeled shoes,
calls us.
We must
answer.

Notes

Chapter 1

1. Richard O. Boyer and Herbert M. Morais, *Labor's Untold Story,* New York, 1970, p. 139
2. Ibid., p. 245

Chapter 2

1. In September 1936, a petition asking Governor Frank J. Merriam to pardon McNamara and Schmidt was initiated by Lincoln Steffens, Clarence Darrow and Mrs. Elinore Herrick, and signed by 48 prominent liberals and trade unionists. In November, McNamara authorized the ILD to organize the campaign on his behalf and the ILD undertook the responsibility of waging a mass campaign for his and Schmidt's freedom; by then McNamara had been in prison for 25 years, Schmidt for 21; McNamara's brother John had been released. Through the years there were numerous articles on the McNamara case in the ILD *Labor Defender.*

   This case was also written about in Louis Adamic's *Dynamite – The Story of Class Violence in America,* NYC, 1931, and extensively by Herbert Shapiro, Dept. of History, Univ. of Cincinnati. Among Prof. Shapiro's articles are "The McNamara Case: A Crisis of the Progressive Era," *Southern Calif. Quarterly,* Fall 1977; "Lincoln Steffens and the McNamara Case," *Amer. Journal of Economics and Sociology,* Oct., 1980; and "The McNamara Case: A Window on Class Antagonism in the Progressive Era," *So. Calif. Quarterly,* May 1988.

Chapter 3

1. ILD Pamphlet, "What Is the ILD?", 1934
2. F. Vager, "The International Red Aid: Its Aims and Tasks," booklet published by Central Committee, Red Aid of USSR, 1931

Chapter 4

1. *Western Worker,* April 16, 1934
2. From the Introduction by Ann Fagan Ginger to the reprint edition of the *IJA Bulletin,* in three volumes, 1932-1942, New York, 1982
3. Ibid.
4. Mark Naison, *Communists in Harlem during the Depression,* U. of Illinois Press, 1983, pp. 86-87

Chapter 5

1. *Western Worker,* Sept. 1, 1932
2. Printed in the May 1933 *Labor Defender*

Chapter 6

1. *Western Worker,* May 8, 1933
2. *California History,* magazine of the California Historical Society, Sept., 1986

Chapter 7

1. Carey McWilliams, *Factories in the Field,* 1971, p. 230
2. Richard Bransten in *New Masses,* May 15, 1934
3. *Western Worker,* December 11, 1933
4. Ibid., Jan. 22, 1934

Chapter 9

1. National Youth Day was the U.S. equivalent of International Youth Day which originated in 1915 in Bern, Switzerland at an International Socialist Conference of Youth. Main purpose was to mobilize youth for the struggle for peace and against imperialist war.
2. San Francisco *News,* May 31, 1934
3. *Western Worker,* June 4, 1934
4. Material on the Auxiliary is from

Elaine's files, which include Auxiliary minutes and a historical review

5. Quin's poem became quite famous and has been reprinted many times. It first appeared in the August 1, 1934 issue of the *Western Worker.*
6. Mike Quin, *The Big Strike,* Olema, 1949, and New York, 1979. p. 130. Page citations are from the 1949 edition.

Chapter 10

1. The Workers Ex-Servicemen's League was a national organization founded in 1930 by World War I veterans; in 1934 it had a membership of approximately 15,000. Its platform called for "unity with the workers in their struggle against the bosses" and "no discrimination against Negroes and single veterans."
2. Mike Quin, *The Big Strike,* p. 142
3. Article by Iris Hamilton, *New Masses,* July 17, 1934
4. Article by Dwight C. Morgan, "Asylum for the Foreign Born," *Labor Defender,* December 1934. Morgan was secretary of the ACPFB.
5. *Labor Fact Book* III, Labor Research Assn., 1936, p. 179
6. Quoted in George Martin, *Madam Secretary, Frances Perkins,* Boston, 1978, p. 323
7. A few years later, in connection with the 1938 Bridges deportation case, Perkins would state that immigration statutes authorized deportation of any alien who "teaches Communism." However, Bridges' attorney Carol King – a New York attorney who often worked with the ILD and was founder of the American section of the International Juridical Association – challenged this interpretation. It was, she wrote in the *IJA Bulletin,* a "misstatement of the law" and provided "positive encouragement to the lawless treatment of radicals." In January 1938, Perkins – in a reinterpretation of the law – told a Congressional Inquiry that "... the various immigration acts do not forbid an alien to organize workers, lead strikes, induce stevedores not to unload ships, or engage in other trade union activities. Nor can such actions be regarded as attempts to overthrow the government."

   The following year, as reported in the April 1939, *IJA Bulletin,* Secretary Perkins and two other officials of the INS were charged by Rep. J. Parnell Thomas of New Jersey with "conspiring against the best interests of the United States by failing to deport Harry Bridges ... " Thomas's resolution attempted – unsuccessfully – to impeach Perkins for "refusing to enforce the immigration laws ... "
8. Frances Perkins, *The Roosevelt I Knew,* New York, 1946, p. 314
9. Ibid., pp. 315-16
10. *Oregon Journal,* Aug. 11, 1934
11. *California Living Magazine,* San Francisco *Chronicle* and *Examiner,* July 8, 1984
12. *Waterfront Worker,* Sept. 14, 1934
13. Ibid.
14. Ibid., Oct. 1, 1934
15. Harry Bridges concluded in an article written in 1984 (excerpted from ILWU Local 10 Special Bulletin, Thursday, July 5, 1990):

    And so they ask, 50 years later, what was it really all about?

    First of all, it was about power. We showed the world that when working people get together and stick together there's little they can't do.

    Second, it was about democracy. We said that the rank and file had the right to decide, and that if you gave them the facts, they'd make the right decision.

    Finally, it was about how people treat one another, it was about human dignity. We forced the employers to treat us as equals, to sit down and talk to us about the work we do, how we do it, and what we get paid for it.

    Pretty basic stuff. But all those gains are today under the most sustained and vicious attack we've seen in more than a generation. They employers, with the connivance of the Reagan administration, made mincemeat out of the rights guaranteed to us by the legislation passed under the New Deal.

It looks as though they've decided that the sky's the limit.

But I believe that the principles for which we fought in 1934 are still true and still useful. Whether your job is pushing a four-wheeler or programming a computer, I don't know of any way for working people to win basic economic justice and dignity except by being organized into a solid, democratic union.

Sure, we may be taking a beating now, as we were in the years before 1934, but that's nothing new. What saved us then was our faith in each other, standing together despite what the employer did to intimidate and divide us, and to discredit our leadership. We showed the world that united working people could stand up against guns and tear gas, against the press and the courts, against whatever they threw at us.

We can do it again.

Part Two
Chapter 11

1. San Francisco *Examiner,* July 21, 1934
2. *Western Worker,* Sept. 10, 1934
3. Ibid., Oct. 11, 1934
4. Ibid., Oct. 15, 1934
5. ILD *Defender,* June 1934

Chapter 12

1. Mike Quin, "The C.S. Case Against Labor – The Story of the Sacramento Trial," published by ILD, Northern California District. Quin was a reporter at the trial.
2. ILD *Defender,* June 1935

Chapter 13

1. *Waterfront Worker,* April 15, 1935
2. Ibid., June 24, 1935
3. Quin, *The Big Strike,* p. 201
4. "Modesto Frameup" – booklet published at the time by Pacific Coast Maritime Unions; quoted in *The Big Strike,* p. 201.
5. Frank Onstine, "The Great Lumber Strike of Humboldt County 1935," 1979, p. 31
6. *Waterfront Worker,* July 8, 1935

Chapter 15

1. LRA, *Labor Fact Book III,* 1936, p. 131
2. *Rural Worker,* October 1936

Chapter 16

1. *Equal Justice, Year Book of the Fight for Democratic Rights, 1936-1937*
2. *IJA Monthly Bulletin,* Vol. 6, No. 3, Sept., 1937
3. Ibid.
4. Ibid., May 19, 1937

Chapter 17

1. *Waterfront Worker,* July 8, 1935

Part 3
Chapter 21

1. From a Gallup Poll taken between Sept. 1939 and May 1940
2. Corliss Lamont, *The Trial of Elizabeth Gurley Flynn by the American Civil Liberties Union,* N.Y., 1968
3. Radio Station KPFK broadcast, "California Union Maids," Feb., 1979
4. "Equal Justice," Winter 1941
5. Ibid., Autumn 1941
6. Ibid., Winter 1942

Chapter 22

1. Carey McWilliams, *Prejudice – Japanese-Americans – Symbol of Racial Intolerance,* New York, 1945, p. 114
2. *IJA Bulletin, Book III, July 1940-December 1942*
3. Michi Weglyn, *Years of Infamy – The Untold Story of America's Concentration Camps,* N.Y., 1976, p. 46
4. This rationale was advanced by CP General Secretary Earl Browder from Atlanta Penitentiary where he was serving a four-year sentence for passport violations. As a result of a mass campaign waged for his freedom, Browder was released by President Roosevelt

in 1942 after serving one year. During World War II Browder led the CP in its own liquidation; the party's May 1944 National Convention revised it into the Communist Political Association. William Z. Foster termed this "the [party's] greatest political mistake in all its history." The Party was reconstituted in July 1945 and Browder was expelled in February 1946.

5. From Elaine Yoneda's FBI files obtained under the Freedom of Information Act
6. Karl Yoneda, *Ganbatte – Sixty Year Struggle of a Kibei Worker,* Los Angeles, 1983, p. 116
7. *People's World,* Jan. 3, 1942
8. Quoted in *Years of Infamy,* p. 288n
9. Dept. of Justice press releases of Dec. 13, 1941 and Feb. 16, 1942, reported in the *IJA Bulletin, Book III,* Vol. 10. No. 8, Feb. 1942, p. 82
10. Ibid. p. 83
11. Ibid.
12. Carey McWilliams, *Brothers Under the Skin,* Boston and Toronto, 1964, p. 142
13. *PW,* Jan. 12, 1942
14. Allan R. Bosworth, *America's Concentration Camps,* New York, 1967, pp. 60-61
15. *Years of Infamy,* p. 68
16. Dorothy Thomas and Richard Nishimoto, *The Spoilage – Japanese American Evacuation and Resettlement,* Los Angeles and Berkeley, 1946, pp. 9-10
17. *PW,* Feb. 10, 1942
18. The Committee was formed in 1919 by V.S. McClatchy, editor and publisher of the *Sacramento Bee,* and sponsored by the Native Sons of the Golden West, the Grange, State Federation of Labor and, when it formed, the Associated Farmers. McClatchy devoted his life to hating the Japanese.
19. Statement presented to the San Francisco Tolan Committee hearing, February 21-23, 1942, p. 11085
20. *PW,* Feb. 3, 1942
21. Ibid., Feb. 13, 1942

Chapter 23

1. *Personal Justice Denied.* Report of the Commission on Wartime Relocation and Internment of Civilians, Washington, D.C., 1982, p. 85
2. Hearings before the Select Committee Investigating National Defense Migration, House of Representatives, San Francisco Hearings, Feb. 21-23, 1942; Problems of Evacuation of Enemy Aliens and Others from Prohibited Military Zones. Hearings were also held in Los Angeles, Portland and Seattle.
3. Allan R. Bosworth, *America's Concentration Camps,* New York, 1967, p. 65
4. Earl Warren was California attorney general from 1939-43; he was elected Governor in 1943 and served until 1953. He was Chief Justice of the U.S. Supreme Court, 1953-1969. Warren, a conservative anti-labor Republican, surprised everyone by leading the Court in many landmark civil rights cases, especially the 1954 *Brown v. Board of Education* case that outlawed school segregation.
5. Michi Weglyn, *Years of Infamy – The Story of America's Concentration Camps,* New York, 1976, p. 299
6. *The Memoirs of Chief Justice Earl Warren,* Garden City, NY, 1977, p. 149; quoted in *Personal Justice Denied,* (see note 1), pp. 375-76
7. Carey McWilliams, *Prejudice . . . op.cit.,* p. 118
8. Ibid., p. 110. Echoing these exact sentiments, and probably inspired by them, was General DeWitt who was quoted in the "Final Report: Japanese Evacuation from the West Coast," May 1942. Absence of sabotage, he said, was "a disturbing and confirming indication that such action will be taken."
9. *PW,* Feb. 25, 1942
10. *New Masses,* March 17, 1942
11. *PW,* March 15, 1942
12. Karl Yoneda, *Ganbatte,* p. 123
13. *PW,* March 4, 1942
14. Ibid., March 6, 1942
15. Ibid., April 3, 1942
16. Quoted in IJA *Bulletin,* June 1942
17. Dorothy S. Thomas and Richard Nishi-

moto, *The Spoilage – Japanese American Evacuation and Resettlement,* Berkeley and Los Angeles, 1946, p. 15
18. *PW,* April 8, 1942
19. Allan R. Bosworth, *America's Concentration Camps,* p. 7
20. Ibid., pp. 211-212
21. *Ganbatte,* pp. 214-15

Chapter 24

1. *Ganbatte,* pp. 129-30
2. IJA *Bulletin,* June 1942
3. Ibid., August 1942
4. Ibid.
5. "Manzanar from the Inside," text of an address before the Commonwealth club of California, San Francisco, July 31, 1942, by Roy Nash, Director, Manzanar War Relocation Project, Manzanar, California.
6. *Ganbatte,* pp. 142-43

Chapter 26

1. *Equal Justice,* ILD, Winter 1942, Vol. XVI, No. 1
2. Ibid., Spring 1942, Vol. XVI, No. 2
3. Ibid.
4. Ibid., No. 3, Summer 1942
5. Carey McWilliams, *Prejudice . . . op.cit.,* p. 233
6. Ibid., p. 234

Chapter 27

1. Pamphlet issued by the Communist Party, USA, "International Women's Day for Victory," 1943
2. ILD Open Letter titled, "For Victory – Support the President's Policies for National Unity"
3. *Afro-American History: Primary Sources, op.cit.,* p. 345. This is an article by Walter White
4. Ibid., pp. 354-55
5. On July 17, 1944, an ammunition explosion razed the Navy depot at Port Chicago, located 25 miles northeast of San Francisco. Of the 320 men killed, 202 were Black. In the segregated Navy, all munition and bomb loaders were Black sailors while all the officers were white. Three weeks later, when Black sailors were ordered to resume loading at Mare Island, 258 refused. Fifty of these were convicted of mutiny in a mass trial, and the rest were given summary courts-martial. In early 1991, members of Congress urged a review of the case in order "to ameliorate an unsavory chapter in the history of the segregated Navy."
6. Vito Marcantonio, "The ILD Looks at the Present, and the Future," ILD pamphlet, 1944
7. ILD pamphlet "For Equality of Military Justice," June 10, 1944, and ILD pamphlet "Equal Justice and Democracy in the Service of Victory – Coninuing the Work of Anna Damon, 1944
8. *Ganbatte,* page 156-157
9. *America's Concentration Camps,* p. 18
10. Ibid., pp. 14-16
11. *PW,* Sept. 5, 1944
12. "The WFTU in the Service of the Workers of All Countries – 1945-1960." Pamphlet by Louis Saillant, WFTU president, WFTU Publications
13. *Ganbatte,* p. 162

Part IV
Chapter 28

1. Included in Elaine's letter to Karl: "Excerpts – County Board Report – 9/8/45 by OCY" Oleta O'Connor Yates
2. *Ganbatte,* p. 210
3. *America's Concentration Camps,* p. 211-12
4. In early 1991, it was announced in Los Angeles that architect Roger Yanagita, whose parents were interned in Idaho, won an international competition for a Japanese American World War II Memorial to be built in the Los Angeles city plaza. Yanagita's design was chosen in a blind competition. The memorial will honor the more than 13,000 Japanese Americans who fought in World War II; the competition called for engraving all their names on the memorial and Yanagita's design will inscribe these in bronze on a circular tapering granite wall.

5. "The Lost Years . . . " *op.cit.,* pp. 12-13
6. ILD pamphlet, "Cry Out America! for Swift Justice to End 'White Supremacy' Murders," 1945
7. Ibid.

Chapter 29

1. William L. Patterson, *The Man Who Cried Genocide, an Autobiography,* New York, 1971, p. 156
2. "Civil Rights Congress Tells the Story," pamphlet issued by the Los Angeles CRC, undated
3. *The Man Who Cried Genocide, op.cit.,* p. 138

Chapter 30

1. *I Vote My Conscience:* Debates, Speeches and Writings of Vito Marcantonio, selected and edited by Annette T. Rubenstein and Associates, The Vito Marcantonio Memorial, 1956

Chapter 31

1. ILWU Auxiliary #16 April-May 1968 Newsletter
2. Communication from Auxiliary #16 to Federated Auxiliaries, 17th Biennial Convention, ILWU, 1975
3. Quoted in the April 1977 Federated Auxiliaries Report to ILWU Convention
4. "The Twenty-Niner," monthly newsletter of OPEU Local 29, June-July 1968
5. February 25 news story reproduced in a leaflet issued by the New Mobilization Committee
6. ILWU Auxiliary #16 Bulletin, April-May, 1970

Chapter 32

1. Charles R. Allen, Jr., *Concentration Camps, USA,* New York, 1966, p. 54
2. Sue Kunitomi Embrey and Warren Furutani were organizers of the Manzanar Committee and led the first pilgrimage in 1969.
3. The Office of Historic Preservation of the California Department of Parks and Recreation has designated as California Historic Landmarks: Assembly Centers, Temporary Detention Camps and Internment [Concentration] Camps at Tanforan Park in San Bruno, and in Fresno, Los Angeles, Merced, Monterey, Sacramento, San Joaquin, San Mateo, Stanislaus, Tulare, Yuba, and at Tule Lake in Modoc County. Plaques – such as one located in the Tanforan Park Shopping Center, El Camino Real, San Bruno – designate the wartime locations of these now non-existent facilities. A designated "historic site must be of lasting significance to the history of the state," according to the Introduction to *California Historic Landmarks,* State of California, Department of Parks and Recreation, 1990.

Chapter 33

1. Quoted in The Dispatcher, ILWU newspaper, June 10, 1988
2. An article on Elaine Black Yoneda as part of a series on Working Women's History, Union WAGE, Sept.-Oct., 1979
3. R. Holliday Cullimore Thesis: "Communist Women Activists in the International Labor Defense of the 1930s: Standard Bearers of Feminism," Berkeley, 1985.
4. Ibid.
5. Quoted in Dexter Waugh's article in the San Francisco Examiner, May 20, 1983
6. Karl Yoneda, "Spring Flows On," a poem to Elaine

Acknowledgements

Grateful acknowledgement is made for permission to quote from the following sources:

From oral history, February and March 1976, and March, May and June 1977, by Lucy Kendall for the Women in California Collection of the California Historical Society, San Francisco.

From the interview by Arthur A. Hansen, March 3-4, 1974 for the Japanese American Project of California State University, Fullerton Oral History Program.

From MADAM SECRETARY by George Martin. Copyright 1976 by George Martin. Reprinted by permission of Houghton Mifflin Co.

From oral history by Kenneth Kann, on Petaluma Jewish Community, October 4, 1977.

From *The Lost Years, 1942-46,* Sue Kunitomi Embrey, Editor. Copyright 1972 by the Manzanar Committee, Los Angeles, CA. 4th printing, 1982.

From YEARS OF INFAMY – THE UNTOLD STORY OF AMERICA'S CONCENTRATION CAMPS, by Michi Weglyn. Copyright 1976 by Michi Nishura Weglyn. By permission of William Morrow and Co., Inc.

From *America's Concentration Camps,* by Allan R. Bosworth, copyright 1967. Permission of W. W. Norton & Co., New York.

From *The Great Lumber Strike of Humboldt County,* by Frank Onstine, Eureka, CA, 1935.

From *The Roosevelt I Knew,* by Frances Perkins, New York, 1946. By permission of Penguin USA, New York.

From *Ganbatte – Sixty Year Struggle of a Kibei Worker,* by Karl G. Yoneda. Resource and Development and Publications Center, Asian American Studies Center, University of California, Los Angeles. Copyright 1983 by the Regents of the University of California.

From Dorothy Thomas and Richard Nishimoto, SPOILAGE: JAPANESE-AMERICAN EVACUATION AND RESETTLEMENT DURING WORLD WAR II. Copyright 1946, The Regents of the University of California.

From *Communists in Harlem during the Depression,* by Mark Naison, University of Illinois Press, 1983.

Bibliography

Adamic, Louis. *Dynamite—The Story of Class Violence in America.* New York: Viking Press, 1931.

Allen, Charles R., Jr. *Concentration Camps USA.* New York: Marzani & Munsell, 1966.

Bart, Philip; Bassett, Theodore; Weinstone, William; and Zipser, Arthur. *Highlights of a Fighting History.* New York: International Publishers, 1979.

Bimba, Anthony. *History of the American Working Class.* New York: International Publishers, 1927.

Bosworth, Allan R. *America's Concentration Camps.* New York: W. W. Norton & Co., 1967.

Boyer, Richard, and Morais, Herbert M. *Labor's Untold Story.* New York: Cameron Associates, 1955.

Civil Rights Congress. *Civil Rights Congress Tells the Story.* Los Angeles, 1950

Commission on Wartime Relocation and Internment of Civilians. *Personal Justice Denied* (A Report). Washington, D. C.: U.S. Govt. Printing Office, December 1982.

Cullimore, R. Holliday. *Communist Women Activists in the International Labor Defense of the 1930s: Standard Bearers of Feminism.* Women's Studies Senior Thesis. Berkeley: Univ. of California Press, 1985.

Donner, Frank J., *The Age of Surveillance—the Aims and Methods of America's Political Intelligence System.* New York: Vintage Books, 1981.

Embrey, Sue Kunitomi, editor. *The Lost Years 1942-46.* La Jolla: Moonlight Publications, 1972.

Foner, Philip S., *History of the Labor Movement in the United States, Volume 8, Postwar Struggles, 1918-1920.* New York: International Publishers, 1988.

Women and the American Labor Movement from World War I to the Present. New York: The Free Press, Div. of MacMillan, 1980.

Foster, William Z. *The History of the Communist Party of the United States.* New York: International Publishers, 1952.

Frazier, Thomas R., ed., *Afro-American History: Primary Sources,* New York, Chicago, San Francisco: Harcourt Brace & World, 1970.

Gentry, Curt. *Frameup—The Incredible Case of Tom Mooney and Warren Billings.* New York: W.W. Norton & Co., 1967.

Ginger, Ann Pagan, ed., *International Juridical Association Bulletin 1932-1942.* In three volumes. New York: DeCapo Press, 1982.

Relevant Lawyers. New York: Simon & Schuster, 1972.

Girdner, Audrie, and Loftis, Anne. *The Great Betrayal.* Toronto: Collier-MacMillan Canada, Ltd., 1969

Hardy, Jack. *The Clothing Workers.* New York: International Publishers, 1935.

International Labor Defender. Publication of the ILD.

ILD Yearbooks, Equal Justice. and various ILD pamphlets.

Jamieson, Stuart, *Labor Unionism in American Agriculture,* Washington, D.C.: U.S. Dept. of Labor Report, Bull. No. 836, U.S. Dept. of Labor Statistics.

Kushner, Sam. *Long Road to Delano.* New York: International Publishers, 1975.

Lamont, Corliss. *The Trial of Elizabeth Gurley Flynn by the American Civil Liberties Union.* New York: Horizon Press, 1968.

Labor Research Association. *Labor Fact Book.* New York: International Publishers, various years.

Martin, George. *Madame Secretary, Frances Perkins.* Boston: Houghton Mifflin Co., 1978.

McWilliams, Carey. *Brothers Under the Skin.* Boston and Toronto: Little Brown and Co., 1964.

Factories in the Field. Santa Barbara and Salt Lake City, Peregrine Publishers, 1971.

Prejudice–Japanese Americans: Symbol of Racial Intolerance. Boston: Little Brown and Co., 1945.

Minton, Bruce and Stuart, John. *Men Who Lead Labor.* Modern Age Books, New York, 1937.

Naison, Mark. *Communists in Harlem during the Depression.* Champaign: Univ. of Illinois Press, 1983.

Onstine, Frank. *The Great Lumber Strike of Humboldt County.* Eureka: 1935.

Perkins, Frances. *The Roosevelt I Knew.* New York: Viking Press, 1946.

Quin, Mike. *The Big Strike.* Olema: Olema Publishing Co., 1940.

Richmond, Al. *A Long View from the Left.* Boston: Houghton Mifflin Co., 1973.

Rubenstein, Annette T., ed., *I Vote My Conscience: Debates, Speeches and Writings of Vito Marcantonio.* New York: Vito Marcantonio Memorial, 1956.

Smith, Louise Pettibone. *The Torch of Liberty: 25 Years in the Life of the Foreign Born in the United States.* New York: Dwight King Publishers, 1959.

Steuben, John. *Labor in Wartime.* New York: International Publishers, 1940.

Thomas, Dorothy S., and Nishimoto, Richard. *The Spoilage–Japanese American Evacuation and Resettlement during World War II.* Berkeley, U. of California Press, 1946.

Vager, F. *The International Red Aid–Its Aims and Tasks.* Moscow, Central Committee, Red Aid of USSR, 1931.

Ward, Estolv E. *The Gentle Dynamiter, a Biography of Tom Mooney,* Palo Alto: Ramparts Press, 1983.

Harry Bridges on Trial, New York: Modern Age Books, 1940.

Weglyn, Michi. *Years of Infamy: The Untold Story of America's Concentration Camps.* New York: William Morrow and Co., 1976.

Yoneda, Karl. *Ganbatte–Sixty Year Struggle of a Kibei Worker.* Los Angeles: Asian-American Studies Center, UCLA, 1983.

Personal Justice Denied

SUMMARY AND RECOMMENDATIONS OF THE COMMISSION ON WARTIME RELOCATION AND INTERNMENT OF CIVILIANS

THE COMMISSION ON WARTIME RELOCATION AND INTERNMENT OF CIVILIANS

Joan Z. Bernstein, Chair

Daniel E. Lungren, Vice-Chair

Edward W. Brooke

Robert F. Drinan

Arthur S. Flemming

Arthur J. Goldberg

Ishmael V. Gromoff

William M. Marutani

Hugh B. Mitchell

Angus Macbeth, Special Counsel

PART 1: NISEI AND ISSEI

On February 19, 1942, ten weeks after the Pearl Harbor attack, President Franklin D. Roosevelt signed Executive Order 9066, which gave to the Secretary of War and the military commanders the power to exclude any and all persons, citizens and aliens, from designated areas in order to provide security against sabotage, espionage and fifth column activity. Shortly thereafter, all American citizens of Japanese descent were prohibited from living, working or traveling on the West Coast of the United States. The same prohibition applied to the generation of Japanese immigrants who, pursuant to federal law and despite long residence in the United States, were not permitted to become American citizens. American citizens and their alien parents were removed by the Army, first to "assembly centers" – temporary quarters at racetracks and fairgrounds – and then to "relocation centers" – bleak barrack camps in desolate areas of the West. The camps were surrounded by barbed wire and guarded by military police. Departure was permitted only after a loyalty review in consultation with the military, by the War Relocation Authority, the civilian agency that ran the camps. Many of those removed from the West Coast were eventually allowed to leave the camps to join the Army, go to college outside the West Coast or to whatever private employment was available. For a larger number, however, the war years were spent behind barbed wire; and for those who were released, the prohibition against returning to their homes and occupations on the West Coast was not lifted until December 1944.

This policy of exclusion, removal, and detention was executed against 120,000 people without individual review, and exclusion was continued virtually without regard for their demonstrated loyalty to the United States. Congress was fully aware of and supported the policy of removal and detention; it sanctioned the exclusion by enacting a statute which made criminal the violation of orders issued pursuant to Executive Order 9066. The United States Supreme Court held the exclusion constitutionally permissible in the context of war, but struck down the incarceration of admittedly loyal American citizens on the ground that it was not based on statutory authority.

All this was done despite the fact that not a single documented act of espionage, sabotage or fifth column activity was committed by an American citizen of Japanese ancestry or by a resident Japanese alien on the West Coast.

No mass exclusion or detention, in any part of the country, was ordered against American citizens of German or Italian descent. Official actions

against enemy aliens of other nationalities were much more individualized and selective than those imposed on the ethnic Japanese.

The exclusion, removal and detention inflicted tremendous human cost. There was the obvious cost of homes and businesses sold or abandoned under circumstances of great distress, as well as injury to careers and professional advancement But most important, there was the loss of liberty and the personal stigma of suspected disloyalty for thousands of people who knew themselves to be devoted to their country's cause and to its ideals but whose repeated protestations of loyalty were discounted — only to be demonstrated beyond any doubt by the record of Nisei soldiers, who returned from the battlefields of Europe as the most decorated and distinguished combat units of World War II and by the thousands of other Nisei who served against the enemy in the Pacific, mostly in military intelligence. The wounds of the exclusion and detention have healed in some respects, but the scars of that experience remain, painfully real in the minds of those who lived through the suffering and deprivation of the camps.

The personal injustice of excluding, removing and detaining loyal American citizens is manifest. Such events are extraordinary and unique in American history. For every citizen and for American public life, they pose haunting questions about our country and its past.

The Decision to Exclude

The Context of the Decision. First, the exclusion and removal were attacks on the ethnic Japanese which followed a long and ugly history of West Coast anti-Japanese agitation and legislation. Antipathy and hostility toward the ethnic Japanese was a major factor of the public life of the West Coast states for more than forty years before Pearl Harbor. Under pressure from California, immigration from Japan had been severely restricted in 1908 and entirely prohibited in 1924. Japanese immigrants were barred from American citizenship, although their children born here were citizens by birth. California and the other western states prohibited Japanese immigrants from owning land. In part the hostility was economic, emerging in various white American groups who began to feel competition, particularly in agriculture, the principal occupation of the immigrants. The anti-Japanese agitation also fed on racial stereotypes and fears: the "yellow peril" of an unknown Asian culture achieving substantial influence on the Pacific Coast.

The ethnic Japanese, small in number and with no political voice — the citizen generation was just reaching voting age in 1940 — had become a convenient target for political demagogues. Political bullying was supported by organized interest groups who adopted anti-Japanese agitation as a consistent part of their program: the Native Sons and Daughters of the Golden West, the Joint Immigration Committee, the American Legion, the California State Federation of Labor and the California State Grange.

Second, Japanese armies in the Pacific won a rapid, startling string of victories against the United States and its allies in the first months of World War II.

In January and February 1942, the military position of the United States in the Pacific was perilous. There was fear of Japanese attacks on the West Coast.

Next, contrary to the facts, there was a widespread belief, supported by a statement by Frank Knox, Secretary of the Navy, that the Pearl Harbor attack had been aided by sabotage and fifth column activity by ethnic Japanese in Hawaii. The government knew that this was not true, but took no effective measures to disabuse public belief that disloyalty had contributed to massive American losses on December 7,1941. **Thus the country was unfairly led to believe that both American citizens of Japanese descent and resident Japanese aliens threatened American security.**

Fourth, as anti-Japanese organizations began to speak out and rumors from Hawaii spread, West Coast politicians quickly took up the familiar anti-Japanese cry. The Congressional delegations in Washington organized themselves and pressed the War and Justice Departments and the President for stern measures to control the ethnic Japanese – moving quickly from control of aliens to evacuation and removal of citizens. In California, Governor Olson, Attorney General Warren and Mayor Bowron of Los Angeles, and many local authorities joined the clamor. These opinions were not informed by any knowledge of actual military risks, rather they were stroked by virulent agitation which encountered little opposition. Only a few churchmen and academicians were prepared to defend the Japanese. There was little or no political risk in claiming that it was "better to be safe than sorry" and, as many did, that the best way for ethnic Japanese to prove their loyalty was to volunteer to enter detention. The press amplified the unreflective emotional excitement of the hour Through late January and early February 1942, the rising clamor from the West Coast was heard within the federal government as its demands became more draconian.

Making and Justifying the Decision. The exclusion of the ethnic Japanese from the West Coast was recommended to the Secretary of War, Henry L. Stimson, by Lieutenant General John L. DeWitt, Commanding General of the Western Defense Command with responsibility for West Coast security. President Roosevelt relied on Secretary Stimson's recommendations in issuing Executive Order 9066.

The justification given for the measure was military necessity. The claim of military necessity is most clearly set out in three places: General DeWitt's February 14, 1942, recommendation to Secretary Stimson for exclusion; General DeWitt's *Final Report: Japanese Evacuation from the West Coast, 1942;* and the government's brief in the Supreme Court defending the Executive Order in *Hirabayashi v. United States.* General DeWitt's February 1942 recommendation presented the following rationale for the exclusion:

> The Japanese race is an enemy race and while many second and third generation Japanese born on United States soil, possessed of United States citizenship, have become "Americanized," the racial strains are undiluted. To concede otherwise is to expect that children born of white parents on Japanese soil sever all racial affinity and become loyal Japanese subjects, ready to fight and, if necessary, to die for Japan

> in a war against the nation of their parents. That Japan is allied with Germany and Italy in this struggle is no ground for assuming that any Japanese, barred from assimilation by convention as he is, though born and raised in the United States, will not turn against this nation when the final test of loyalty comes. It, therefore, follows that along the vital Pacific Coast over 112,000 potential enemies, of Japanese extraction, are at large today. There are indications that these were organized and ready for concerted action at a favorable opportunity. The very fact that no sabotage has taken place to date is a disturbing and confirming indication that such action will be taken.

There are two unfounded justifications for exclusion expressed here: first, that ethnicity ultimately determines loyalty; second, that "indications" suggest that ethnic Japanese "are organized and ready for concerted action" – the best argument for this being the fact that it hadn't happened.

The first evaluation is not a military one but one for sociologists or historians. It runs counter to a basic premise on which the American nation of immigrants is built – that loyalty to the United States is a matter of individual choice and not determined by ties to an ancestral country. The second judgment was, by the General's own admission, unsupported by any evidence. General DeWitt's recommendation clearly does not provide a credible rationale, based on military expertise, for the necessity of exclusion.

In his 1943 *Final Report* General DeWitt cited a number of factors in support of the exclusion decision: signaling from shore to enemy submarines; arms and contraband found by the FBI during raids on ethnic Japanese homes and businesses; dangers to the ethnic Japanese from vigilantes; concentration of ethnic Japanese around or near militarily sensitive areas; the number of Japanese ethnic organizations on the coast which might shelter pro-Japanese attitudes or activities such as Emperor worshipping Shinto; and the presence of the Kibei, who had spent some time in Japan.

The first two items point to demonstrable military danger. But the reports of shore-to-ship signaling were investigated by the Federal Communications Commission, the agency with relevant expertise, and no identifiable cases of such signaling were substantiated. The FBI did confiscate arms and contraband from some ethnic Japanese, but most were items normally in the possession of any law-abiding civilian, and the FBI concluded that these searches had uncovered no dangerous persons that "we could not otherwise know about." Thus neither of these "facts" militarily justified exclusion.

There had been some acts of violence against ethnic Japanese on the West Coast and feeling against them ran high, but "protective custody" is not an acceptable rationale for exclusion. Protection against vigilantes is a civilian matter that would involve the military only in extreme cases. But there is no evidence that such extremity had been reached on the West Coast in early 1942. Moreover, "protective custody" could never justify exclusion and detention for months and years.

General DeWitt's remaining points are repeated in the Hirabayashi brief, which also emphasizes dual nationality, Japanese language schools and the high percentage of aliens (who, by law, had been barred from acquiring American citizenship) in the ethnic population. These facts represent broad social judgments of little or no military significance in themselves. None supports the claim of disloyalty to the United States and all were entirely legal. If the same standards were applied to other ethnic groups, as Morton Grodzins, an early analyst of the exclusion decision, applied it to ethnic Italians on the West Coast, an equally compelling and meaningless case for "disloyalty" could be made. In short these social and cultural patterns were not evidence of any threat to West Coast military security.

In sum, the record does not permit the conclusion that military necessity warranted the exclusion of ethnic Japanese from the West Coast.

The Conditions Which Permitted the Decision. Having concluded that no military necessity supported the exclusion, the Commission has attempted to determine how the decision came to be made.

First, General DeWitt apparently believed what he told Secretary Stimson: ethnicity determined loyalty — that it was impossible to distinguish the loyal from the disloyal. On this basis he believed them to be potential enemies among whom loyalty could not be determined.

Second, the FBI and members of Naval Intelligence who had relevant intelligence responsibility were ignored when they stated that nothing more than careful watching of suspicious individuals or individual reviews of loyalty were called for by existing circumstances.

Third, General DeWitt relied heavily on civilian politicians rather than informed military judgments in reaching his conclusions. The civilian politicians largely repeated the prejudiced, unfounded themes of anti-Japanese factions and interest groups on the West Coast.

Fourth, no effective measures were taken by President Roosevelt to calm the West Coast public and refute the rumors of sabotage and fifth column activity at Pearl Harbor.

Fifth, General DeWitt was temperamentally disposed to exaggerate the measures necessary to maintain security and placed security far ahead of any concern for the liberty of citizens.

Sixth, Secretary Stimson and John J. McCloy, Assistant Secretary of War, both of whose views on race differed from those of General DeWitt failed to insist on a clear military justification for the measures General DeWitt wished to undertake.

Seventh, Attorney General Francis Biddle, while contending that exclusion was unnecessary, did not argue to the President that failure to make out a case of military necessity on the facts would render the exclusion constitutionally impermissible or that the Constitution prohibited exclusion on the basis of ethnicity given the facts on the West Coast.

Eighth, those representing the interests of civil rights and civil liberties in Congress, the press and other public forums were silent or indeed supported exclusion. Thus there was no effective opposition to the measures vociferously sought by numerous West Coast interest groups, politicians and journalists.

Finally, President Roosevelt, without raising the question to the level of Cabinet discussion or requiring any careful or thorough review of the situation, and despite the Attorney General's arguments and other information before him, agreed with Secretary Stimson that the exclusion should be carried out.

The Decision to Detain

With the signing of Executive Order 9066, the course of the President and War Department was set: American citizens and alien residents of Japanese ancestry would be compelled to leave the West Coast on the basis of wartime military necessity. For the War Department and the Western Defense Command, the problem became primarily one of method and operation, not basic policy. General DeWitt first tried "voluntary" resettlement: the ethnic Japanese were to move outside restricted military zones of the West Coast but otherwise were free to go wherever they chose. From a military standpoint this policy was bizarre, and it was utterly impractical. If the ethnic Japanese had been excluded because they were potential saboteurs and spies, any such danger was not extinguished by leaving them at large in the interior where there were, of course, innumerable dams, power lines, bridges and war industries to be disrupted or spied upon. Conceivably sabotage in the interior could be synchronized with a Japanese raid or invasion for a powerful fifth column effect. This raises serious doubts as to how grave the War Department believed the supposed threat to be.

The War Relocation Authority (WRA), the civilian agency created by the President to supervise the relocation and initially directed by Milton Eisenhower, proceeded on the premise that the vast majority of evacuees were law-abiding and loyal, and that once off the West Coast they should be returned quickly to conditions approximating normal life. Governors and officials of the mountain states objected to California using the interior states as a "dumping ground" for a California "problem." They argued that people in their states were so bitter over the voluntary evacuation that unguarded evacuees would face physical danger. Again and again, detention camps for evacuees were urged. The consensus was that a plan for reception centers was acceptable so long as the evacuees remained under guard within the centers.

The War Relocation Authority dropped resettlement and adopted confinement. Notwithstanding WRA's belief that evacuees should be returned to normal productive life, it had, in effect become their jailer. The politicians of the interior states had achieved the program of detention.

The evacuees were to be held in camps behind barbed wire and released only with government approval. For this course of action no military justification was proffered. The WRA contended that these steps were necessary for the benefit of evacuees and that controls on their departure were designed to assure they would not be mistreated by other Americans on leaving the camps.

It follows from the conclusion that there was no justification in military necessity for the exclusion, that there was no basis for the detention.

The Effect of the Exclusion and Detention

The history of the relocation camps and the assembly centers that preceded them is one of suffering and deprivation visited on people against whom no charges were, or could have been, brought.

Families could take to the assembly centers and the camps only what they could carry. Camp living conditions were spartan. People were housed in tar-papered barracks rooms of no more than 20 by 24 feet. Each room housed a family, regardless of family size. Construction was often shoddy. Privacy was practically impossible and furnishings were minimal. Eating and bathing were in mass facilities. Under continuing pressure from those who blindly held to the belief that evacuees harbored disloyal intentions,the wages paid for work at the camps were kept to the minimal level of $12 a month for unskilled labor, rising to $19 a month for professional employees. Mass living prevented normal family communication and activities. Heads of families, no longer providing food and shelter, found their authority to lead and to discipline diminished.

The camp experience carried a stigma that no other Americans suffered. The evacuees themselves expressed the indignity of their conditions with particular power:

> On May 16,1942, my mother, two sisters, niece, nephew, and I left ... by train. Father joined us later. Brother left earlier by bus. We took whatever we could carry. So much we left behind, but the most valuable thing I lost was my freedom.

* * *

> Henry went to the Control Station to register the family He came home with twenty tags, all numbered 10710, tags to be attached to each piece of baggage, and one to hang from our coat lapels. From then on, we were known as Family #10710.

The government's efforts to "Americanize" the children in the camps were bitterly ironic:

> An oft-repeated ritual in relocation camp schools... was the salute to the flag followed by the singing of "My country, 'tis of thee, sweet land of liberty" — a ceremony Caucasian teachers found embarrassingly awkward if not cruelly poignant in the austere prison setting.

* * *

> In some ways, I suppose, my life was not too different from a lot of kids in America between the years 1942 and 1945. I spent a good part of my time playing with my brothers and friends, learned to shoot marbles, watched sandlot baseball and envied

the older kids who wore Boy Scout uniforms. We shared with the rest of America the same movies, screen heroes and listened to the same heart-rending songs of the forties. We imported much of America into camps because, after all, we were Americans. Through imitation of my brothers, who attended grade school within the camp, I learned to salute the flag by the time I was five years old. I was learning as best one could learn in Manzanar, what it meant to live in America. But, I was also learning the sometimes bitter price one has to pay for it.

After the war, through the Japanese American Evacuation Claims Act, the government attempted to compensate for the losses of real and personal property; inevitably that effort did not secure full or fair compensation. There were many kinds of injury the Evacuation Claims Act made no attempt to compensate: the stigma placed on people who fell under the exclusion and relocation orders; the deprivation of liberty suffered during detention; the psychological impact of exclusion and relocation; the breakdown of family structure; the loss of earnings or profits; physical injury or illness during detention.

The Decision to End Detention

By October 1942, the government held over 100,000 evacuees in relocation camps. **After the tide of war turned with the American victory at Midway in June, 1942, the possibility of serious Japanese attack was no longer credible; detention and exclusion became increasingly difficult to defend.**

Determining the basis on which detention would be ended required the government to focus on the justification for controlling the ethnic Japanese. If the government maintained the position that distinguishing the loyal from the disloyal was possible and that exclusion and detention were required only by the necessity of acting quickly under the threat of Japanese attack in early 1942, then a program to release those considered loyal should have been instituted in the spring of 1942 when people were confined in the assembly centers.

At the end of 1942, over General DeWitt's opposition, Secretary Stimson, Assistant Secretary McCloy and General George C. Marshall, Chief of Staff, decided to establish a volunteer combat team of Nisei soldiers.[1] The volunteers were to come from those who had passed a loyalty review. To avoid the obvious unfairness of allowing only those joining the military to establish their loyalty and leave the camps, the War Department joined WRA in expanding the loyalty review program to all evacuees.

This program was significant, but remained a compromise. It provided an opportunity to demonstrate loyalty to the United States on the battlefields; despite the human sacrifice involved, this was of immense practical importance in obtaining postwar acceptance for the ethnic Japanese. It opened the gates of the camps for some and began some reestablishment of normal life. But with no apparent rationale or justification, it did not end exclusion of the loyal from the

1 For a further review of the military contributions of the 442nd Regimental Combat Team, 100th Battalion and MIS, see the CWRIC Report Chapter 10, "Military Service," pages 253-260.

West Coast. The review program did not extend the presumption of loyalty to American citizens of Japanese descent, who were subjected to an investigation and review not applied to other ethnic groups.

Equally important, although the loyalty review program was the first major government decision in which the interests of evacuees prevailed, the program was conducted so insensitively, with such lack of understanding of the evacuees' circumstances, that it became one of the most divisive and wrenching episodes of the camp detention.

After almost a year of what the evacuees considered utterly unjust treatment at the hands of the government, the loyalty review program began with filling out a questionnaire which posed two questions requiring declarations of complete loyalty to the United States. Thus, the questionnaire demanded a personal expression of position from each evacuee – a choice between faith in one's future in America and an outrage at present injustice. Understandably most evacuees probably had deeply ambiguous feelings about a government whose rhetorical values of liberty and equality they wished to believe, but who found their present treatment in painful contradiction to those values. The loyalty questionnaire left little room to express that ambiguity. Indeed, it provided an effective point of protest and organization against the government, from which more and more evacuees felt alienated. The questionnaire finally addressed the central question of loyalty that underlay the exclusion policy, a question which had been the predominant political and personal issue for the ethnic Japanese over the past year; answering it required confronting the conflicting emotions aroused by the relation to the government.

> Well, I am one of those that said "no, no" on it, one of the "no, no" boys, and it is not that I was proud about it, it was just that our legal rights were violated and I wanted to fight back. However, I didn't want to take this sitting down. I was really angry. It just got me so damn mad. Whatever I do, there was no help from outside, and it seems to me that we are a race that doesn't count. So therefore, this was one of the reasons for the "no, no" answer.

The loyalty review program was a point of decision and division for those in the camps. The avowedly loyal were eligible for release; those who were unwilling to profess loyalty or whom the government distrusted were segregated from the main body of evacuees into the Tule Lake camp, which rapidly became a center of disaffection and protest against the government and its policies – the unhappy refuge of evacuees consumed by anger and despair.

The Decision to End Exclusion

The loyalty review should logically have led to the conclusion that no justification existed for excluding loyal American citizens from the West Coast. Secretary Stimson, Assistant Secretary McCloy and General Marshall reached this position in the spring of 1943. Nevertheless, the exclusion was not ended until December 1944. No plausible reason connected to any wartime security has been offered for this eighteen to twenty month delay in allowing the ethnic Japanese to return to their homes, jobs and businesses on the West Coast.

Between May 1943 and May 1944, War Department officials did not make public their opinion that exclusion of loyal ethnic Japanese from the West Coast no longer had any military justification. If the President was unaware of this view, the plausible explanation is that Secretary Stimson and Assistant Secretary McCloy were unwilling, or believed themselves unable, to face down political opposition on the West Coast. General DeWitt repeatedly expressed his opposition until he left the Western Defense Command in the fall of 1943, as did West Coast anti-Japanese factions and politicians.

In May 1944 Secretary Stimson put before President Roosevelt and the Cabinet his position that the exclusion no longer had a military justification. But the President was unwilling to act to end the exclusion until the first Cabinet meeting following the Presidential election of November 1944. The inescapable conclusion from this factual pattern is that the delay was motivated by political considerations.

By the participants own accounts, there is no rational explanation for maintaining the exclusion of loyal ethnic Japanese from the West Coast for eighteen months after May 1943 — except political pressure and fear. Certainly there was no justification arising out of military necessity.

The Comparisons

HAWAII: When Japan attacked Pearl Harbor, nearly 158,000 persons of Japanese ancestry lived in Hawaii — more than 35 percent of the population. **Surely, if there were dangers of espionage, sabotage and fifth column activity by American citizens and resident aliens of Japanese ancestry, danger would be greatest in Hawaii, and one would anticipate that the most swift and severe measures would be taken there. But nothing of the sort happened.** Less than 2,000 ethnic Japanese in Hawaii were taken into custody during the war — barely one percent of the population of Japanese descent. Many factors contributed to this reaction.

Hawaii was more ethnically mixed and racially tolerant than the West Coast. Race relations in Hawaii before the war were not infected with the same virulent antagonism of 75 years' agitation. While anti-Asian feeling existed in the territory, it did not represent the longtime views of well-organized groups as it did on the West Coast and, without statehood, xenophobia had no effective voice in the Congress.

The larger population of ethnic Japanese in Hawaii was also a factor. It is one thing to vent frustration and historical prejudice on a scant two percent of the population; it is very different to disrupt a local economy and tear a social fabric by locking up more than one-third of a territory's people. And in Hawaii the half-measure of exclusion from military areas would have been meaningless.

In large social terms, the Army had much greater control of day-to-day events in Hawaii. Martial law was declared in December 1941, suspending the writ of habeas corpus, so that through the critical first months of the war, the military's recognized power to deal with any emergency was far greater than on the West Coast.

This policy was clearly much more congruent with basic American laws and values. It was also a much sounder policy in practice. The remarkably high rate of enlistment in the Army in Hawaii is in sharp contrast to the doubt and alienation that marred the recruitment of Army volunteers in the relocation camps. The wartime experience in Hawaii left behind neither the extensive economic losses and injury suffered on the mainland nor the psychological burden of the direct experience of unjust exclusion and detention.

The promulgation of Executive Order 9066 was not justified by military necessity, and the decisions which followed from it —detention, ending detention and ending exclusion — were not driven by analysis of military conditions. The broad historical causes which shaped these decisions were race prejudice, war hysteria and a failure of political leadership. Widespread ignorance of Japanese Americans contributed to a policy conceived in haste and executed in an atmosphere of fear and anger at Japan. A grave injustice was done to American citizens and resident aliens of Japanese ancestry who, without individual review or any probative evidence against them, were excluded, removed and detained by the United States during World War II.

Many of those involved in the exclusion, removal and detention passed judgment on those events in memoirs and other statements after the war. **Henry Stimson** recognized that *"to loyal citizens this forced evacuation was a personal injustice."* In his autobiography, **Francis Biddle** reiterated his beliefs at the time-. *"The program was ill-advised, unnecessary and unnecessarily cruel."* **Justice William O. Douglas**, who joined the majority opinion in Korematsu which held the evacuation constitutionally permissible, found that the evacuations case *"was ever on my conscience."* Milton Eisenhower described the evacuation to the relocation camps as "an inhuman mistake." **Chief Justice Earl Warren**, who had urged evacuation as Attorney General of California, stated, *"I have since deeply regretted the removal order and my own testimony advocating it because it was not in keeping with our American concept of freedom and the rights of citizens."* **Justice Tom C. Clark**, who had been liaison between the Justice Department and the Western Defense Command, concluded, *"Looking back on it today [the evacuation] was, of course, a mistake."*

PART II: THE ALEUTS

During the struggle for naval supremacy in the Pacific during WWII, the Aleutian Islands were strategically valuable to both the United States and Japan. Beginning in March 1942, U.S. military intelligence repeatedly warned Alaska defense commanders that Japanese aggression into the Aleutian Islands was imminent. In June 1942, the Japanese attacked and held the two westernmost Aleutians, Kiska and Attu. American military commanders ordered the evacuation of the Aleuts from many of the islands to places of relative safety.

Eight hundred seventy-six Aleuts had been evacuated from Aleut villages west of Unimak Island, including the Pribilofs. Except in Unalaska the entire population of each village was evacuated, including at least 30 non-Aleuts. All of the Aleuts were relocated to southeastern Alaska except 50 persons who were either evacuated to the Seattle area or hospitalized in the Indian Hospital at Tacoma, Washington.

The evacuation of the Aleuts had a rational basis as a precaution to ensure their safety. The Aleuts were evacuated from an active theater of war; 42 were taken prisoner on Attu by the Japanese. It was clearly the military's belief that evacuation of non-military personnel was advisable.

The Aleuts' Camps

Aleuts were subjected to deplorable conditions following the evacuation. Typical housing was an abandoned gold mine or fish cannery buildings which were inadequate in both accommodation and sanitation. Lack of medical care contributed to extensive disease and death.

The Funter Bay cannery in southeastern Alaska where 300 Aleuts were placed was one of the worst camps. The majority of evacuees were forced to live in two dormitory-style buildings in groups of six to thirteen people in areas of nine to ten feet square. Until fall, many Aleuts were forced to sleep in relays because of lack of space.

In the fall of 1942, the only fulltime medical care was provided by two nurses who served both the cannery camp and a camp at a mine across Funter Bay. Doctors were only temporarily assigned to the camp. Medical supplies were scarce.

Epidemics raged throughout the Aleuts' stay in southeastern Alaska; they suffered from influenza, measles, and pneumonia along with tuberculosis. Twenty-five died at Funter Bay in 1943 alone. It is estimated that probably 10% of the evacuated Aleuts died during their two or three year stay.

The standard of care which the government owes to those within its care was clearly violated by this treatment, which brought great suffering and loss of life to the Aleuts.

Return to the Islands

The Pribilovians were able to get back to the Pribilofs by the late spring of 1944, nine months after the Japanese had been driven out of the Aleutian chain. The return to the Aleutians did not take place for another year The delay may be attributed to transport shortage and problems of supplying the islands in order to resume a normal life. But the government's record, especially in the

Aleutians, reflects an indifference and lack of urgency. Some Aleuts were not permitted to return to their homes; to this day, Attuans continue to be excluded from their ancestral lands.

When they first returned, many Aleuts were forced to camp because their former homes (those that had still stood) had not yet been repaired and were now uninhabitable. The Aleuts rebuilt their homes themselves. They were "paid" with free groceries.

The Aleuts suffered material losses from the government's occupation of the islands for which they were never fully recompensated, in cash or in kind. Devout followers of the Russian Orthodox faith, Aleuts treasured the religious icons and other family heirlooms that were their most significant spiritual as well as material losses. They cannot be replaced.

In sum, despite the fact that the Aleutians were a theater of war from which evacuation was a sound policy, there was no justification for the manner in which the Aleuts were treated in the camps, nor for failing to compensate them fully for their material losses.

Economic Losses

The excluded people suffered enormous damages and losses, both material and intangible. To the disastrous loss of farms, businesses and homes must be added the disruption for many years of careers and professional lives, as well as the long-term loss of income, earnings and opportunity. It is estimated that, as a result of the exclusion and detention, in 1945 dollars the ethnic Japanese lost between $108 and $164 million in income and between $11 and $206 million in property for which no compensation was made after the war under the terms of the Japanese American Evacuation Claims Act. Adjusting these figures to account for inflation alone, the total losses of income and property fall between $810 million and $2 billion in 1983 dollars.[1]

Recommendations

Japanese Americans

[The remedies, which the Commission on Wartime Relocation and Internment of Civilians issued on June 16, 1983, are based upon their fact-finding report and economic impact study.]

1 An analysis of economic losses was performed for the Commission by ICF Incorporated. According to their study titled, "Economic Losses of Ethnic Japanese as a Result of Exclusion and Detention, 1942-46, total uncompensated economic losses of the ethnic Japanese adjusted for the corporate bond rate range from $1.2 billion to $3.1 billion, and at a 3% interest rate and inflation, from $2.5 billion to $6.2 billion.

Each measure acknowledges to some degree the wrongs inflicted during the war upon the ethnic Japanese. None can fully compensate or, indeed, make the group whole again.

The Commission makes the following recommendations for remedies as an act of national apology.

1. That Congress pass a joint resolution, to be signed by the President, which recognizes that a grave injustice was done and offers the apologies of the nation for the acts of exclusion, removal and detention.

2. That the President pardon those who were convicted of violating the statutes imposing a curfew on American citizens. The Commission further recommends that the Department of Justice review other wartime convictions of the ethnic Japanese and recommend to the President that he pardon those whose offenses were grounded in a refusal to accept treatment that discriminated among citizens on the basis of race or ethnicity.

3. That the Congress direct the Executive agencies to which Japanese Americans may apply for the restitution of positions, status or entitlements lost in whole or in part because of acts or events between December 1941 and 1945.

4. That the Congress demonstrate official recognition of the injustice done to American citizens of Japanese ancestry and Japanese resident aliens during the Second World War, and that it recognize the nation's need to make redress for these events, by appropriating monies to establish a special foundation.

The Commission believes a fund for educational and humanitarian purposes related to the wartime events is appropriate and addresses an injustice suffered by an entire ethnic group.

5. The Commissioners, with the exception of Congressman Lungren, recommended that Congress establish a fund which will provide personal redress to those who were excluded, as well as serve the purposes set out in Recommendation #4.

Appropriations of $1.5 billion should be made to the fund over a reasonable period to be determined by Congress. This fund should be used, first, to provide a one-time per capita compensatory payment of $20,000 to each of the approximately 60,000 surviving persons excluded from their places of residence pursuant to Executive Order 9066.[1] The burden should be on the government to locate survivors, without requiring any application for payment, and payments should be made to the oldest survivors first. After per capita payments, the remainder of the fund should be used for the public educational purposes as discussed in Recommendation #4.

1 Commissioner William M. Marutani formally renounces any monetary recompense either direct or indirect.

The fund should be administered by a Board, the majority of whose members are Americans of Japanese descent appointed by the President and confirmed by the Senate.

Aleuts

The Commissioners agree that a claims procedure would not be an effective method of compensation. Therefore, the sums included the Commission's recommendations were chosen to recognize fundamental justice.

1. The Commissioners, with Congressman Lungren dissenting, recommend that Congress establish a fund for the beneficial use of the Aleuts in the amount of $5 million. The principal and interest of the fund should be spent for community and individual purposes that would be compensatory for the losses and injuries Aleuts suffered as a result of the evacuation.

2. The Commissioners, with Congressman Lungren dissenting, recommend that Congress appropriate funds and direct a payment of $5,000 per capita to each of the few hundred surviving Aleuts who were evacuated from the Aleutian or Pribilof Islands by the federal government during World War II.

3. That Congress appropriate funds and direct the relevant government agency to rebuild and restore the churches damaged or destroyed in the Aleutian islands in the course of World War II.

4. That Congress appropriate adequate funds through the public works budget for the Army Corps of Engineers to clear away the debris that remains from World War II in and around populated areas of the Aleutian Islands.

5. That Congress declare Attu to be native land and that Attu be conveyed to the Aleuts through their native corporation upon condition that the native corporation is able to negotiate an agreement with the Coast Guard which will allow that service to continue essential functions on the island.

The Commission believes that, for reasons of redressing the personal justice done to thousands of Americans and resident alien Japanese, and to the Aleuts — and for compelling reasons of preserving a truthful sense of our own history and the lessons we can learn from it — these recommendations should be enacted by the Congress. In the late 1930's W.H. Auden wrote lines that express our present need to acknowledge and to make amends:

We are left alone with our day, and the time is short
and History to the defeated
May say Alas but cannot help or pardon.

It is our belief that, though history cannot be unmade, it is well within our power to offer help, and to acknowledge error.

Index